W9-BZJ-528

Children of the Dream

Children of the Dream

Our Own Stories of

Growing Up Black

in America

Laurel Holliday

POCKET BOOKS

New York   London   Toronto   Sydney   Tokyo   Singapore

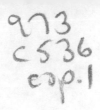 POCKET BOOKS, a division of Simon & Schuster, Inc.
1230 Avenue of the Americas, New York, NY 10020

Contents

Contents

Contents

Contents

Introduction

> *Now is the time to make justice*
> *a reality for all of God's children. . . .*
> *I have a dream my four little children*
> *will one day live in a nation where*
> *they will not be judged by the color*
> *of their skin but by the content of*
> *their character. I have a dream today!*
>
> — Dr. Martin Luther King, Jr.,
> "I Have a Dream,"
> delivered at the March on Washington
> for Civil Rights, August 28, 1963

In this, the fourth volume in the international Children of Conflict series, African-Americans from across the United States invite us into their childhoods. Carrying on a long-standing black autobiographical tradition, the thirty-eight writers in this anthology recount the struggles, as well as the joys, of growing up in twentieth-century America. In poignant, personally revealing, and often highly entertaining true stories (nearly all of them published for the first time in this book), they tell us what it was like to grow up stigmatized by the color of their skin, yet often very proud of their heritage, their culture, and their community.

Exploring the roots of their racial awareness, they describe turning points in their youths that changed their lives forever: the shock of the first time a white child called them "nigger," the agony of wanting to be friends with a white child but "knowing" that they weren't "good enough," the humiliation of being told that they were "dirty" because they didn't wash their hair every day and that they were "ugly" because their facial features and skin color were different from the majority.

In one of the stories, a writer describes a group of white adults chanting "Two, four, six, eight, we don't want to integrate" at her and her black classmates when they were just barely old enough to climb up the steps of their Brooklyn elementary school for the first time. Another writer depicts the utter humiliation and even physical torture he suffered at the hands of racist Los Angeles County sheriffs. Another tells us what it was like to live every day in fear of starvation because welfare did not provide enough food to sustain him and his sixteen brothers and sisters. And yet another describes the anger that rose in him in response to the blatant racism of his elementary school teacher—an anger that, when full-blown, would eventually lead to his being incarcerated on death row in San Quentin Federal Penitentiary.

Some of the writers describe the difficulties *not* of being black and suffering at the hands of white racists, but of being found not black enough by their own peers. To be judged the wrong shade of black by other blacks, they say, or to be found "uncool" by those of one's own race for not being able to afford the "right" athletic shoes, is as excruciating, sometimes even more so, than to be bullied by insensitive whites.

Tenderly, yet precisely, these writers point out how blacks perpetuate prejudice by insisting on certain hairstyles and ways of speaking, for example, and by disrespecting those of different educational and economic experience from their own. Several of them describe the double bind of feeling trapped between two colors:

Why did they hate me for being a little different? Sounding educated and being interested in different things than they were didn't make me any less "black," did it? It seemed that I was too black for the white people, yet not black enough for the black people.

(Charisse Nesbit)

The early blows to my psyche were not black or white. They were black and white. And I loathed them equally.

(Bernestine Singley)

Ranging in age from eleven to seventy-five and raised in twenty-two states, the writers in this volume provide a wide window on the experience of growing up black in the United States. Born about the same time as Dr. Martin Luther King, Jr., one writer's coming of age took place in Boston against the backdrop of the Great Depression. Another grew up in the 1950s and writes about her admiration for her father, a famous bootlegger in New Jersey who was proud of being able to support his family without working for white people. Three describe their efforts to integrate previously all-white schools in the 1960s: one in Brooklyn, one in Boston, and one in South Carolina. Three more describe the enormous effort and expense of trying to maintain their hair in a way that would be acceptable to the majority culture and their black peers. And several write about adolescent racial challenges that they are still in the midst of: one in Birmingham, Alabama, and three sisters living in a small town in Georgia.

Polls indicate that the lives of black children have not improved since Dr. Martin Luther King, Jr., proclaimed his dream for children in 1963. At that time, one out of five black teens was living below the poverty level, and black teens had the lowest rate of suicide of any teenage racial group in the United States. Now, as we near the turn of the century, one black teen in two is living below the poverty line, and black teen suicide rates surpass those of all other racial groups.

In this book, in the context of the writers' own personal experiences, we learn of the persistent racial inequities that black youth have been faced with over the course of this century. At a time in their lives when they might need to simply focus on the ordeal of growing up, they are forced to deal with racism.

But the writers also write about their resilience and how they learned to transmute such injustices into determination to achieve racial justice. As such, the writings here are a testament to the endurance of Dr. Martin Luther King, Jr.'s dream, the courage of black youth and the role of *creativity* in the redemption of racism.

Even though this anthology spans eight decades and includes a wide range of black experiences from coast to coast, it is not a history book; nor is it a sociological account of African-American childhood and adolescence. What you will find here are the true, intimate, and finely crafted accounts of thirty-eight black people's coming of age during what, if he had not been assassinated, would most likely have been the lifetime of Dr. King. Most of the writers tell me they have written their stories with a desire to extend racial understanding and to increase, in whatever way they can, racial justice and equality in this country. But they speak for themselves and of themselves; none would presume to speak for all African-Americans. And, similarly, there is no attempt on my part to have this book be representative of the full range of African-American cultures, lifestyles, and experiences in the twentieth century.

As with all the anthologies in this series, this book could not have been created without the help of many, many people. I would like to sincerely thank all the people who submitted stories for this anthology, all of the writers published herein who have worked so hard with me to make this the best book we could make, and all of the people around the country who have helped me with research, making connections with writers, library materials, etc. I would especially like to thank Millicent E. Brown, Ph.D., who gave me the benefit of her opinions on this introduction and supplied me with very helpful resources for the chronology, and Sam Fulwood III, who also reviewed the introduction and the chronology. Finally, I would like to thank those at Pocket Books who helped make this dream a reality.

Children of the Dream

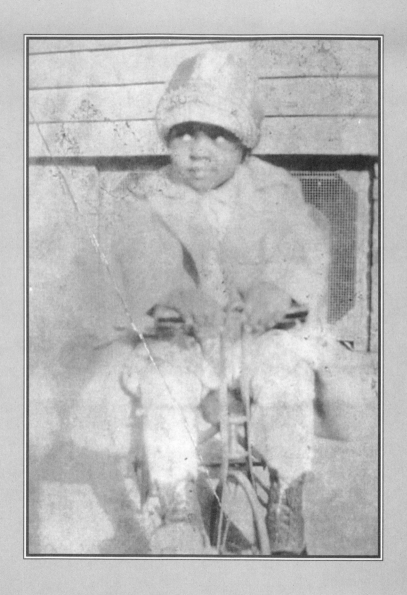

Arline Lorraine Piper

In this heart-stoppingly honest and beautiful account of four generations of challenge, resilience, and generosity, Arline Lorraine Piper, who will turn seventy-five this year, takes us back to the time of the Great Depression, when she was just beginning first grade at a mostly white school in Boston, Massachusetts.

"From my very first engagement with white people when I went to first grade," she says, "I came to understand that to be black in America was to live in two worlds, to experience two selves, to play two sets of roles, and to struggle to preserve sanity and surety when those two realities collided. When I left home for school the first day I was excited and expectant because . . . in my world I was *somebody*. But when I went to school and faced the prejudice, the contempt, and the downright meanness of which others are capable when they do not see you as human in the way that they are, I was made to feel as if I was *nobody*. And in every encounter with white people since,

1

I have had to strive to establish and sustain the true experience and expression of my worth."

Looking back on her life, Arline sees herself as a resourceful person, persistent and resolute in whatever she has done. She started college in the late 1940s, but, unable to finish because she was poor and had the responsibility of raising five daughters, she finally received her degree in elementary education at the age of sixty-four.

Despite her impressive accomplishments, however, Arline insists that she is "an ordinary black woman." So often when we hear about those who have overcome incredible hardship or impossible odds, she says, we think of them as somehow different, outside the bounds of normal life. "If I am at all extraordinary," she tells you, her readers, "it is in my willingness to expose my truth to myself, so that my truth can also be accessible to you. But this effort on my part to be ruthlessly honest with myself will only have full significance for you if it empowers you to the same honesty with yourself, and if that honesty finds its expression in your gifts, and your giving to others."

Surely the following story about the importance of giving— even in the midst of extreme poverty—is a gift itself, from Arline Lorraine Piper.

THE QUESTION

My nine-year-old grandson is asking the question that echoes in my memory. He tells me that he and his mother, my daughter, had been driving along the streets near their home in Los Angeles when she spotted a man lying on the sidewalk. Other people had been passing by on that sidewalk, hurrying to their important wherevers; in fact, my daughter and grandson were, themselves, a little late to somewhere. But she pulled over and got out of her car and helped the older white man up on his feet and over to a nearby bench. She had my grandson flag down a passing police cruiser, and before they returned to their car, she left her card with the old man and assured him that he would get help.

"Mom," my grandson asked her, "why did you stop for that guy? Wasn't he just drunk?"

"No, son," his mother replied. "Although I guess that's what everybody figured as they were passing him by. I think that he was lost and disoriented. Anyway, even if he *was* drunk, I would still have wanted to help him."

"But why?"

"Because he needed my help. He was partway into the street and he could have gotten hit. He needed help."

"But why should *we* help him, Mom? He wasn't none of ours."

A small smile skittered across my daughter's face. "Why don't you ask Grandmother? You know how she can always explain stuff like this."

This child is so like his mother, was my first thought. My daughter is a psychological anthropologist specializing in the inner representations of racism, sexism, and classism in America. As an African-American intellectual who has degrees in the study of the history of our people in America, she knows intimately the contradictions and complications, the inconsistencies and indiscretions, that plague race relations in this country. She is deliberately and unfailingly African-American in her thinking, her behavior, and her approach to life.

My grandson's questions reflect his understanding of this. At nine years old, he cannot fathom why his educated, scholarly, and often radical mother would stoop to help a fallen white man in the street. And I, too, was at first a little curious until I remembered that once in *her* childhood—I think she must have been very close to the age my grandson is now—she had asked me why I had helped an old white man who had become lost in our neighborhood. She could not understand either, back then in the 1960s, why I would do that, until I told her about Mumma. Perhaps this bit of my childhood would also help my grandson. . . .

I am the first grandchild of my maternal grandparents. In those days it was not uncommon for young girls to marry in their teens, and because of this I was born while my grandparents were still having their children. Consequently, I have eight aunts and uncles who are younger than I am. My grandmother,

Mumma, as her children and grandchildren called her, was a quiet woman who gave birth to more than twenty children. She was always at home when I was growing up. Although she was a devout Christian, she didn't go to church much because she was always pregnant and felt more than a little awkward about it. But even that was not so unusual in those days.

Our house was on Murdock Street in Cambridge, Massachusetts. There were not many black families in that area during the early 1930s, but we lived in a fairly mixed neighborhood. There were four other black families, along with five or six white families, on our street. Because there were so many of us, there was always something going on at our house. There was always someone to play with, always someone interested in whatever you wanted to do. I guess that's why it didn't strike me as odd that I almost never went farther than two doors down from our house on either side. My parents and grandparents were careful to keep us all close to home; it was not safe for us beyond our street because the white people then were somehow dangerous to us. It's hard for me to say how I knew about race and race relations by the time I was four or five years old, but I did.

Some of my clues came from how whites acted around us in Boston. On the rare occasion that my mother would take me downtown to buy something for me, I would get the great treat of riding the bus. I would wait at the bus stop, my hand in my mother's hand, dancing around beside her, impatient for the ride. When the bus pulled up, I could sometimes hear people talking to each other through the open windows. But when we got on the bus, it would grow silent in a menacing and eerie sort of way. Some people would stare at us soundlessly; others would look beyond us, acting like we were not there. They would refuse to make eye contact. They did not speak to us.

My mother bore these terrible acts of rudeness with no outward sign of displeasure or disquiet. She treated these breaches of human civility as if they were normal. Somehow that frightened me all the more, and I would press even closer to her as I walked down the aisle to our seat, squeezing my eyes shut against the contemptuous, invasive silence. We would find a seat, and soon I would be in another world, happily peering out the window.

My mother and I never talked about those rides on those buses, or the behavior of the white people on board, but I wondered . . . and feared.

Some of my ideas about race relations in those days came from the way my parents and other adults acted around white people. When black people congregated at church socials and backyard get-togethers, oh, what a time we all had! There was always plenty of food, but there was something else too—*fun!* Such clowning and joking around as you never did see anywhere else. It was pure joy to see the adults whooping and hollering and laughing like us kids. It made me want to clap my hands together and laugh for the sheer happiness of laughing. Even the more straitlaced, sober-faced, citified adults—most of whom were women—could be seduced into a smile, coaxed into a laugh by the determined jokesters—most of whom were men.

But around white people, even the most perpetually crazy black folks grew withdrawn and subdued. Even when they were thrown together socially they did not mingle freely and easily. When black people were with white people they could laugh, but it was like they could not get it all out. They could smile, but the truth of their cautious difference peered out of their shuttered eyes. Something about white people shrouded the natural sunlight of black people's dispositions. White people were dangerous, and I knew it, even at five.

There was even more frightening evidence of danger from whites. One day I overheard my mother tell her family that the white man who owned the mattress factory where she worked had tried to "get fresh" with her. I could not be certain what this meant, but I knew to the marrow of my being that my mother had been in deadly danger among all those fluffy mattresses. I believe she stopped working there soon after that.

I really learned firsthand about race relations from my own experiences at school. On my first day of school I was so excited. My uncle Ernest—the one that is only four months younger than I am—and I were going to school together. We had all new clothes on and eager hearts, bouncing along the sidewalk on either side of my mother. We were too young to realize that we were going to be part of a very small and unpopular minority that day, but we began to get nervous when we grasped that the school was farther than we were allowed to travel on our own. Our apprehension grew with each step away from our neighborhood.

We streamed into the school with all the white children and their parents. I had never before had to stay in a place where black people were not in the majority. We found my room and waited for the first-grade teacher to finish with some children who were ahead of us. She was welcoming all the parents and children individually. She bent down to speak to the little ones and reassured their nervous parents, but when she saw me and my mother her greeting changed. Her smile was gone and she did not bend down to talk to me. She didn't really look at me at all. She looked through me, as if I were a specter instead of a flesh-and-blood child.

Moving away from my mother, I took the last seat in the back of the room, which the teacher had pointed out for me. It seemed like every step I took carried me farther away from my family and the world of black people and deeper into white people's distrust and distaste, aversion and insensitivity. I was too young to understand that my mother would have to leave me there. And by the time I did realize it, it was too late. I would have run screaming from that seat in the back of the room if I had not been too terrified to move. That whole first day—in fact, the first week—I moved in a kind of frightened fog, from one look of suspicious repugnance to another. I was no one, a nonperson, in that place. In time, the total immobility went away, but the certainty of my teachers' disfavor and disregard never did. In their behavior and their words, they made it clear that little black children were not of any real value to them.

Even the children made their view of race relations clear to me. One day in that first school year, I was standing near the fence next to a little white classmate at recess. We had played together before and, in the way of all children, we had become instant friends. I was shyly delighted to have a school friend, and I approached her to see what we might play.

An acquaintance of hers passed by on the other side of the fence, and they struck up a conversation. The one on the outside looked over at me and declared that Negroes certainly did look different.

"Well, she's got pretty eyelashes," she said, as if she had to search every inch of my entire body to find an acceptable feature.

"Yes, she does," replied my classmate. "But I'm glad I don't have anything else about her."

"Me either," the outside one confirmed.

In that moment I knew that, as far as they were concerned, I was the only true outsider.

There were always two worlds—home with black people and out there with white people—and I adapted my behavior and attitudes to these two worlds, which never mixed. Even when they collided, as they sometimes did on the front steps of my house, they swirled around one another like oil and water and then oozed back into their own separate streams.

Because we had so much family, all kinds of kids came to our front steps. The white kids sat down and joined us, recounting raucous stories and laughing at the stories of others, and they seemed to enjoy themselves, but there was no bond. They would stay and talk and laugh with the others, but then it was like they went back to being white. We never lingered on their front porches. We weren't invited to eat in their homes. When we passed their houses, we hurried to pay our respects and leave.

White people never came into our house through the front door. They never came and sat in the parlor and sipped tea or hot milk. They never socialized in our big kitchen like family and friends. So you cannot imagine my shock when I dashed into the kitchen one day during my first summer vacation from school and saw Mumma dishing up food for a white man who was eating at our table! I stood stock still, my suddenly soundless mouth wide open. I couldn't believe it. It felt like the universe had just split open and trapped me in a place that made no sense. Before I could rudely blurt out the surprise that was evident all over me, Mumma looked up and saw me.

"Lorraine," she said, "you go on back outside and play till I call you."

"Yes, ma'am," I replied without question. In those days polite obedience was immediate, instantaneous.

I turned around and went outside. But the puzzled confusion and utter bafflement stayed with me. What was that white man doing in the house? Eating at the table. With Mumma. I asked the other children, but they didn't know any more than I did. Mumma had shooed them out too, and like the restless, happy-go-lucky little people we were, we soon got back to the business of shouting, running, and screaming around the neighborhood.

But I never forgot that incident, and I started keeping my eyes open, so to speak—becoming aware, for the first time, really, of what was going on around my house. I started noticing that from time to time during that summer of 1929, several white men ate at our house. I never saw anyone of them more than once, and I was convinced that none of us had ever seen them before. Where did they come from? What were they doing here? I was too young to know about the Great Depression. I had overheard some adults talking about it, but its effect on us didn't seem to be too great. I did not know then that we were so poor already that we didn't really feel the significance of the crash. All I knew was that these white men were getting into our house somehow, and I was determined to figure out how—and why.

It didn't take long to determine that they were coming in the back door; if they had come through the front everybody would have seen them. I started playing in the back more regularly, engineering little games with my aunts and uncles so that I could keep a vigilant eye on the door.

One day I noticed a white man coming down the alley. He was dressed casually, in clothes that had once been fine for that era, though by then they looked a little worn. All in all, he looked respectable, which is what made me watch him carefully. He did not belong in the back alley. I stayed in my hiding place around the corner of the house until the man walked up to our back door and opened it—it was never locked—and then I rushed stealthily in behind him.

Our back door, like the back door to all the houses on our street, was at ground level, but the kitchens was up a flight, so you had to feel your way up the dimly lit back stairs and knock on the door upstairs to get in. I followed the white man up the stairs; I stopped when I heard him knock on the kitchen door. The door opened and Mumma stood there, calm and serene, wiping her hands on her apron.

The man had taken off his hat when he had come in the downstairs door. Now, looking down at it, he spoke respectfully to Mumma.

"Good afternoon, ma'am."

"Good afternoon, sir." Mumma's quiet voice floated down the stairs like a soprano saxophone, her West Indian accent a colorful counterpoint to the man's baritone.

"It sure is nice weather we're having."

"Yes." She took in a deep breath and let it out slowly. I could have spent the whole afternoon listening to my grandmother's sighs. "But it is uncommon warm this summer."

The man looked up. It seemed a matter of honor, a mark of

respect shown to my grandmother, that he should not be servile and groveling. His courage made it possible for her to refuse him if she had to, with a dignity equal to his own. "Ma'am, I am mighty hungry. Could you spare me a little supper?"

I was beyond movement and speech. I crouched in the lower hallway and watched this human drama unfolding before me as if I were in a theater. It was so remarkable to me that I could hardly take it all in. The white man had just asked a black woman, with at least ten dependent children, to feed him. I could not comprehend it.

Mumma pulled the door open a little wider. "Of course," she replied. "Come right in and sit down at the table. Supper will be ready in a few minutes." She shut the door after he came in, but I scooted up the stairs and pushed it back open just a hair so that I could see.

We didn't have a lot of furniture in our kitchen, just the table and chairs and some basins for washing up. The white man sat down and waited patiently. They didn't talk much, he and Mumma, but the silence wasn't hard or sharp. It flowed in and out of the kitchen like a breeze. It was a peaceful, composed silence, like a well-trained child who knew how to behave himself in public.

Soon the food was ready, and Mumma dished it onto a plate. The man ate greedily, but he used good table manners. A couple of the children burst into the room, but Mumma ran them right back out again, just as she had done to me. The white man had put his fork down when the children entered, but when he realized that they weren't staying, he took up eating again as if it were his religion. At one point he complimented Mumma on one of the dishes, probably her peas and rice, which really was something. He finished the meal, thanked Mumma profusely, and turned to leave. I flew back down the stairs and around the corner, and I watched him come out the back door, close it carefully, and continue down the alley.

Over and over again that summer I snuck up the stairs to watch my grandmother feed hungry white men. Hungry black folks came sometimes too, but they came in the front door and ate with the family. The white men always came to the back. I don't know why they chose our door. Maybe they passed the word around that Mumma had food and a willingness to share it—I don't know. I don't even know how it is that we always *had* some kind of food. I only know that Mumma never turned any of them away. White men came to the house, they would ask politely for food, and they were grateful for anything they got. They acted toward this black woman the way that blacks were expected to act toward whites—respectful and considerate, courteous and mannerly. They thanked her profusely and they left.

Mumma never explained why she did what she did. She was a woman who rarely gave explanations as answers. In those days we children rarely asked questions. Those summer evenings during the end of the Depression, when white men walked down the small alley between our house and the next and knocked on our back door asking for food, we never asked why we should feed them. My grandmother would not have added the impoliteness of us staring at them to the humiliation of having to beg for food, so she would not often allow us to remain in the kitchen while they ate. She just fed those men and we took it as a natural routine.

In my childhood, like my daughter in hers and now my grandson in his, I wondered how black people could exhibit such trust and gracious hospitality in the midst of devastating racial oppression. Even as a small child, I knew to be careful because white people were "different." I knew that they could be dangerous, that they might hate us and act on their hatred with impunity. We were taught to be warily silent, to be carefully courteous in the presence of these people.

But my grandmother's kindness did not stem from her sense of danger. She fed white men food that had to be shared with her ten children because of something entirely different from fear or wariness. Her legacy became my mother's, and mine, and my daughter's, and now my grandson's. My mother went on to continue to perform what I consider to be acts of unusual generosity. One time she allowed a homeless white woman and her daughter to share our house for three weeks.

She tried to explain her philosophy about this to me, but her explanation seemed short and inadequate to the circumstances. I asked my mother why she let that white woman come into our house. Her only answer was, "Everybody's got to expect some trials if you want to get through this life." But that didn't make sense to me then.

I am fascinated by how this tradition, so important to my family, has been passed down through four generations without us really talking much about it. We learned kindness to strangers through the acts of my grandmother and my mother—acts that were not considered extraordinary or remarkable. It was something that you just did because it was part of you, normal because it was right. We were taught by example that you were obliged to those less fortunate than you, no matter how temporary the misfortune. We were taught that this responsibility and our willingness to assume it was what made us human in our own eyes, even if we were somehow less than human in the eyes of others. Our oppression became a unique perspective from which to view the oppression of others.

My grandmother fed those men, my mother housed that woman, I helped that sick man, and my daughter lifted that transient off the street because we understand hunger and need in the eyes and heart as well as in the stomach, and we minister to those needs because we see ourselves as most fully human when we are most humane.

My daughter and my grandson have asked me the question, "Why?" but there really is no answer. I do not help people for a specific reason; I just do it. It is part of the natural contours of my being, and I am proud to know that my daughter and her son have inherited the legacy of my mother and grandmother. I know that I can care, even in the context of being uncared for. I can learn compassion for people who are not always compassionate. I know that because my kindness is normal for me and not dependent on another person's response.

It is important to know that life reaches beyond the black and white categories we have created for it. There will always be inconsistencies and complexities in our lives. I know now that it is within these paradoxes and contradictions that we learn to see ourselves as whole people.

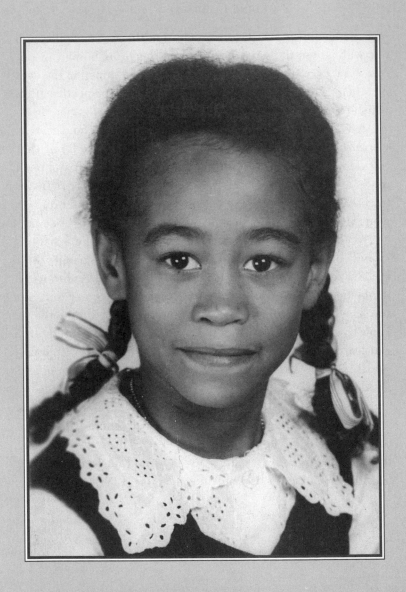

Amitiyah Elayne Hyman

A minister in the Presbyterian church for eighteen years, Amitiyah Elayne Hyman began her own company called SpiritWorks in Washington, D.C., in 1998. Consulting with individuals and institutions, she designs prayers and rituals that assist people with self-acceptance, self-love, and the ability to be open and vulnerable to others. As a "mixed-blood woman," she brings African, Native American, and European traditions together in her rituals.

Amitiyah's writing also serves as a healing ritual. "Racism fed a cycle of abuse in which I was trapped as a child," she says, "and writing out this story helped me to heal from that abuse." In this true story she revisits the horror she felt in 1948, when she was first forced to defend herself against a racial epithet.

When I asked Amitiyah for her thoughts about Dr. Martin Luther King, Jr.'s dream, she said that it is no longer applicable. "The twenty-first century will be the time for people of color, the earth's majority, to come into their own. King's dream is *too small* for the future."

STICKS AND STONES
AND WORDS AND BONES

We only met outside, in air that was cold and stung our faces, or in warm breezes that invited us to catch lightning bugs before bedtime. We cherished these sidewalk encounters, escapes from overheated kitchens and sun-starved hallways, an older sister's bossiness, and forced afternoon naps. They made us feel special, adventurous, beyond the limits imposed on kindergartners in a steel-workers' town on the Ohio River in 1948.

We would sit on the steps of the house between our two houses—a buffer zone that held our little end of the block, of blue collars and rednecks and black professionals, together. Swaddled in maroon corduroy leggings or knee-padded overalls, blue wool peacoats, rubber boots, and mismatched mittens that never wanted to stay on our hands, we enjoyed each other.

Passersby might have guessed that we were the best of friends, or cousins perhaps, from the way we whispered and laughed into each other's faces in the middle of winter. They would have missed that our faces were the colors of sweet vanilla and caramel cream, that my thick dark braids were rebelliously unraveling in the moist heat of my scalp, and that her short, straight blond hair was stringy and wet in the dampness. Our heads were hidden, sweating inside earmuffs and knitted caps, which taunting boys, from across the street, dusted white with well-aimed snowballs.

Our shovels, wooden sleds, and buckets lay nearby. Once we began to talk, they seemed to fall away, forgotten in the rush of intimacy. We discarded imaginary playmates, birthday gifts, and Christmas favorites as if they had been leaky boots or outgrown sweaters. Somehow we understood that as long as we stayed in the safe zone between our two houses and came when mothers clapped or called, we could continue the giggling and tickling and the whispering games we'd grown to love. We played patty-cake and hopscotch back and forth, first on one leg, then on the other, in foot-high mounds of snow.

> *Little Sally Walker, sitting in a saucer,*
> *Wipe your weeping eyes.*
> *Rise, Sally, rise.*

At first we didn't notice that our mothers kept their distance. They never ventured out of shaded doorways or warm kitchens to chat or to see what was going on. They didn't join in our laughter and whispering. Instead, they vigilantly kept themselves apart, watching for us through screened doors and upstairs bedroom windows. We made an unspoken pact with them—if they allowed us to cross yards and fences, then no one else need go beyond the boundaries or break invisible barriers set up by city sidewalks, conforming siblings, and disapproving fathers. Our little-girl forays compensated for grown-up dislikes and distances, for long held habits of fear.

She first said the words, after we marveled about the storm the night before and the way the moon said "hush" over the blanketed street. They fell out of her lips like jacks from her hand, plopping haphazardly onto the brick-and-concrete steps that had been shoveled earlier in the day. The sting of them sent tremors through my body that found a resting place in the soft tissues of my heart. They froze the spot and sent chills down my arms. They numbed my fingers.

"NIGGER. My daddy says that you're a NIGGER."

"Never let anyone call you NIGGER," was the mantra my father had drilled into my head.

Hot tears swirled up from somewhere deep, spilled out onto flushed cheeks, dripped into my lap. They warmed my hands and released my stiff fingers. I began to shake uncontrollably as I reached for a piece of brick, lying near the stoop, to steady myself. I snatched off my mittens. My fingers tore at the stone. Curling themselves around it, they locked onto its sharp, frozen hardness.

> *Sticks and stones can break my bones*
> *but words can never harm me . . .*
> *Sticks and stones can break bones and words . . .*
> *Break bones and words can . . .*
> *Harm me . . .*

She saw the impact her words had upon my body as they flew from her thin lips, forming tiny darts of puffy gray-white air. They seemed to hang suspended in the stinging cold for an instant before they pierced my flesh. Then they disappeared into the frost. As if to prolong their power, she fired them rapidly, over and over again:

NIGGER, NIGGER, NIGGER, NIGGER,
Nigger, niggerniggerniggerniggernigger
niggerniggerniggernigger . . .

It was the way we played; we repeated grown-up words, trying them on for size the same way we donned dress-up clothes and pretended we were adults. If one word was sufficient, then we'd say ten for rhythm's sake. They tickled our mouths. It was fun, we thought, repeating grown-up words.

But I couldn't laugh with her. This word had hit its mark. I was impaled on it. In the background, I heard the drone of numerous warnings, the veiled threat of my gruff-voiced father. From that moment on, I believed that something terrible was going to happen to me. I knew I had set an unalterable chain of events into motion. I feared that they would avalanche, burying me in shame. I was cursed, doomed. I had let somebody call me "NIGGER." It wasn't just any old body, either; it was my friend. That really hurt.

Before I could stop myself, I wrenched out the loosened brick, heavy in my little girl's unmittened hand, and lifted it to her head, smashing it into her face. I heard the crack as it connected with her forehead in a well-positioned strike. The boys across the street howled and hooted their approval. She screamed in pain. Blood began to spread over her eyebrows, dripping into her eyes, rolling off her nose, down her snotty lips, and over her trembling chin. It pooled, making large polka dots on her play clothes.

For a moment we were freeze-framed by the clash of energies. Her words and my well-aimed brick had done what wary mothers could not do. The safe zone between our houses melted like snow, evaporating in the scorch of this ancient bat-tle, begun by great-grandparents centuries ago. Now we played out the script. We ran to our mothers, scrambling in terror, falling in and out of snowdrifts. Skidding over the porch, I leapt into the vestibule, scattering icy wetness everywhere. I hurled myself through the doorway into the outstretched arms of my mother. She'd heard the wailing and had seen me coming from the lace-curtained living room window.

My father, who had been working in his second-floor study, raced downstairs to us. I was sobbing, and I didn't want to tell him what had happened. I was fearful of his wrath; after all, had-n't I let someone call me "NIGGER"? I had survived her teasing, but could I stand up to his hot anger? Too many tongue-lashings and belt strappings told me that was impossible.

My heart was hammering. I could have exploded. My chest wall, brains, and clenched teeth wanted to shatter like icicles into sharp pointy pieces. My father tried to wrench me loose from my mother. I tried to avoid his grip. Gasping for air, I twisted toward my mother and buried my face in her aproned belly.

The glass door of the house began to shake. My father whirled around in response to the pounding and the pacing on our porch. I saw her father's red menacing face. His shirttails flew from unbuttoned pants that he hadn't bothered to cover with a jacket. The two men glared at one another, straining shoulders, flexing arms, rocking back and forth on their heels. My father wore his slippers; her father had on metal-clipped boots. My mother peeled me loose from around her waist and took up a position at my father's side. Together they formed a phalanx, an impenetrable wall against him. Her father yelled and paced, threatening me and my parents.

Standing tall with stone-still faces, they held their ground. They refused him access to me. My father snarled as he spit words out: "I've told Elayne never to let anyone call her NIG-GER. She was obeying my instructions."

What he didn't say in that moment was that he himself had called me "little nigger" more times than I care to remember. It was a mean "pet" phrase, handed down from one generation of colored to another. It migrated, in their mouths, from the deep south of Edisto Island, South Carolina, to Pittsburgh, Pennsylvania. It took up residence in his mouth. He used the phrase like a stick, stalking me and my older sister. Whenever we displeased him, he struck us with it. I felt helpless in those moments, unable to defend myself, knowing that I could not go up against this big man's insults with my little girl's body, my little girl's hate, my little girl's hurt.

All of those "little niggers" coalesced around the big one I'd heard just moments before. Together they formed a tight fist, knotting beneath the surface of my skin. The knot remains. That brick-bearing little girl stays with me. She is vigilant and available, should the need arise, to explode against taunts and bullies. Now she has a well-stocked arsenal and seldom wears mittens.

Our friendship ended on a day when brooding clouds swirled past steel mills, sullied snow drifted into puddles and onto porches. Our intimacy terminated with her father's insolent retreat from our porch. She traveled through icy streets, past snowbound buildings, to the hospital where doctors stitched her face. I cried, watching the empty street from my bedroom window. Cold wind stirred cruel words and frigid rage into a witches' brew of sticks and stones. Together they erased the spot where we had laughed and whispered, before the blood ran down.

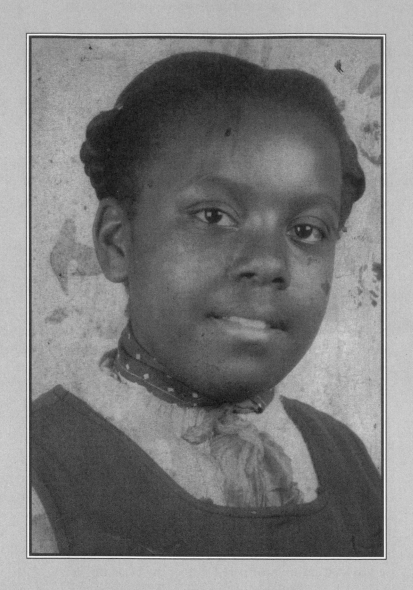

Staajabu

In this loving look at her father and his "life of crime," Staajabu takes us back to the beginning of the 1950s, when she was eight years old and living in racially divided Camden, New Jersey. "My father was very proud and did everything he could to keep us from having to deal with white people altogether," she says. "I was always under the impression that they were inferior to us, or that something was wrong with them . . . ." Nevertheless, when she was old enough to go to kindergarten, she became best friends with a white girl named Darlene. "Our friendship caused a lot of whispers," she recalls.

In her fifties now, Staajabu has coauthored four books of poetry and stories with her daughter, V. S. Chochezi. The books are entitled *Crucial Comments and Vicious Verses* (1990), *BAMM!* (1992), *This Queendom Come* (1994), and *Taking Names and Pointing Fingers* (1997).

255 SYCAMORE STREET

"How many left?" I heard Mr. Benny ask, as Daddy handed him another gallon of moonshine.

"Eight or ten," Daddy said. "We be thu inna minute."

Mr. Benny was standing in a knee-deep dirt hole, and he gently laid the jug down next to the others that were lying in four long rows, side by side, with the dirt all around them providing a cushion.

We had been burying liquor since the sun went down that warm fall evening. Mom said to wait so the neighbors couldn't see exactly what was going on. We had gotten the word just before breakfast. We were going to be raided, and the whole family and some of Mom and Daddy's friends were working as hard and fast as they could to take the huge whiskey still down from the third floor of our house on Sycamore Street. They had to help dismantle and haul off the vats, barrels, tubes, hoses, hot stoves, bags of barley, hops, corn, and sugar. Then the funnels, buckets, tables, stands, and who knows what all else, using wheelbarrows and Daddy's and Mr. Wash's big old trucks. Then they had to shut off all the drainage hoses and water pipes, cap them, and bury twenty-eight glass gallon jugs full of corn whiskey in the back yard. They were buried real deep, too—at least two-and-a-half feet—all in one big wide hole covered with the richest, blackest, sweetest-smelling dirt you could imagine. After the last jugs were put in and covered up, we put all the tools and equipment on top of where the liquor was buried in the left corner of the yard, at the back, near the fence that was between us and the Smiths, and where we also kept the woodpile.

There were different crops growing during different times of the year in the rest of the yard. Not long before, it was okra, tomatoes, squash, and string beans. The right side of the yard had a huge fig tree. We loved the figs, but Mom used switches from the tree to whip us when we got too far out of hand. My sister, Kitty, and I got so many whippings that once she was talking about burning the tree down. But the figs were so sweet she said she just couldn't do it.

Daddy never did talk much unless he was telling stories about his family (he had twenty-four brothers and sisters) or explaining how to do something like lay bricks, hammer nails, mix cement, or fix a car, and that night he was really short on talk and long on thought. Everybody was so tight you could feel it in your bones. Mom had that "I tole you dis was gonna happin" look all over her, and that wasn't good. We children just stayed out of the way unless they needed us for something. We had already done most of the digging and had been running up and down the stairs carrying what we could out to the trucks till the third floor back room was cleaned out and looked like a regular bedroom again, with some of the best secondhand bedroom furnishings black folks could afford in 1951.

Gone was the bubbling, cooking, steaming, dripping whiskey still that had filled that room for as long as I could remember. Gone! No more watching the magnificent spectacle for hours on end after school, or hearing the regular rhythmic thumps of the pipes and hoses letting out steam with gurgles and hisses. Gone was the unmistakable odor of sweet, poignant, intoxicating spirits, which seemed to be with me all the time— in my clothes, following me, surrounding me like an aura.

My daddy was a bootlegger. He wasn't just a bootlegger; he made the best whiskey in the area. At least that's what I over- heard at some of the "likka taystin' pardees" Daddy would give at 255 Sycamore Street. Everybody would be all dressed up, and Kitty and I would sneak a peek through the stair railing. There would even be white folks there, and everybody in Camden, New Jersey, knew my daddy didn't like no white folks coming around our house "for nuthin'."

We finished around eight that night, and everybody just kind of looked around to make sure things would look normal when the police came. "I'll start gittin' the chillun ready now," Mom said. She was taking us to Toledo so we wouldn't be there when the raid happened. Too exciting! We were going to ride on a train—me, my sister Kitty, and my big brother, Hubert. Next to Daddy, Hubert was my favorite person in the whole world. He was sixteen and all my girlfriends could talk about was how cute he was!

"Great goodness, D," Mr. Benny said. Daddy's close friends called him D, D.P., or Boot. Uncle Andrew said they called him that because he was so black. Some of my aunts said they called him Boot because he made bootleg liquor. "These chillun sure have grown. How old 'er you, Vicki?"

"Eight," I replied, looking up into Mr. Benny's round, red- dish-brown face and pleasant smile as we were walking toward the back porch. Mr. Benny always smiled with his mouth closed, and his eyes twinkled like my daddy's. He liked us and it showed, but I never was too long on talk, either.

"I'm eleven." Kitty spoke right up. "Had my birthday in May." Kitty was usually long on talk and short on thought, but even she was kind of quiet tonight.

"Know anybody want to marry 'em?" Daddy asked Mr. Benny. "They eat'n me outa house and home. Got me wearin' ovaraws f' draws."

We all laughed for the first time since getting news of the raid. Somebody on the syndicate's payroll told them, I found out in later years. At the time, all I knew was we were going to be raided, and my folks knew the date and the time and had everything organized so we were able to cover everything up in half a day.

Hubert was sixteen, but he had asthma so bad that, after helping move the wood back, he went to take his medicine. Everyone else started heading for their homes or cars. "Thanks, yawl!" "Night," Mom and Dad called to Mr. Benny, Mr. Arbry, and Mr. Wash.

Mr. Benny had the stub of a cigar in the corner of his mouth and the smell of moonshine all around him. With his gloves in his back pocket, he was headed for his '51 black Pontiac parked at the curb in front of the house. One by one we went up the concrete steps, across the concrete porch Daddy built the summer before.

Daddy built the front steps too. They had a ledge on either side where we could sit. He'd had a construction company for a while and built houses all over south Jersey. The men walked down the five concrete steps and across the red brick sidewalk to Mr. Benny's car. Daddy's car was parked in front of his. Mr.

Wash's truck was in front of Daddy's black 1951 Cadillac. The street lights lit the way, illuminating Daddy's six-foot, muscular frame in its white coveralls. Daddy drove a lot of different cars. He worked as a chauffeur when he wasn't working construction, during the winter. In Jersey, construction work was scarce from November through March, so Daddy did a lot of other things then, and he traveled a lot. There were rumors, and I heard Mom tell this to Miss Sis one day over the back fence, that he was hooked up with the Mafia driving stolen cars across state lines, and that was why he was gone so much.

"Don't forget to play that number I gave ya, Grace," Mr. Arbry told Mom. "Eight in the lead. Play it straight. Just like I dreamed it. Checked the dream book. When you dream eights like I did, means money for sho."

"Soon's Joe's or Harry's open tamarra," Mom said. Mr. Arbry was tall and lean. He ran a gas station in Philly where we would stop whenever we took liquor over there. Sometimes he did work on Daddy's cars. He had chestnut-brown, close-cut nappy hair, light brown eyes, and always wore blue coveralls and smelled like gasoline. He gave me and Kitty a dollar whenever he saw us because he said we were so black and pretty.

"Better you play it with Henry when he comes round. He pays off by six," said Mr. Arbry.

Mom just nodded. She was tired. We were all tired. Daddy took my hand as we walked back to the house. He had big, rough black hands that looked like they were carved from old tree bark. He picked me up under my arms, leveled his eyes with mine, and looked at me.

"You too big for me to be pickin' up, yuh know?" Then he hugged me tight and I hugged him back.

The men left in their cars and trucks. We went back in the house, and Daddy lit a kerosene lamp and sat down in the big green chair next to the pot-bellied coal stove in the middle room. He pulled out his guitar from behind the chair and started strumming and humming. He was looking down at the guitar with me standing right next to him. His big eyes looked up at me as he sang "Am I blue? Am I blue? Ain't these tears in my eyes tellin' you?" Daddy was home and nothing else in the whole world really mattered to me. No police raid, no whiskey, nothing.

When Kitty and Mom came in we fixed dinner—one of my favorites—corned beef hash and cabbage with cornbread. After cleaning up the dishes, we sang and played hand games, with Daddy cheating and letting us catch him, the rest of the evening. When he put us to bed he told us he wanted us to be good for Mom when we went to Ohio, and he told us again about what we could and could not say to other people if we were asked any questions about "yo daddy making whiskey." We had heard this so many times, we just nodded our heads and agreed that we were not to answer any questions or talk to anyone about the raid or the whiskey still. We didn't ask questions about anything. That just wasn't done. Children did not ask questions about "grown folks' business."

Mom hit the number the next day with Slick Henry, the numbers man, and we left for Toledo that night. She played 809 boxed for five dollars and played the eight as a lead for five. We went to Ohio wearing all new clothes and carrying all new suitcases. Mom says now that after she won the five hundred dollars she was seriously thinking about not coming back to Jersey at all. But we would have had to live with her family in Ohio, and at least in Jersey she had her own home.

The raid was in all the newspapers two days later. It didn't make front page headlines, but they had a picture of Daddy and another man being led to a police car. Miss Sis sent us a copy of the article. There was no evidence to confiscate, the article said, and, after the suspects were picked up and held for questioning, they were released.

When we returned two weeks later, Daddy wasn't there. After helping get all the luggage out of the cab, I bolted up three flights of stairs as fast as I could to see what was on the third floor. I was running as fast as my fat, short, brown eight-year-old legs would carry me, and my barrettes were bouncing up and down, beating me all upside my head, but even so, I heard the thumping of the pipes, the hissing of the valves, the bubbling of the vats, and I smelled the sweet corn whiskey welcoming me home.

Arthur B. Arnold

Now retired and living in Warren, Ohio, where he grew up, Arthur Arnold has worked as a truck driver, a steelworker, a supervisor, and a manager in various industries.

"I'm not a self-made man," Arthur says. Quick to credit others for their help with his career, his happy family life, and his writing, he says of his story, "My father gave me the words, my family gave me the motivation and support, my childhood friends gave me their camaraderie. I am only the vessel."

Having grown up in a racially integrated environment, the painful reality of racism did not hit Arthur until he was a teenager. "Watching professed 'Christians' partake in race-hate acts," he says, "stripped me of my naïveté and convinced me that the hereafter population will be small."

FIELD OF BEANS

It was the summer of 1954 when I first began to understand segregation and racism. Really understand it. I was just shy of my twelfth birthday. Maybe, for some reason I've yet to understand, my friends and I had been chosen to remain ignorant for so long.

We lived in a small, mixed community called Bolindale. It's just southeast of Warren, Ohio. Every aspect of my life was integrated—from the community, to Bolindale Grade School up on the hill, to the church my family attended.

Of course, my folks had told me about segregation and racism. My mother, aunts, and uncles, and all the older black people I knew, had been born in the south. They understood it up close and personal. I'd listened intently as they talked about their experiences "down south." I'd sat on the steps leading upstairs, out of sight, and eavesdropped as they relived the horrors of racism.

They'd talked about the hangings, the burnings, and so many other things I couldn't understand. What I couldn't comprehend was how so many white people had enough hate in their hearts to act worse than animals. Animals killed for food. These white people killed for pleasure.

But hearing how bad things were down south wasn't like experiencing it. Some things can be taught. Other things have to be lived to be really understood. Such was the case with segregation and me.

I had three close friends—two colored and one white—and we wanted to make some money. The pocket change our parents gave us from time to time never came anywhere near meeting our childish expectations. Our parents just didn't have it to give. We knew that. We weren't destitute. Just poor. All of us. Black and white.

In an effort to make some money, we found and cashed in soda bottles. It was something, but it didn't help much. Two cents for the small bottles and a nickel for the large bottles. And even they were hard to find because most people kept their empties and turned them in for credit when they bought groceries.

Egg cartons were another source of revenue, if you could get your hands on them. Mr. Coast, the little old white man who had the store up on the avenue, would pay three cents for each usable carton. His son had a small chicken farm and was always in need of used egg cartons to help cut his costs.

Getting a job at one of the neighborhood stores was out of the question. They're referred to now as mom-and-pop stores. Mom and Pop did everything for themselves. Most of them lived in the back of, or upstairs over, their stores. They had their own kids who did the sweeping, unpacking, running errands, and everything else that was needed. We had the energy and the desire, but we just couldn't find any jobs.

Elmore Jones, one of our small group of friends, came up with the answer. He lived just inside the city, about three miles from us. He told us about the truck farms. I thought he was just kidding. Trucks were made in a factory. They certainly weren't grown on a farm. Even a fool had to know that. He explained that the farmers grew vegetables. They paid thirty-five cents a basket for picking beans.

Thirty-five cents! We had to hunt bottles and cartons all day long to come up with enough to make thirty-five cents. Once we were convinced that he was telling us the truth, visions began to dance in our heads. We sat down and figured it out.

There were four of us. Robbie, Poochie, Elmore, and me. We could each pick ten baskets (so we thought) easily. At thirty-five cents a basket, that was three dollars and fifty cents. There were four of us, so that meant we would bring home fourteen dollars. Fourteen dollars! That was more than a lot of grown-ups made in one day. In a week we would have seventy dollars!

Our thoughts were skyrocketing. Thumm's bike shop had some nice bikes for around thirty dollars. In just two weeks we would have enough money to buy each of us a new bike. And beyond that, after we had the bikes, the potential was unlimited. We were so excited we couldn't wait to get started.

It was time for us to learn that nothing is as simple as it seems. The first pin to prick our bubble filled with dreams came from Poochie's older brother. After hearing our plan, he told us that Robbie couldn't go. We stood with mouths agape as he explained that the bus sent to pick up the bean pickers wouldn't take him because he was white.

I'd heard about colored people in the south not being able to get on a bus. And when they did they had to sit in the back because white people got the seats in the front. It didn't make any sense to me. A white not being able to get on a bus? We rode the city buses all the time. Black and white. And we sat wherever we wanted to sit. It was all too confusing.

Poochie's older brother went on to explain that all the pickers were colored. And the whites who worked on the farm didn't pick. They worked in the barns, drove the tractors and trucks, and did the better-paying jobs. And none of them ever got on the pickers' bus.

I could see that Robbie wanted to cry. He held his tears back, though. All of our wonderful plans, and now he was being excluded. He said, in a choked voice, that it didn't matter. But I knew it did. I was hurt too. It was like we were going to be separated from a family member. Like we would never see him again. The ways of the world were forcing themselves into our lives, splitting us apart.

We decided that we wouldn't go either. Not if Robbie couldn't go with us.

"Suit yourself," Poochie's older brother said. "But you may as well get used to it. If you want to make some money you have to go where the money is."

We talked for a long time after he left. It was decided that we would go to the bean fields and work. It would take a little longer, since Robbie couldn't be included, but we would make the money to buy the bikes. And we were going to buy one for Robbie too.

Robbie's part, once we got the bikes, was to take care of them while we were at work. He was to keep them washed up and make sure none of the other kids got anywhere near them. Robbie was happy to play a part. Any part. It was all settled.

The three of us got permission from our folks to go pick

beans. We found out where the bus stopped and what time. There were two farms sending out buses. Beech's Gardens and Rutherford's Gardens. They paid the same, but Rutherford's bus came closer to where we lived, so we chose that one.

The second pinprick to our bubble of dreams came when we were told how the game was played. Often, there were more pickers than the bus could carry. Miss Bertha was the field boss over the pickers, and she chose who would get on the bus. She normally picked the older people. The people she could count on to do a good job.

We knew that we needed to prove that we were good workers. But to do so, we had to get on that bus.

Monday morning was the best time to get selected, so we were told. On the weekends, a lot of the older people went out to the nightclubs in the Flats, an all-black area of the city. Monday morning hangovers, the remnants of a weekend of getting drunk, prohibited many of them from making the early morning rise to pick beans all day in the hot sun. That was the best time for the unproven, us, to get a chance to go to the fields.

It was four-thirty in the morning when the alarm startled me awake. I shut it off quickly so it didn't disturb anyone else. My tired eyes, which felt like there was sand under my eyelids, made me question my desire to work. The bicycles didn't seem so important at that hour of the morning. It was the first time in my life that I'd ever gotten up so early, that I could remember.

I rolled out of bed and dressed in the dark. I went downstairs, washed my face and hands, brushed my teeth, and prepared my breakfast. It consisted of two hot dogs hurriedly washed down with a glass of Kool Aid. It was strange being up at that time of the morning, with everyone else sleeping.

I took the lunch I'd prepared the previous night out of the Coldspot—two baloney sandwiches, store-bought banana cake, and an apple. I filled an empty wine bottle with cold water from the tap. I'd removed the label, but there was no doubt that it was a Wild Irish Rose bottle. After some effort, I managed to crack a few ice cubes and force them down the neck. I figured the ice wouldn't last long, but it was better than nothing.

Elmore knocked on the door. Softly. Looking up at the clock, I noticed it was five minutes after five. We were late. It took half an hour to walk to the bus pickup point. And we had to stop for Poochie along the way. We left the house running. Missing the bus, after getting up so early, was something we didn't even want to think about.

Poochie was sitting on his porch, in the dark, when we arrived. Having made up lost time by running, we began the long trek down Deforest Road to the Pine Avenue Extension.

In total darkness—there were no streetlights—we walked through the silence and early morning dew, each lost in our own thoughts. And all a little bit nervous. This was our first independent venture into the world at large.

The morning air was moist and cold. Even with our heavy jackets on, we were chilled to the bone.

As we approached the pickup point, we could see silent forms standing there beside the road. The older people. The regulars. They eyed us suspiciously as we stood off to the side, not really joining them. We were feeling out of place. Not wanted.

"There's a lot of them," Elmore whispered. "Maybe we won't get on." We knew that we were standing at the last stop. Perhaps our dreams of making money were going to end right there. We stood in silence for a long time.

Headlights appeared in the distance. Finally, the old yellow school bus reached us and squealed to a stop. The grown-ups forced their way to the door, leaving us standing in the back of the crowd. I looked up at the windows. There weren't many people on the bus. Perhaps the Flats crowd had been smaller than normal. Just as we had been told.

A surly-looking little white man was driving the bus. Standing on the step nearest the door was Miss Bertha. I'd seen her before. She was a very big, tall woman with skin almost as dark as burnt cork. Her expression, always hostile, made her even more imposing. And her lower lip was always poked out by the wad of snuff forced into it.

I remembered she had three scars: one on her forehead, one on her left cheek, and one on her left forearm. They were long scars. Old scars. Scars from cuts that should have been sutured and weren't, leaving them raised like small puffy mountain ranges on otherwise smooth skin. Her hair was covered with a huge bandanna that was tied in a knot at the nape of her neck. On top of her head, pulled down until it touched the tips of her ears, was a wide-brimmed straw hat.

The thing I remembered most about her was that she would "kick your ass" if you messed with her. I had also heard that she could punch so hard she could knock men out. Big men.

She spoke to a few of the older people as they entered the bus. Her voice sounded like a rasp being drawn across a large piece of metal. Most of the people she just ignored.

Everyone was on the bus except us when she blocked the doorway. "You boys look awful little to me," she accused. "How old are you?"

"We're twelve," Elmore answered. He and Poochie were twelve. And I was almost twelve.

"Y'all ever picked beans before?" she asked.

"Yes, ma'am," Elmore said. And he was right. We had all picked beans in our folks' gardens. We'd never done it for money, though. I was happy he didn't volunteer that bit of information.

She eyed us suspiciously. "I'm going to let you boys on this bus. But y'all better pick a lot of beans, and you better not be playin' around either. Y'all's folks know you're here?"

"Yes, ma'am," we said in unison.

All the seats had been taken and there were already people standing in the aisle. We stood, holding on to the sides of the seats, all the way to the farm. It seemed to take forever. We had no idea where we were, or in which direction we were heading. "To the bean fields." That's all we knew.

Daylight was breaking when the bus slowed and pulled off the road. It followed a dirt path for a while. Then it ground to a stop. I'd never seen a bean field so big before. At least not up close. Perfectly straight rows of bean plants almost as far as the eye could see.

We laid our lunches on one of the seats and left the bus. On the left edge of the field sat a large truck. It was half filled with baskets. Miss Bertha led the way like a mother hen, with us chicks following close behind her.

Each picker was given two baskets. "Remember," the man handing out the baskets hollered out. "Thirty-five pounds in each basket. Fill 'em up." I noticed the scale sitting right behind him.

People grabbed their baskets and followed Miss Bertha. Single file. She led the way to the beginning of the rows. "You take these," she said, indicating each person's assignment. We each got three rows. Since we were at the back of the line, the others were already picking by the time we started to work. We noticed the others straddling the center row, picking that row and the rows to either side. We knew we were expected to do the same thing.

I looked down at my cold feet. We had walked through the dew-dampened weeds and grass, getting our shoes wet. Stepping into the dirt in the field turned our soles into cakes of mud. I bent over at the waist and began to pick.

"You can't pick like that, boy!" Miss Bertha's voice rang out. I was embarrassed. I was getting hollered at and I hadn't even picked more than three beans. "I thought y'all told me you'd picked before. Get down on them knees and git to picking like you got some sense!"

The cold, damp soil immediately stuck to the knees of my pants. I could feel the moisture seeping from my hands and wrists up through the sleeves of my coat as soon as I shoved them down into the first bean plant. And beyond the first plant, the moisture from the beans I hadn't already picked wet my pants between the legs. I looked like I had peed myself. Bean picking wasn't what I'd expected. As a matter of fact, I hadn't thought about it much at all except for the money we were going to make. And the bicycles.

I'd been trying to keep an eye on Miss Bertha. She'd already hollered at me once. I certainly didn't want to displease her again. "Ya'll lagging behind." Her voice came from behind us, making me jump. I glanced over at the rows to our left, where everyone else was. Yes. They were yards ahead of us. Damn, I thought. I didn't know this was a race. "Y'all better quit talking so much and start to picking." We hadn't said a word to one another. I imagine it was the shock of the whole situation. We were overwhelmed, for some reason. We started to pick faster. My fingers, still numb from the cold, began to burn a little from pulling the beans.

"I don't know." Poochie was the first to complain. "This bean picking ain't what I thought. Just look at me. I'm all wet and muddy. My feet and hands are freezing. And it's going to take forever to fill up these damn baskets."

He was expressing my feelings too. "And that old woman keeps hollering at us," I said.

"Us, hell," Elmore said. "She was hollering at you."

"Not just me," I protested. I needed to share the blame and the sting of my humiliation.

"You all better quit talking," Poochie said. "You know she don't want us talking." We continued picking, suffering, and mumbling to one another like the convicts did in prison movies, trying to talk to one another without turning our heads or moving our lips. I felt like a prisoner. In the middle of that bean field in the middle of who knew where. No way to leave even if we wanted to. That old yellow retired school bus wasn't going anywhere until almost dark. All of a sudden I really missed home. And my mother. And Robbie. I wondered what he was doing.

"Quiet. There she is," Elmore said.

Looking up, I saw Miss Bertha coming down our rows. I glanced over and saw that we had lost even more ground to the other pickers. They had a full thirty yards on us. Oh hell, I thought. She's going to get us again. We kept our heads down, clamped our lips shut, and picked as fast as we could.

She stormed right past us. I didn't look up, but I could feel her staring daggers into me.

"Damn it all to hell!" she shouted, her voice leaving us quaking on our knees. "Y'all can't pick for shit. Look at this!"

We turned our heads in unison, like they were wired together, and she looked directly at me. She was straddling my middle row and bending a bean plant over with her foot. "Y'all missing too damn many beans. Git your narrow asses back here and pick these."

I felt some solace in the fact that she had said "Y'all," even though she was examining a bush I had picked. "And you! The yellow one! You're worse than them other two. Look here. You missed more beans on this one plant than you got in that damn basket."

My heart sank. She had singled me out. I knew she was referring to me because both of my buddies were chocolate colored. "If y'all can't do no better than this, then get your narrow asses on that bus and sit there until we go home. And don't bring your no-picking butts back out here no more!"

She stormed away and we began to grumble in that prisoner-like way we had just learned, while we tried to pick faster. Poochie started to chuckle. "She got all in your ass, Bo." We called each other Bo when we were deviling one another.

"She was talking to all of us," I said, trying to share the blame.

"Well," Elmore said. His daddy was a preacher, and Elmore mocked his pulpit-speaking style when he really thought he was being funny. "She done already damned you to hell. And hell ain't no laughing matter. But you got a bigger problem, Bo. The next time she check your rows and find they ain't picked right, she's likely going to put one of her big foots dead up in your ass."

I was mad and I wanted to fight them. Both of them. But I knew better. Miss Bertha was after me already. She probably didn't like light-skinned people, I surmised. (That's how I referred to myself. I hated being called yellow or high-yellow.) If she saw us fighting, she would surely take it out on me. I bit my lower lip until it pained me and kept on picking. As usual, Elmore and Poochie soon stopped deviling me. We were friends again.

We were still behind the others, but Miss Bertha seemed to be ignoring us. It was near noon. The stinging rays of the sun, once it had decided to make its grand appearance, burned the backs of our necks and penetrated the backs of our shirts. The mud on our trousers hardened in the heat and stiffened. The wet crotches of our trousers dried, hard, and made uncomfortable carrying cases for our family jewels.

Sweat dripped from our faces and ran into our eyes. We were miserable. Our hands were sore, as were our knees. And my back ached something awful. We had long since shed the coats that we'd worn that morning, and they were tied around our waists since we dared not take the time to walk back to the bus and fall further behind with our picking.

Quick trips to the woods to relieve ourselves were the only breaks we'd gotten. And even they had been the subject of ridicule from Miss Bertha.

"Y'all ain't got to go at once," she had shouted when she saw us heading for the woods. "What? Y'all need help to take care of your business?" All of the workers broke into laughter. Much to our embarrassment.

Finally, we had baskets of beans. Elmore was the first to smooth out his beans. Yes. They were level with the top of the basket. He was ready to take his beans over to the truck. "Seventy cents," he announced proudly. He scooped up his baskets, one in each hand, and headed out across the field. Poochie and I picked even faster, trying to fill our first baskets.

A few minutes later Elmore returned with what looked like two empty baskets and a look of dejection on his face.

"What's the matter?" I asked.

"Man," Elmore said, shaking his head from side to side. "Those folks ain't hardly right. That man took my first basket and put it on the scale. He said it didn't weigh thirty-five pounds. Then he started taking my beans out of the other basket and piling them on the first one until the needle said thirty-five pounds. He had the beans heaped up all around the handle." Elmore held one of the baskets out for us to see. "See this little bit of beans in here? That's what's left over after he filled the first basket."

My jaw dropped. As did Poochie's. Elmore had worked all morning and had only made thirty-five cents. He took the money out of his pocket and held the quarter and the dime in the dirt-stained palm of his hand. They looked lonely.

"Maybe if we put all our beans in one basket," I reasoned out loud, "we could do better."

Poochie looked at me as if I were retarded. "It's still the same amount of beans, fool." I didn't argue because I knew he was right.

Miss Bertha called everyone out of the fields to have their

half-hour lunch break. We went back to the stifling bus and retrieved our lunch bags. We then headed up on a little rise to sit under a large oak tree.

My lunch—hot, soggy baloney sandwiches—wasn't a treat. The mayonnaise that I had liberally applied had soaked into the bread, turning the sandwiches into a soggy mess. I ate half of one of them and threw the other half away. My apple looked tired and uncomfortable in the stifling temperature. I took two bites and threw it away too. Even the banana cake, something I usually cherished, wasn't pleasing to my palate. I forced it down. And my wine-bottle water container had succumbed to the temperature too. The water was hot enough to make a tepid cup of tea. It took only one sip to convince me that hot water was wet—nothing more.

Sitting in the shade of the tree, lunches hardly touched, we spotted a barn. Outside of it, we saw the white kids. They were driving tractors, unloading the baskets of beans, laughing, and having a good time. What Poochie's brother had said came to mind. I looked at the pickers sitting in the shade of a line of trees. Not one white person among them. Not one. It all began to make sense to me. Colored people got on their knees, got hollered at, and had all their beans poured into one basket. The white people took the baskets of beans and put them into the barn.

I wondered how they got paid. By how many tractors they drove? By how many baskets of beans they took out of the truck? Elmore seemed to know more than Poochie, so I asked him.

"How them white kids playing over at the barn get paid?" I asked.

"They get paid by the hour," Elmore replied. "At least that's the way I hear it."

"How much they get paid?" My interest was piqued.

"I hear tell they get paid thirty-five cents an hour," he said.

I wasn't a mathematician by any means. But it didn't take much math to figure out that Elmore had picked all morning and had thirty-five cents to show for it. And those white kids, being paid by the hour, had made a buck forty. And besides, they were having fun. I would have loved to drive a tractor or a truck—drive anything—and get paid for it.

Poochie's brow was furrowed, as it always was when he was thinking real hard. He finally spoke. "We ain't nothing but slaves. Only difference is that we're picking beans instead of cotton. And that's only because they can't grow cotton up here. Too damn cold." He thought for a while and then spoke again. "I got it," he said, a smile on his face. "Here's the plan. We put rocks in the bottom of the baskets. I know there's a lot of them out there in the bean field because my knees are sore from kneeling on 'em."

I thought about my knees. I was sure that all the skin had been worn away. My fingers were sore. And my back hurt. My mother had said, every time I had complained about stooping over in our own garden, that children didn't have backs. I now knew better, for sure.

Poochie went on. "The rocks will make the baskets heavier. We won't have to pick as many beans."

The plan sounded good. "Do they dump the beans out?" I asked Elmore. I was cautious. I didn't want to get caught.

"No," he said. "They just weigh 'em, make sure they're thirty-five pounds, and set 'em in the back of the truck."

A penny a pound, I thought. We were picking beans for a lousy penny a pound. And they probably had the scale fixed. They had set it so the needle said thirty-five when there were fifty or sixty pounds in the basket. We were being cheated. Well. We'd get them.

We saw Miss Bertha waving. We were so far away that we couldn't hear her voice too well. But we knew that it was time to go back to work. As soon as we reached our rows, we looked around cautiously, just like the convicts in the movies. Seeing that Miss Bertha was nowhere in sight, we began to empty Elmore's few beans into our baskets. After carefully lining the bottoms of his baskets with stones, we filled them with beans. We repeated the procedure until we had four level baskets of beans.

Smiling, Poochie and I headed for the bean truck. He rushed ahead of me to get there first. I didn't object. After all, it had been his idea. Besides, I reasoned, if anyone got caught it should be him, since it was his idea.

Poochie handed the baskets up to the white man on the truck. The white man sat the first basket on the scale and reached for the second basket, ready to add beans to the first one. "Bullshit!" he hollered when the first basket registered fifty-three pounds. He dumped the basket out into the bed of the truck. Out tumbled the rocks.

"Bertha! Bertha!" he shouted across the field. Miss Bertha got out of the bus and headed for the truck.

My mind was a blur. Well, at least she couldn't blame me. It wasn't my basket. "Look at what this boy is doin'," the white man shouted down to Miss Bertha. He pointed to the rocks resting atop the pile of beans. Then he picked up Poochie's second basket and dumped it out—with the same results, of course. I wanted to drop my baskets and run. But I was frozen with fear.

Miss Bertha glared at Poochie and then at me. I turned, attempting to make my way back to my rows. "Come on back here, yellow boy!" she said. Not seeing any options, I turned back. She snatched my baskets and emptied them onto the bed of the truck. There, for all to see, was the clear evidence that I was a thief too. "Give 'em thirty-five cents each!" she demanded of the man. He handed Poochie and me a quarter and a dime.

Miss Bertha scowled at both of us. "Get your sorry little asses on that bus!" she said. "And don't ever try comin' back out here! I ain't got no time for y'all's no-good, can't-pick-for-shit, sorry asses! And go get that other boy too. The one what's with you. Get the hell out of this field!"

Of course all the other pickers looked up when they heard the commotion. We hung our heads and walked back to get Elmore. We could hear the reprimands and see the eyes of the regular pickers "Damn kids ain't worth a shit." And, "Need to keep y'all's sorry asses out of these fields unless you want to work." And, "Y'all ain't nothing but shameful. No wonder we can't get no decent jobs." And, "Ain't nothing but little crooks."

We did as Miss Bertha had demanded. We got Elmore and headed for the bus. "I knew y'all was going to git y'all's butts caught," he said. "I knew it all the time. I knew that white man wasn't goin' to pay y'all for pickin' no rocks."

Elmore was like that. He went along with any idea until it went sour. Then he always pretended that he knew what the outcome was going to be ahead of time.

And I wasn't any better. I was the one who had tried to skulk off when Poochie had gotten caught. It was only the eagle eyes of Miss Bertha that had prevented me from leaving Poochie to suffer alone.

We had made one dollar and five cents for all of our pain and misery. The white kids had made a lot more than that, each one of them, for just playing around.

The rest of the afternoon we spent under a shade tree at the edge of the woods. The bus was so hot that we couldn't stay on it.

We made excuses for our actions. We said we'd just fought back because we were being ripped off. And that the white kids made more money for just playing in the barn. Mostly, we spent the time burying our dreams of bicycles among the trees that lined the field of beans.

Robbie was waiting when we got off the bus. "How much we make?" he asked excitedly, visions of bicycles dancing in his head.

"We ain't made shit," Poochie said. "What's this 'we' shit anyway? You ain't picked nary a bean." He was in a surly mood.

Robbie looked confused. He came up to me as we began our walk home. "No kidding around," he said. "How much did we make?"

"A dollar five," I said. I knew that Robbie would have been there too if they'd let him on the bus. It wasn't his fault.

"That's not too bad," he said, evidently trying to cheer us up. "It was only the first day." He counted in his head. "At least we got three dollars and fifteen cents. And we're just getting started."

I hated to burst his bubble. "No, Robbie," I said. "A buck

five for all of us." Robbie smiled, like he knew I was playing a joke on him. Then his face fell.

"You serious? You ain't funnin' me? We could have made a buck five cashing in pop bottles. You guys must not pick beans for crap."

It was just past five-thirty in the afternoon. We'd been gone for more than twelve hours and had a measly dollar and five cents to show for it. Miss Bertha was never going to let us on that bus again. Even if we'd wanted to go. And we didn't.

Ordinarily someone would have whopped Robbie upside the head for making such a comment. But what was the use? He wouldn't have understood it anyway. We'd just experienced something horrible. Our dreams were dashed. And we were too tired to fight.

Bernestine Singley

At almost fifty years of age, Bernestine Singley has had a life full of twists and turns. She worked her way up from welfare and the clutches of overzealous social workers in the south to being an attorney, a corporate executive, and a published author. Currently she is married, "child-free," as she says, working as a management consultant, and living in a Dallas suburb. Two of her short stories have appeared in recently published anthologies, one in *Kente Cloth* (1998) and the other in *¡Tex!* (1998).

"I see myself as one who has emerged victorious from a life of mental and spiritual assaults, both intra- and interracial," Bernestine says. In the true story that follows, she uses humor, irony, and finely tuned dialogue to depict her childhood discoveries about the attitudes that whites and the black middle class have in common. "By hearing and seeing the meanness of bourgeois black folks early, when I saw similar traits in white folks, it became clear that oppression was not race-specific."

Although Bernestine has enjoyed considerable academic and business success, she says her "primary identification is and will always be with the oppressed, especially people of color, and women and children around the world."

WHITE FRIENDS

"How can you be friends with them?!" my friend sputtered indignantly. She jammed her hands in her pockets, but still managed to shake a verbal finger in my face.

We were talking about white people and, consequently, about slavery, lynchings, segregation, poverty, violence, racism. It was the season of Clarence Thomas and Rodney King.

How can you be friends with them?

The answer has everything to do with the circumstances under which I was born. Having started out with things so far out of kilter, I suppose it was just a matter of time before I added white friends to the collection of paranormal phenomena that make up my life. Perhaps I can explain.

When I was around six months in the making, my grandmother beat my mother so brutally that my mother and my sister, then four years old, fled town with Uncle Tommy's help. I was born three months later, a birth not widely heralded. At least not by my grandmother and her side of the family. Although we were living with my father's sister and her husband, I have no recollection of them and so I can't speak to what their reaction might have been to my arrival. Except to say, of course, they knew I was coming. And then there I was.

I didn't arrive completely without fanfare, though. Right there in the delivery room, I literally used my entry into this world as an occasion to show my ass. There are those who would argue today that this approach marked me for life, that indeed it became my signature. But in this instance, I literally mean my ass, because my butt was where my head should have been, giving some who know me cause to claim that my head and my ass have often been juxtaposed in ways that defy nature and defeat my best interests.

Anyway, this was not a normal position. So, as my mother, Odessa, told it, the doctor reached in and turned me around. Straightened me out. This turn of events might have something to do with my subsequent experiences with men along the way who have felt the need to turn me around in an effort to straighten me out.

In any event, several days after my arrival, my sister had an idea and approached my mother. "You see," she told Odessa, "we don't need another baby in this house. So you can just take her right on back to that hospital."

The honesty and directness of that approach inspires me to this day. My sister was not confused.

Though I was born in the south, in the summer, as 1949 wended its way toward 1950, things did not fall into the easy, slow pace often associated with that time and place. My problems started when, from the beginning, Odessa forced me to understand my power to disagree with the general populace about who I am in relationship to them, the rest of the world.

Even though I was a precocious, stubborn child, I did not welcome this burdensome responsibility, this task of self-definition and, consequently, of self-defense. I wanted to be like everyone else. But I had no choice. Odessa said it was to be. And so it was.

Black, female, poor, and confident in the apartheid south of the U.S. was a heady recipe for danger, a brew sure to produce only one thing: a crazy nigger. A crazy baby nigger—I got off to a very early start.

When I was four, we moved out of the room we shared in the home of Bertha and Major Bunch and into a public housing project, a place where poor people and their families were bricked in and roundly despised.

Shortly afterward, a small white social worker came to our two-story flat, which had paper-thin, vomit-green walls, to verify the information that had previously submitted and was required to determine the amount of government subsidy—the welfare check—we were to receive.

Early on, the issue of my parentage ambled into the conversation and plopped down on the table, exposing the questionable origins of my existence and therefore my worthiness for government support. "So the Youngest Recipient is illegitimate," the social worker said, glaring at me, cutting me down to a millimeter.

"No," Odessa responded utterly remorselessly. "Bernestine is not illegitimate. I just wasn't married to her father." She was not one to lie or to shadow the truth.

"My baby is not illegitimate because, you see, God gave her to me just like He gave me my oldest daughter. And nothing that is the work of God can be illegitimate. Illegitimate is a man-made thing. My children come straight from God."

Instantly, I shot up to six feet tall.

The social worker raised her eyes to meet Odessa's steady

gaze, snorted, rolled her eyes back down to the form, and wrote in the block next to my name: *Illegit.*

I leaned against Odessa. She put her arm around me and saved me from being swallowed whole in that abbreviation.

That was the first of many visits from the social worker, every one of them unannounced. She cruised our home, eyeing cupboards for contraband ("No sugared cereal? No sodas? Good. They cost too much for what *you* have to live on"), pulling back the curtains in front of the closets, seeking the merest hint of a male presence ("Not even *one* boyfriend for such a good-looking woman like yourself?"), fingering my skirt or my sister's blouse while Odessa looked on silently ("Did Mother make these for you or did we go shopping and *buy* them *downtown?*").

By the time I reached kindergarten, I was diagnosed as severely anemic. Had low blood. Needed iron. Consequently, I was routinely at the health department, where the government corralled poor sick folks of all colors for the convenience of dispensing whatever medical attention was our due. I was poked and prodded and stuck and pulled by strange, always white, always male hands.

These trips contained their own lessons for a black child in 1950s Charlotte, North Carolina. After riding in the back of the bus to get to the health department, we signed in and then took our seats in the back of a huge hall, the part of the room reserved for coloreds. There I learned to sit and wait for my name to be called for services to be rendered on a first come, first served basis, unless you were lucky enough to be white, which meant that no matter how late you arrived, you always came before every single black person.

Our relationship with the welfare department and the health department lasted about eight years, during which my life seemed in constant peril. Time after time, Odessa was ordered to deliver me up to doctors who barely spoke English, which is really beside the point because, of course, they had no need to talk to us. They were doctors. We were poor, black, female. What could we tell them—even about ourselves—that was important to know?

Before I could be cured of "low blood," I developed "heart trouble": a nonspecific set of alleged irregularities that might be curable, they surmised, after a bit of cutting-edge surgical technology administered by the hands of young doctors in training. Without it, they warned, I would die before I reached the age of ten.

Without it, I turned ten, at which point it was determined that I needed eye surgery to correct a problem that they could see, though not explain.

But Odessa kept getting in the way of those icy-eyed doctors in stiffly starched green cotton jackets who never once spoke directly to us or even called us by our names, the ones who were desperately seeking to use me as a guinea pig. Each time they offered a surgical cure, Odessa turned to me and said, "Honey, do you want this operation?"

Her statement could easily have been mistaken as a question. Instead, in each instance, I understood that I was being called upon to speak up for myself.

So, each time, I surveyed the forces arrayed before me: my mother, who would not presume to grant or withhold permission for such an invasion of my body without first consulting me; the doctors, jaws slackened in disbelief, scowling disapproval.

And, each time, I just said, "No."

The second time I exercised my right to choose, they practically threw us out of the welfare department. Those wardens of the public trough accused Odessa of being crazed, an unfit mother who would let her ten-year-old daughter's voice be heard above those of doctors who knew what was medically required.

They said they would take me and my fourteen-year-old sister away from her. At the very least, they said, they would cut off our welfare check. That was not the end of it, they warned. We would see. A crazy nigger and her crazy nigger child.

One night during our weekly family meeting, the three of us voted unanimously to take ourselves off welfare. We decided the thirty-dollar-a-month welfare check was not enough to make up for the stigma, the invasions, the assaults that came in tow.

It was around this time that I came to loathe white people. Odessa, a fervent believer with impeccable Christian credentials, was not pleased. "Judge not lest ye be judged," she frequently admonished. Considering what I was working with, I decided I was willing to take my chances, though I was wise enough to keep all these thoughts strictly to myself.

Up to that point, what I had learned of white folks I learned from Odessa, books, and magazines. Raised in a home purposely devoid of television—"the stupid box"—I looked to Odessa as my primary source.

White folks were the people whose houses she cleaned. You can't wash shit from a man's drawers and not learn a lot about him in the process. And what she learned, we learned. Every nuance.

Many days, Odessa came home exhausted—not from the physical labor, but from the mental toil of constantly deflecting the arrogance of adults and children drenched in the rightness, the mightiness of their relentless whiteness. Hers were not a victim's tales, just tiresome examples of white folks who believed the only way to rise was to first step in her black face.

In 1961, a few reasonably prudent white leaders in our town struck a deal with middle-class black leaders and thus began inching toward desegregation of the public schools. As agreed, at first the black leaders offered up their own progeny, thinking them the best representatives of our race: colored children with two college-educated parents, members of Greek letter societies, holders of a mortgage and two car loans, regular churchgoing, paid-up members of the NAACP. These were children who came from something and were, therefore, best qualified to go places.

But native intelligence and academic stamina were irrelevant when it came to tracking the number of families and household income needed to provide a large enough pool from which to draw the Race Warriors. So it wasn't long before the circle of the deserving had to be substantially widened. The black leaders went back and dutifully broke off a larger piece of the pie that contained their best, brightest, and most well-behaved children and offered us up, a handful of talent to be cast upon a sea of white mediocrity. For their part, the white leaders refrained from unnecessary talking.

I was among the first to be courted as part of the larger group for this social experiment, another opportunity to become a guinea pig but for a different cause. At first, I was intrigued, even flattered to be seen as a worthy warrior in The Fight for Racial Justice and Equality. Then we had a family meeting and together explored my options.

For one year, I had attended a junior high school that had been an all-white school in an all-white working-class neighborhood the year before we showed up. But when the propertied white leaders decided to send the poor black folks to sit in classes beside the poor white folks, the poor white folks fled and took their children with them, leaving all of us mostly poor black students and solidly middle-class black teachers to our completely black selves.

One night, after attending the first monthly parent-teachers' meeting of the year, Odessa came home mad as hell. My English teacher, technically black but proudly bearing the genes of the oppressor, had smiled into my mother's face, the mirror image of her own, and said, "We were so surprised to find out that Bernestine is a recipient." In Odessa's fury, the word came out "ree-SIP-yunt."

"Recipient?" Odessa repeated, puzzled.

"Yes. On welfare!" The English teacher whispered sympathetically. "Bernestine is so well dressed, so well mannered. She speaks so beautifully and carries herself so tall. We just never would've thought . . . You can imagine our surprise . . . " Her voice trailed off.

Odessa inhaled the insult, tucked it away inside her gut, and finished listening to the glowing reports from the English teacher and all of my other teachers. And then she came home fit to be tied.

Less than a year later, my sister and I both got summer jobs. At thirteen, I earned the same thirty-dollar weekly salary as Odessa, who, at forty-three, had been in the workforce for thirty-three years. Because she refused to let me or my sister clean white folks' houses ("*I* do it so *you* won't have to do it"), I had found an office job doing typing and filing.

Then it was time to choose schools again, the Fight for Racial Justice and Equality having ground slowly on.

In the end, the decision was left up to me. I chose to leave the Race War to those who knew they had the money for the clothes and thought they had the money for the weapons.

The next fall, I transferred to a brand-new school in a black community made up of a mix of poor, working-class, middle-class and even upper-middle-class black neighborhoods. There, left to our own devices, we Children of the Dream brilliantly mimicked the ways of the oppressor, endlessly creating, refining, dismantling, and recreating hierarchies of class and skin color and hair texture that would scar us forever after.

It was around this time that I came to loathe middle-class black people, while I continued my life as one who was different, unusual, not an easy fit.

Like my name, my fatherlessness and other differences—some real, some imagined—grew into a source of strength, even as they remained an easy target for those who saw them as one more reason to try to bludgeon me into conformity.

Eventually, I awoke to the liberation of a life led hugging the periphery—a status quo that granted me no allowances, and commanded no allegiance in return. So when college presented me with the first real opportunity to break free of my black oppressors, I grabbed it with no thought of ever looking back.

Finally, I would stand toe-to-toe with and fight the first people whom I had hated long and hard: white folks. I marched off, brave under the banner of my own personal declaration of war.

I had long ago grown accustomed to being set apart. So, free to haunt quarters and form alliances that, under normal circumstances, would have been taboo. Courageously different for that moment, I continued skirting the rim of convention, consorting with others who pleased me.

This is how, once I reached college, I came to have white people as friends. And to simultaneously understand that whiteness was a character defect.

Gruesomely visible in a sea of colorless faces, I was deluged by an endless mass of centuries of wrongs that had to be stomped, burned, smashed into sixties and seventies rights; I was deluged by white folks, one-dimensional obstacles to be overcome, jack-boot forces in control of the world, yet so mean, so small, so scared, so threatened. It nearly drove me mad.

Until I remembered that I had seen something like them before.

Long before I ever saw a white person in the flesh, I remembered, there were middle-class black folks who sat in judgment on me. The black mothers who, upon meeting me with their children, especially their sons, would stop me in my tracks with their threshold inquiries, challenging my right to enter: *Where do you live? Who are your parents? What do they do for a living?* Perched atop their pedestal in our black, segregated world, they and their offspring were the first who were mean, small, scared, threatened by my difference.

So, years later, in my near madness, adrift in the raging white sea called college, I reached back and saved myself by remembering: The early blows to my psyche were not black or white. They were black and white. And I loathed them equally.

How can you be friends with them?

That is a very good question.

Marion Coleman Brown

$\mathbf{N}$ow in her forties and working as a counseling psychologist, home-based publisher, and writer, Marion Coleman Brown has devoted much of her life to helping the handicapped. "I look ahead and plow paths for those who have given up on life," she says, "people who are hurting, sick, neglected, abused, misunderstood, depressed." Particularly important for her is helping children to realize their full potential. "I am an encourager, a planter, a waterer," she says, "and I believe in children first, always."

In this very moving story of her relationship with her first playmate and friend, "blond-haired, blue-eyed Linda," Marion shows how internalized self-hatred, passed on from one generation of blacks to another, can be just as destructive to children as white prejudice and bigotry.

"Because of my childhood experiences, I am who I am today," Marion says. "But it took me forty years to get here, to a life of self-love and self-respect."

MY FIRST FRIEND
(My Blond-Haired, Blue-Eyed Linda)

Who was your first playmate? Do you remember? And who was your first friend? Were they one and the same? It doesn't often happen that way. But to me it did. I remember mine—I can't help but remember her. She was blond-haired, blue-eyed Linda. I had never seen a white girl up close before, and she had never seen a black girl up close before. Getting to be with her was like being with the Queen of England. So it seemed, at least by my grandmother's standards.

I belonged to my grandmother during the summer months, to have and to hold for better or for worse. Everybody called her by her nickname, Big Mama. I often wondered why such a name was given to such a scrawny little woman. I guess part of it was how she could have her way with you. When you heard that raspy voice, you'd think thunder and lightning were about to strike you dead. She was always towering over me like she was some cousin of the mighty King Kong, assessing my every move and emotion.

I never could understand how quiet and humble she became when Linda and her parents came up the hill to see her. I had never seen my grandmother that way before—so submissive, and every sentence she uttered ending with, "Yes, ma'am, Miss Thelma," "Yes, sir, Mr. Ancil," and "Yes, ma'am, Miss Linda." "Miss Linda!" I said to myself, almost choking from what I'd heard. Why in the world was Big Mama calling her Miss Linda and answering her with "Yes, ma'am"? Linda was as young as I was—no more than six or seven years old. For the life of me, I couldn't understand what Big Mama was doing.

She was scaring me to death. Where was the woman I knew? Vanished without a trace. I've seen dried-up prunes with more spirit!

"Ugh, ugh," I said. These people must be something awful special. Got Big Mama acting strange. Who were they to command such respect? They must be people to be feared.

"Pearleane" (that was my grandmother's real name), "I want Miss Linda here to have a friend and a playmate," Linda's mother squawked out the car window in her evangelical voice. "And, since you've got so many grandchildren underfoot, I thought we could have one of them during the day to play with Miss Linda and keep her company. Do you think you can get one of them for us now?"

Big Mama looked around the yard nervously and impatiently. She seemed totally rattled. I think for the first time she was in a heaping pile of ants, so to speak, trying to step out of it before the biting started. She looked around and spotted me.

"Ohhhh, my Lord! Save me!" I said. I had been peeking out from behind an old oak tree in the front yard. My cousins and I played hide-and-seek there. We sometimes pretended we were climbing Jacob's ladder and building a tower to heaven. The tree was just that tall.

At first I could barely hear her calling me. "Gal, come here!"

I hid my body behind the tree, trying with all my might to be still.

"Come here, gal. You hear me calling you."

Her weather-beaten hands took hold of my arms, and before I knew it I was standing in front of Miss Linda. I mean right smack in front of her face.

"Here's one of my grandchildren. Take her. But let me send her over after a while. I just need to clean her up a bit first."

"Wait a minute, here!" I said to myself. "I am cleaned up!"

I couldn't make heads or tails of things. And there was Linda, standing in front of me, inspecting me as though I were a side of beef, trying to determine if I was grade A or throwaway. "She looks all right to me, Mama. I want to play with her now."

"I don't want to send her without a bath," Big Mama said. "It won't take long, ma'am. She'll be right over."

Good Lord, what was going wrong with my grandmother? Had she lost her mind? I'd just had a bath that morning. And I smelled fine.

That's when it all started. I just knew being friends with this girl was going to cost me my soul. I knew it the moment Big Mama started grappling with her words, crumbling right in front of me. I knew for sure that these people were royalty. And Linda was a princess. I knew I had to conduct myself in a manner worthy of being in her presence, the same way Big Mama did. I knew I couldn't get cross with Linda. Or her family. If by chance I did so, I would, without a doubt, die by their hands. Or they'd make Big Mama kill me.

The next thing I knew I was in my red-and-white polka-dot Sunday school dress with my nice polka-dot socks to match and my black patent-leather shoes that my mom had ordered through the Sears catalog.

There was a burning smell coming from the kitchen. The odor was strong, overpowering. Then Big Mama called me to the kitchen. "Sit down over here," she directed. On top of her black-and-white granite stove was something black, fiercely smoking. My heart landed in my lap.

All I could think was, "Run, run for your life!" I heard Big Mama calling me, but it was a chance I had to take. I couldn't go back. I just couldn't.

I could hear her marching through the house trying to find me. "Marion, come on out. It's not going to burn you. I'm going to be real careful, I promise. You must be pretty when you go to play with Miss Linda."

"Pretty," I said, moving my lips silently. Now how do you think that made me feel? So now I discover I'm not even pretty. I crawled deep under Big Mama's bed, where there were stacks of old boxes filled with whatnots.

She heard the boxes sliding around under the bed. "I'm too old for this kind of foolishness," she said. "Them folks waiting for you, so come on and let me straighten your hair."

Suddenly things were quiet. I could hear her storming out of the house through the front door. Minutes later she was back, tapping on the bedspread, then on the walls, then the floors. I recognized that sound. It was a switch. She'd gone out front and broke a limb from my oak tree. She pushed the switch under the bed, slapping and swatting it about, until she tagged me several times good, driving me from under the bed.

Now please don't think I went without putting up a kickin' fit. But of course she won.

That straightening comb scared me as much as those strange people did. I smelled of grease and smoke. What was happening to my life—my soul? Tears painted my face as I tried to escape the hot iron. Screams of rage bellowed from deep within me.

"No, Big Mama, don't do this to me," I'd cry out. But there was no end in sight. Day after day, I'd dart to the left and then to the right, each time hoping to escape the pain of this indignity. But to no avail. Burns plastered my ears. My scalp was covered with blisters. My forehead was impaired for life. And all for what?

Linda was intriguing to me. Every day she'd ask about this burn and that burn on my skin. But I never replied. She was always fascinated with the ribbon bows I wore in my hair, asking, "How did you get your hair that way?" Again, I was close-mouthed. I never could explain because I didn't know myself.

The moment came when I decided I would touch her hair and inspect it as she so often did mine. Her silky blond hair swayed like the wind, dancing back and forth across her head and shoulders. I was mesmerized by it. It seemed so nice to have hair that would move so gracefully. Almost floating on air. I said to myself, "Ohhh, so maybe that's what my grandmother is trying to do with mine. Make it dance like the wind. But why did it have to hurt to get it that way?" I inspected Linda for burns. I didn't detect anything remotely resembling a burn. I even cupped a handful of her hair, smelling it for that foul grease and smoke. Again there was nothing. I asked her how she got her hair that way. She looked at me with no reply.

The friendship between Linda and me grew. I began to

enjoy the times we spent together—learning to ride horses, exploring the woods that surrounded their sixteen-hundred-acre ranch, fishing, bike riding, going into town with her and her mother, watching her dad smoke meat in a smokehouse . . . I even went to vacation Bible school a couple of times with her.

But I was so tired of dressing up. My patent-leather shoes were killing me. So I started taking them off when Linda and I would play in her dollhouse and putting them back on right when it was time to go home. Linda didn't seem to mind. She didn't seem to mind about anything I did. She was just happy to have me there to play with and be a friend. But I knew Big Mama would have had a fit if she knew how relaxed I'd become around Linda.

Summer passed, and Linda and I were still playing together. But something was beginning to happen to my hair. I was losing it. It was all burnt out. Big Mama was still using the sizzling-hot comb on my hair. Then she heard about perms and decided that there would be no more straightening combs. So she took me to a hairdresser who claimed that she knew how to do it. She put lye, full strength, on my head. My hair stiffened, my head was infested with boils and blisters, my hair stuck to my scalp. We had to get scissors to cut it away from my head. It bled for hours. Within three days it all had come out. I couldn't stand to touch my head or have anyone else touch it.

By the time I was twelve, I was wearing wigs. Wig stores were cropping up all over the place, and Big Mama had bought me one. "You need something to cover your bald head. You don't have enough hair to do anything with, so I bought you a wig to wear."

My heart broke. I knew I would never be whole again. My life had ended. I was forced to put that wig on my head—hot and uncomfortable. What was a twelve-year-old child doing with a wig on her head? What was it all for?

I began to operate as though the wig were my hair. But I was always afraid that I'd play too hard and it would come off. Or some mean-spirited person would snatch it off.

Sitting next to the wig on my dresser was a small container my grandmother had bought for me marked BLACK AND WHITE OINTMENT: BLEACHING CREAM FOR THE SKIN. Putting it on my face had become a nightly ritual, as had the sweating and burning it caused and having to sleep on my back so the grease would stay on my face and not rub off onto the pillows.

So my grandmother was trying to bleach the black away from my skin. What was going on here, I wondered. Did Linda care about my skin? She never tried to rub the blackness from it. Big Mama would say things like, "It's time for you to use it; it's not too strong for your skin." I wondered what she meant about "it's time."

She was always fixing something on me. Patting here and tucking in there. Pulling and wiping. Still making a fuss over those strange people across the way. And there I was, caught in confusion. Was I ever good? Or was I only as good as what I presented myself to be in this friendship with Linda?

Linda and I had always attended public schools. "Separate but equal." Suddenly I was assigned to her school. But she was no longer there. Her parents took her out and placed her in Sillman's, a private school in a nearby town. She said I was her best friend forever. And I said she was mine. Why couldn't we go to the same school?

Each summer Linda and I continued to play together. We

became such friends that her parents began to allow her to break bread at my house the way I did at hers. We never stopped being friends until she wanted to date my brother and my brother wanted to date her, and our friendship, as we knew it, ceased. I'll remember Linda always. I believe she didn't care about the color of my skin as much as Big Mama forced me to care about it.

And now I must live with the struggle of loving myself for who I am, without all the fixing and patting and tucking; without the wiping and the pulling; without the bleaching, without all the hair. I brave the world with my short knots of hair between the scars that are permanent fixtures on my scalp.

Years passed and finally I saw Linda again. Just for a few fleeting moments, we stood side by side in a polling place, waiting to cast our votes. Still blond-haired, blue-eyed Linda. She moved closer to me and whispered in my ear. "Marion," she said, "our doll house is still there. Your name is up there too."

Then she pulled away without saying another word. Tears drenched my soul as I stood there, my heart racing wildly, uncontrollably. My hands jammed against my breasts; it was all I could do to keep from bursting. But I could say nothing. The curtain on the voting booth swung open and I stepped inside. I could feel her watching my every step. Once I was inside the booth, I broke down and wept. Attempts at composing myself were futile. Somehow I managed to cast my vote. I pulled the lever and the curtain swung open. I stepped out and looked for her, but she was gone.

• • •

Lost in silence are the hot summer months. Sometimes I feel the strong urge to stop in and say hello. I wonder if she is thinking of me too. I have a feeling she is.

Not a day goes by without me wondering if Linda had an inkling of what I went through to present myself to her. Was she as confused as I was? I believe so. She was caught in something that neither of us had any control over. On some hot summer days I hear her voice. I see her face staring back at mine.

Now I sleep with my comfort quilt pulled tightly over my head. I feel Linda's heart tugging, trying to loosen the quilt's hold on me. Scared of what she will see, what she will know, I need to let her in my comfort quilt because it wasn't she who did this to me.

Linda was my very first playmate. My very first friend. I will never forget my blond-haired, blue-eyed friend. Linda. I long for her still.

Millicent Brown

Millicent *F. Brown-v.-School Board District #20* was the official name of the NAACP-backed court case that led to the desegregation of a public school in Charleston, South Carolina, when Millicent was in tenth grade. Along with one other black student, Jackie Ford, she was to cross the threshold of racial equality at her new school on September 4, 1963, a stalwart representative of her race and a source of pride to her family and friends.

Her father was a "major player" in the NAACP, and Millicent grew up fearing violence. Her family had received death threats and had crosses burned at their home. But, as she so humorously reveals in this story, the day before the Big Day, on which she would attempt to desegregate the schools of Charleston, she had far more pressing concerns on her mind.

As we read her story, Millicent would like us to remember how "*ordinary* most of the movement people were." Growing up, she had deep respect for the way her parents and their

NAACP friends were standing up for what they believed, but, she says, "hero/heroine worship was not needed." Before she was twenty-one, she was personally influenced by being in the company of Thurgood Marshall, Septima Clark, El Hadjj, Malik el Shabazz (Malcolm X), H. Rap Brown, and many others who were advocating for social justice. From them she learned that one must step to one side of the line or the other, or as some would say, people must walk the walk, not just talk the talk. To this day she is "intolerant of inconsistency of talk and action" and a strong proponent of "congruence."

Now a college professor, Millicent lives in Greensboro, North Carolina, with her fifteen-year-old son, Akil, and her life partner, Daniel McDuffie. She has worked as a college counselor, a marriage and family counselor, a medical educator, and an education and exhibits director for an African-American research center.

THE DIPPITY-DO REVOLUTION, OR
GROWN-UPS DON'T HAVE A CLUE

Johnette was Mama's best friend. She, her husband, John, and their children, Don and Cornelia, made up a regular flank to our nuclear family of five. It was an odd alliance—these two families—with none of the total of seven children being the same age, and with a wide span even in the four adults' ages.

John was quiet and reserved, and my dad, J. Arthur, anything but. It was J. Arthur who engaged Johnette, many years his junior, in heated debates about politics and public affairs. They seemed, to my adolescent mind, to challenge each other to "contests of sacrifice" as to who spent more time being of service to the broadest segment of the black community of Charleston, South Carolina. Johnette probably had a longer list of affiliations than did my father—everyone knew his single passion was the NAACP. But devotion to one or many didn't matter; these two gave unlimited time and energy to addressing racial inequities and social setbacks that were accorded black folks (respectfully called Negroes in the times described here).

Whenever our two families converged at one another's homes, John and Mama passed the time fixing food. I'm sure my earliest attitudes about marriage were formed while observing that in both couples there was a quiet one and a talkative one, a brash one and a shy one, the person's sex notwithstanding, and that did a marriage make. (In retrospect, my lack of success with the sacred institution may have something to do with these oversimplified conclusions drawn from childhood observations.)

Our Labor Day backyard feast in 1963 had all the usual bustle about corn and potato salad and grilling techniques. There always seemed to be somebody's "new" grilling technique for hot dogs and chicken. But as long as John and Mama gave directions and nurtured their pots, the younger ones took little notice, and that day was hardly different from any of our other back-to-school, end-of-summer gatherings. I tuned out any of the speculations about what tomorrow might bring.

From my perch on Johnette's porch, I could see the top and the back of the new school I would be attending as I began tenth grade. Our family lived many blocks away, and the school was out of sight and virtually unknown to me. But as I sat there, gazing at its red bricks and multiple stories, the school and the next day—*the* day—seemed closer than I needed or wanted.

It didn't seem worth worrying or speculating about because there was nothing to compare it to—little black children had never crossed the racial divide in the state's public schools, and the unthinkable was just that. As one of two black students going to the school under the watchful eyes of who knew who, awaiting who knew what responses, I'd be confronting the unknown, unblack, unfamiliar. I figured most tenth graders had the same kind of uncertainties—at least I hoped so. Besides, for that day, I had only one thinkable thing to concern myself with.

I had decided what dress to wear, and my shoes had been bought on sale two weeks earlier. What I was worrying about was whether or not I'd made a big mistake in putting too much faith in my older sister, Joenelle. I had given her, a college student, the most important, potentially disastrous, part in deciding my fate the next day; I had entrusted her with my hair.

Joenelle had washed my hair earlier that morning, and instead of "pressing" the thick, long stuff with a straightening comb (our method of processing hair all our lives) or applying any of the chemical permanents that found favor among early-sixties moderns, she had a new method, called Dippity-Do, of taming the tangled web. This sky-blue, jelly-like substance was supposed to soften and manage my hair into the total respectability and beauty befitting my grand entry into the new school. I paced the backyard in my three-inch rollers pinned with plastic holding rods pushed deep into my scalp. At some dreadful moment—I think it was during the ambrosia pig-out—I realized that Joenelle's hair was a softer grade than mine. Maybe *she* could Dippity-Do her way to freedom, but why had I been so easily convinced that I could? It made the corn and potato salad extremely hard to enjoy.

Daddy and the others offered reassurances about the number of policemen bound to be on hand, including FBI agents, deemed more reliable than our local protectors. But toward the end of the afternoon, there were mainly jokes, light chatter, and off-the-wall conversations intended to keep the tension level down. Mama needed the diversion more than I did, since I was showing little or no interest in the political significance of any of this. Inwardly I envisioned being a mockery to my entire race when my Dippity-Do tresses failed to act affirmatively.

At some reasonable time in the early evening, we parted company—the two socially conscious families whose children were all destined to walk in their parents' footsteps as spokespersons for justice and racial integrity, challenging status-quo U.S. hypocrisy.

But that day, all the challenge I could summon was pitted against my fear of a failed revolution of an entirely different sort.

J. K. Dennis

Born in Milledgeville, Georgia, J. K. Dennis has lived in many places and still travels a lot, "trying to see how other folks live." Currently he is living in Carbondale, Illinois.

In this story from his childhood, J. K. explores the tensions between girls and boys, blacks and whites, in the elementary school he attended. In the surprise ending, we see how one feisty little girl named Margaret Ray was able to change him and his school forever.

SILVER STARS

We all noticed just how different Margaret Ray was when she refused to be punished by Miss Weatherhead. Miss Weatherhead was our teacher. She was a tall white woman with big feet and a big gray hairdo that she lost pencils in all the time. She wore sandals and a pair of black cat-eyed glasses on the edge of her pointed nose. The glasses were attached to a thin gold chain around her neck. Miss Weatherhead would hit us on our hands with a ruler for "misconducting ourselves," as she would call it. She hit so hard that it made the skin inside our hands turn blood red. But Margaret Ray would not let Miss Weatherhead hit her with that wooden ruler for anything in the world.

"Hold out your hand, Margaret Ray Johnson. You have been here at Groover Elementary long enough to know my policy on misconduct."

"No! You ain't gone hit me with that stick."

"Remember, little girls should be seen and not heard," said Miss Weatherhead.

"I'm a woman!" hollered Margaret Ray.

This is when Nasty Boy looked at me and I looked at L. Bugg. We knew it was a good thing Margaret Ray was out of our group before she caused any more trouble for us. It would have been different if she hadn't discovered our secret hiding place, which was under Nasty Boy's house in the south end of town. His house stood almost three feet from the ground on stacked concrete blocks. We were having a meeting to see who would collect the money for the ice cream cones that we would buy over at Marvie's. We picked L. Bugg because he was the only one during math hour who could count by threes without pausing to use all of his fingers and other people's fingers who sat close to his desk. Miss Weatherhead always put a little silver star in the middle of his forehead when he got A's on his math tests. Since the busing of blacks to the white school, L. Bugg had been the only one of us to ever get one. He walked around school all day looking like a fool with that silver star on his head. When it refused to stick any longer, L. Bugg pasted it to his forehead with glue. He quit when Nasty Boy and I threatened to kick him out of the group. But he made things just as bad when he sided with Margaret Ray. She was smart to find us squatting under the house, and she would not leave us alone until we let her in our group.

"I know who went over and stole all Miss Tillie's apples off her apple tree, and I know how you been making good marks in math hour too."

"We don't want you in our group!" I screamed.

"You shut up, Jerry Roach. I'll tell your momma you pushed me down and messed up my new dress the other day at school."

"He ain't did no such thing to you at school!" yelled Nasty Boy.

"You shut up, Nathan, or I'm gone tell your momma you throwed rocks at me the other day."

"No he didn't," said L. Bugg.

Then Margaret Ray had to start that fake crying business. Nasty Boy's momma rushed down the steps to the backyard. A long switch was in her hand. Within seconds, she squatted under the house and whipped the switch across our backs and shoulders and legs. We flew away like birds that had been shaken out of a tree. We stood on the sidewalk on the other side of the street listening to Nasty Boy scream for his life. And that was all Margaret Ray's fault too.

It was a two-to-zero vote. L. Bugg and me both decided to hold our meeting deep in the woods by the creek that flowed just off the dirt road that led to Mr. Cooper's house. We tried to swim, but the water stopped above our ankles. We sat in the water on our behinds.

"Ooooooh . . . wee! I'm gone tell. Y'all ain't suppose to be out here." Margaret Ray stood by a tree with her hands covering her eyes. We sat still like dark rocks. "I won't tell if you let—"

"No! You a girl. We don't want no girls in it," I said.

"Okay, then I'm telling." She marched away, dodging tree limbs.

L. Bugg whispered, "Roach, you know what happened to Nasty Boy, and we don't get to see him no more except in school."

At first, it was a one-to-one vote. Then I gave in.

"OK." I stood up. Before I could say anything, Margaret Ray sat behind me in her blue dress.

"You not suppose to wear your clothes in the water, stupid!"

"I ain't stupid! I'm a lady. Move out the way, Jerry Roach. Get over, Leonard Bugg. I want to try to dive in. Move!"

"You can't dive in a creek."

"So!" I said.

"So my big toe, Jerry Roach!" She splashed water in my eyes.

"Stop now! That wasn't a dive. I can dive better than anybody. I been swimming longer than you have anyway, now, 'cause girls can't swim."

"Can too! My uncle taught me how to swim in the Pacific Ocean."

"You a storyteller. She telling a story, L. Bugg."

"Ask my Aunt Sara, then." She raised her nose in the air and stuck out her tongue. It just so happened that Margaret Ray came to live with her aunt, Miss Sara, a month before the busing started. Miss Sara lived around the corner from my house. I wanted to go ask her because I knew Margaret Ray was a big storyteller.

"And when I used to live in Louisiana with my Aunt Cora, I knew a black man who dived into the Gulf of Mexico."

"You for real?" L. Bugg's eyes were big.

"You can't even spell Gulf of Mexico," I told her.

"Yes I can too."

"What it look like, Margaret Ray? Is it big? What color it is?"

"Shut up, L. Bugg. She can't spell it cause Miss Weatherhead told me our kind have a harder time with words than numbers, and I believe that go double for a girl."

"It is real blue and real cold."

"Everybody know that. Now spell it!" I told her.

"Roach, shut up cause you just mad cause you ain't never been nowhere," said L. Bugg.

"So!"

"Ess oh."

"That don't spell Gulf of Mexico," I told her.

"Where else you been?" L. Bugg made me hot in my face.

"I ain't never dived in it, but I saw Lake Michigan when I used to live up there with my uncle and his mean wife."

"She telling a . . ."

"Shut up and let her talk," said L. Bugg.

"No, 'cause she a storyteller, a big old storyteller."

I stood for a second time. Little chill bumps crawled up and down my arms. I kicked water in L. Bugg's face. He tried to rush me from the side. I swung at him but missed. He fought the air. Margaret Ray jumped on my back and strangled my neck. "Jerry Roach, you better leave Leonard Bugg alone!" She choked my neck and bit my ear so hard that I screamed for my momma. We stopped fighting after I faked death. L. Bugg walked Margaret Ray home like she was some kind of queen. I just sat there in the water thinking about the whole thing and how maybe Miss Weatherhead might not have been right after all.

"Hold out your hand, Margaret Ray. I don't want to have to send you to Mr. Abney's office. Little girls of all colors should be seen and not heard. You have been invited to this school to improve yourself. You do want to be one of the little girls who improves herself, don't you, Margaret Ray?"

"I'm a woman, you stupid lady you!"

Since L. Bugg was so good at math and Nasty Boy and I weren't, Miss Weatherhead gave him permission to move from the back of the class to the middle, right behind Margaret Ray with her storytelling self. She could count a little bit for a girl. But none of us except L. Bugg believed her when she said she could count to a hundred before she was four. Knowing he would get attention, L. Bugg raised his hand.

"Yes, Leonard."

"Is there any math homework tonight?"

"No math homework tonight, Leonard. Now hold out your hand, Margaret Ray." Miss Weatherhead's voice bounced off the walls into everybody's ears.

"No! You ain't gone hit me with no stick, white lady."

"Can you say Miss Weatherhead, Margaret Ray?"

"No, 'cause I hate you and I hate this white school and I hate this white part of town too."

Margaret Ray could not even take a joke. Once I played a joke on Nasty Boy by hiding his clothes in the bushes while he practiced diving in the creek. Nasty Boy then tricked me into believing that the earth was going to be invaded by aliens from Mars, and I couldn't sleep that whole night. I asked Miss Weatherhead in class the next day. It was during quiet hour. I raised my hand. Miss Weatherhead was grading papers at her desk. She had her glasses on, and the gold chain dangled at the sides of her face. She had two yellow pencils sticking out of her hair.

"Yes, Jerry."

"Will aliens be coming here from Mars any time soon, Miss Weatherhead?"

Laughs rolled toward me from every direction. I felt small, with Miss Weatherhead's blue eyes staring at me from behind her glasses. There was no sound for a long time. She frowned too. I could feel the bad coming.

"I can't seem to find your spelling homework here anywhere, Jerry. Did you do it?"

L. Bugg turned around to stare at me. Margaret Ray leaned over to see past L. Bugg's head. Nasty Boy, who had his head tucked in his folded arms, suddenly popped up and made a fist with one of his hands. I wanted to lie. I had to. But I couldn't. I knew the truth. And I knew Miss Weatherhead knew the truth too but was just waiting to see what I would say. It took me a while before I finally told her no. L. Bugg let out a long breath. Margaret Ray whispered to him how she was going to tell my momma. It seemed like I dropped every book I had and woke the dogs.

"Didn't they teach you all anything at that school! My goodness, that just proves what I have always known. You will never receive a silver star for spelling if you all can't even do homework."

The others in the class snickered. Nasty Boy reached over and punched me on my shoulder for asking such a dumb question in the first place. When he told me I was stupid, I put my head on my desk and cried.

His momma allowed him to join us as we walked down the sidewalk from Marvie's with our ice cream cones. The change that was left rattled in L. Bugg's pocket as he attempted to walk in the exact spots Margaret Ray stepped out of. Nasty Boy switched his chocolate for Margaret Ray's vanilla. Then he let her lead the group home. I tried to protest but Nasty Boy and L. Bugg said they needed some time to like me again, especially after that stupid question about aliens and the extra homework assignments the four of us had to do. They let Margaret Ray do anything she wanted. Then Nasty Boy punched me on my shoulder the same way he did when I asked about the aliens.

"Okay, me and L. Bugg forgive you, so I guess I can tell you the secret now. I stuck something in her ice cream. That's why I traded with her. That'll get her out of our group for good."

"What?"

"I put a dead fly in her ice cream." Nasty Boy pulled L. Bugg out of Margaret Ray's tracks.

"You did it yet?"

"Shush." L. Bugg had a big mouth. Margaret Ray twisted herself around toward us. Chocolate ice cream was around the outside of her lips. Nasty Boy and I both laughed like it was the funniest thing we ever saw.

"Nasty Boy, she probably ate it already," I whispered.

Margaret Ray looked at us and laughed as if she knew what we were giggling and holding our stomachs about. We laughed so much we started faking it.

"What's so funny?"

Ice cream ran down L. Bugg's hand and dripped on the sidewalk, creating little white spots. I stepped forward so I could see Margaret Ray's face.

"A fly was in your ice cream, and you done ate it already, and you gone turn into a fly in your sleep, and you gone look just like one of them aliens from Mars."

"And it was one of them big juicy flies too," said Nasty Boy. He licked his cone on the left and the right and circled his tongue all around it. L. Bugg finally laughed.

"It wasn't no fly in my ice cream."

"Mmm hmmm," I moaned.

"Who did it, Leonard Bugg?" She grabbed the neck of his shirt.

"Don't look at me!" said L. Bugg. "I didn't do it."

I thought the earth was shaking. But I was shaking. Margaret Ray freed L. Bugg, and he tried to lick and look innocent at the same time. Nasty Boy's tongue was rotating back and forth on his ice cream cone. Margaret Ray was the only one shaking. She tried to hold back her tears. Her eyes reddened. They filled with water. Then a tear hit her jaw. She dropped what little was left of her ice cream and ran.

"Look at her, everybody," I said. "She is a big old crybaby. Go on back to the Pacific Ocean. Go on back to the Gulf of Mexico. And you can't even spell it. G-U-L-F-O-F-M-E-X-I-C-O." I licked the ice cream that ran down my hand. Nasty Boy dug into his pocket and pulled out a tiny black something. I squinted my eyes to see if it was what I thought it was. It was.

"That's the fly, ain't it? You said you were going to put it in her ice cream. Nasty Boy, you a storyteller, a big old storyteller," said L. Bugg. L. Bugg dropped his ice cream and swung at Nasty Boy but hit me. L. Bugg had one coming from me anyway, so I rushed him. We both fell backward and thumped against the sidewalk. I couldn't hurt L. Bugg the way I wanted to because Nasty Boy was on top of us. L. Bugg was stuck in the middle, just as was when he sat in Miss Weatherhead's class.

"All right, Margaret Ray Johnson! I have had about enough of you for one day." Miss Weatherhead raised the ruler above her head and slammed it down on Margaret Ray's desk. The ruler cracked. Margaret Ray rushed Miss Weatherhead from the side.

"Somebody help me! They are attacking me. John . . . Billy . . . somebody go get Mr. Abney! Hurry!"

We sat with our eyes wide and our mouths open. The chain that was attached to Miss Weatherhead's glasses broke. The glasses cracked as they hit the floor. One of the lenses rolled under Mary Harper's desk. Her pink hands covered both her eyes. Margaret Ray swung and swatted at Miss Weatherhead's face. Miss Weatherhead tried to control her by holding her shoulders, but Margaret Ray twisted and jerked her body so much that poor Miss Weatherhead didn't know what to do besides scream that she had always done good for little black children and that it was unfair for us to be attacking her when all she ever wanted to do was improve us.

"I hate you! I hate you! I hate you! You white lady you! I'm a woman! Nobody hit me with a stick! You stupid lady you! I tried to tell you one time, you stupid lady!"

L. Bugg, Nasty Boy, and I were on the playground about a month later drawing sticks to see who would be responsible for collecting the money to pay for hot fudge sundaes at Marvie's. I looked over at Margaret Ray, who was sitting at the top of the slide. She wouldn't move. Her arms were folded, while the other special children ran wild below her under strict supervision. Then I wondered if she was learning how to spell any big words. Miss Weatherhead retired, and Mrs. Franklin, our new black teacher, told me I was born to spell words. I had made all A's on the spelling test she gave. And, unlike L. Bugg, I wore the silver star that Mrs. Franklin put in the middle of my forehead everywhere I went. I didn't care what anybody said. I wasn't stupid. I was proud of myself.

Toni Pierce Webb

Written as a letter to her white great-great-grandfather, "Warmin' da Feet o' da Massa" is part of *Hand-Me-Down Stories,* an unpublished collection that documents seven generations of Toni Pierce Webb's family. The questions she poses in this letter to Massa John are not just personal, she says, but are intended to address the immorality of slavery in general. "If the brutal honesty of the letter is disturbing, it is only because the consequences of slavery are disturbing!"

The mother of four children and the grandmother of five, Toni lives with her husband and two sons in Columbus, Georgia, where she works as a media specialist and librarian. She has had stories for children and stories for adults published, and is currently working on a collection of writings about women entitled *Flashin' and Other Significant Changes.*

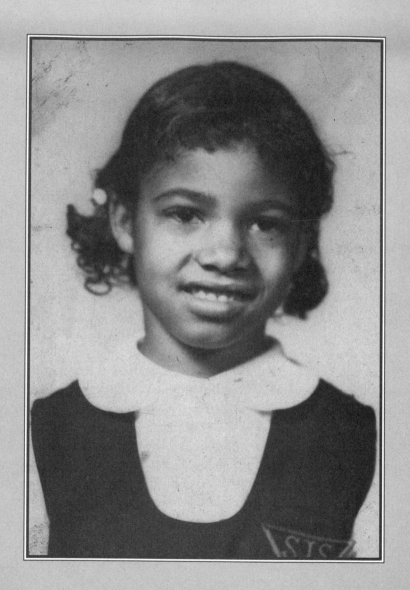

WARMIN' DA FEET O' DA MASSA

Any home I've had
Any city I've lived in
Any day of my life

Dear Great-Great-Grandpa Massa John,

Let me begin this letter by telling you that if we, by chance, had ever met, I would not have known what to call you, an affectionate name or Massa John or just plain Massa. Not only are you a stranger to me, but the relationship we share is bizarre. What other American ethnic groups have massas for grandfathers? Do Native Americans or Spanish-Americans have massas for grandfathers? How about Japanese or Irish-Americans— was the white man their massa? Who in this country, besides slaves and masters, shared such an inherently ambiguous and conflicting family structure?

My sisters and brothers and I have known of your relationship with our great-great-grandmother for as long as we can remember. You are as much a part of our genealogical and ethnic heritage as any other ancestor, yet for some reason I have never made my peace with you.

In the past I have been, and sometimes still am, slow to claim you as a forefather. I find it impossible to imagine that you ever felt affection or love for my great-great-grandmother, your captive Missy Pierce. I cannot, no matter how hard I try, envision you as a loving father and grandfather.

Tell me, why did you force yourself upon Missy? (Of course, "force" is putting it genteelly. "Rape" would be a more accurate term.) You had a wife. What sociopathic or neurotic need did you seek to fulfill with my African kin? Was it power over a person whom your sick society told you was not as good as you, less than human? Maybe you were frustrated . . . or was it just simple lust for a black woman? Regardless of your motive, rape was unjustifiable.

Were you cruel toward Missy in other ways, or were you considered a "good master"? Hah! Good master! Now that's an oxymoron if ever there was one. Massa John, only a fool would believe that he could be the master of another human's soul.

How many children of yours did Missy bear? I know only of John, your namesake and my great-grandfather, who was born in August of 1858. Amazingly, his name is John Pierce, like yours, but he does not have the honor of being a junior. He is listed in the 1880 census as a mulatto. You would recognize him anywhere. He carried your genes boldly. Your grandson Sidney, who is my grandfather, also bears the trademark blue eyes, fair skin, and straight hair with which your act of rape burdened him. How did you feel about your first-born son? Did you acknowledge him, love him, accept him—or was he just another Georgia "nigra" to you? Were you proud, ashamed, indifferent? I would love to know!

My memories of my grandmother and grandfather are loving

and pleasant, but I often wonder what they thought of you and their other grandfathers—slave holders who raped Granny's and Papa's grandmothers, captives. Was love exchanged between the white fathers and mulatto children and grandchildren? What was the grandfather-grandchild relationship like? Were you affectionate with your eleven grandchildren born of John Pierce and Eliza Maunds Pierce? Did you even know their names?

Massa John, what can you tell me of your relationship with your grandson Sidney R. Pierce, my grandfather? Enlighten me. All I know is that on cold Georgia nights, Papa had to sleep at the foot of your bed to keep your feet warm so you could sleep comfortably.

Massa John, who is to pay for your sins and the sins of others like you? Did you ever consider there would be retribution, payback, judgment, consequences? It's been one hundred and thirty-two years since the Emancipation Proclamation was signed, yet deep-rooted racism and discrimination still permeate this country like an incurable disease. Who pays for your sins, Massa John? We do. I'm sure you do, too.

How should I end this letter, Massa John? Shall I say, "With love, your great-great-granddaughter, or would it be more appropriate to close . . .

With grave misgivings,
Toni Pierce Webb

Robert E. Penn

Now in his early fifties, Robert E. Penn is a widely published writer of fiction, nonfiction, and poetry. He has worked as an administrator for several nonprofit organizations, including Gay Men's Health Centers, NOW Legal Defense and Education Fund, and Save the Children. His most recent book is *The Gay Men's Wellness Guide: The National Lesbian and Gay Health Association's Complete Book of Physical, Emotional, and Mental Health and Well-being for Every Gay Male* (New York: Henry Holt and Co., 1998).

In this story, Robert uses the present tense to engage readers with his efforts, as a teenager growing up in Gary, Indiana, to learn about the role of his father and other black soldiers in World War II. Along the way, he explores his sexuality and his own feelings about the morality of war.

Asked for his thoughts about the future of race relations in the United States, Robert said, "I have to hope that understanding will improve; otherwise, I get depressed. . . . But the prospect of parity is dim. The widespread recognition that slavery and the slave diaspora still hurts is not likely to occur in my lifetime."

WAR

Daddy got me a scholarship to a private school. It's a military academy. Uniforms and the full regalia. The buildings remind me of Windsor Castle in Canada. Stone, tall rooms, and cold. Our steps echo as we walk down a corridor to the admissions office.

They are very polite white people. They show me pictures of the last graduating class and of last year's sophomore class. There are no black students in either class. (Not even a caramel, ginger, or cream-tinted one.) Would I be their first? We walk through the buildings: the science lab, the swimming pool, the dormitories. If I accept the scholarship, I would live here. They give me pamphlets and forms and look forward to hearing from me about my decision very, very soon.

"The military taught me discipline." Daddy looks at me from behind the wheel every once in a while. It is two hours by car back home. "I was an officer. The training and my service to this country made it possible for us to live comfortably today. The GI Bill paid for my master's degree. Veterans Administration mortgage rates helped us buy our house. I was a captain. You could do better than I did if you go to a good military academy like this and West Point."

Daddy's not even teaching math anymore, so why does he need a master's? "Yes, Daddy."

I flip through the pages of the brochures. The other boys are cute. Is it true that when you go to a boys' school, there is lots of hanky-panky? Is it different to mess around with white boys than with the kids in my neighborhood? They say white boys are really fairies. I mean really. Not just fooling around like us.

"Chief, you may not realize what an opportunity this is."

"Daddy, what about my friends?"

"You can come home every weekend to see them."

"Not until the second semester." I show him the paragraph that says so.

"But it's exciting. You will have a better education, especially in the sciences. You like biology and math, don't you? And you can get a head start on meeting people who will be the military leaders of the future. If you work hard, you could be one of those leaders."

I have never really told Daddy this, but I think war is stupid. A lot of people get killed. A lot of things—houses, cars, farms, and stuff—are ruined. All because some presidents and generals disagree over who gets what.

"I made some very good friends in the service, son. Other Negro soldiers as well as the natives of Burma and India, where I was stationed most of my tour of duty."

"Was there a lot of jungle?"

"Yes."

"Is the bridge over the River Kwai near there?"

"Not far."

"I don't remember seeing any black soldiers in that movie. Were there other black soldiers besides you?"

"Chief, there were black soldiers in every major effort during World War II. Absolutely every one. We were called the Negro troops back then. Everything was segregated, except many of the officers with the black battalions were whites."

"Why couldn't black officers like you run the black battalions?"

"Some did. But mostly there was a shortage of black officers."

"But why aren't there black soldiers in the movies or in history books? I never read about them. All I have is your word." He complains about the unjust laws of this country. Why would he fight for this government overseas?

Daddy turns and looks at me. He is making himself smile. "My word is all you need."

Maybe. He was the first person to tell me about Benjamin Banneker and Harriet Tubman. Then he gave me books about them, too. Maybe not. Even the worst racists can't change the historical facts. Why doesn't Daddy have a history book with black soldiers in it, if he's telling the truth?

The uniforms at the military academy remind me of the Boy Scouts. It could be good to all wear the same thing: belonging to a group. But I don't know about eating square meals three times a day: They want you to lift your fork at a ninety degree angle to the table, till it's at the level of your mouth, then shovel it parallel to the table into your mouth. Why? Another rule.

"What about girls, Daddy?"

He looks at me like I've done something wrong, betrayed someone. "There's a girls' boarding school near the academy, but . . ." He glances at me again, wearing a sly smile. "But you'll be home on weekends to see Tanya."

"Yes, sir." And Charlane, too.

I guess I would get good and strong exercising every morning. But I can do that at home. The thought of sleeping with white boys is exciting. They're cute. They're blond. Like television characters. But if they're like some of the white Boy Scouts at summer camp, they'll mess around but won't become pen pals. I don't know for sure. And what if I get caught sleeping with another boy? Probably will be worse than if I get caught at home.

The people at my school are my friends. Even though I have to keep some things secret and nobody, not even the younger guys, who should be glad to have my attention, wants to spend enough time with me. But they all trust me and we're mostly black with some white and Mexican.

I'll go to a white college. Dillard Smith from church went to Yale. My college prep advisor at school said if I keep my grades up I could get into the Ivy League, too. Guess I'll get away from home soon enough. Be the only black soon enough. For now, I'll spend three more years with Tanya, Spider, Sharon, Maynard, everybody else, and Miss Williams, our new French teacher. She's even more gorgeous than Charlane!

There is no military history class at our high school. I am curious about the black soldiers in World War II. Is Daddy making that stuff up? He says he isn't. I saw war pictures of him. In the Philippines, I think. He looked good in his uniform, handsome. He wore his officer's insignia with pride and he was thinner then. There were some other black men in uniform at a church service. I don't think they were officers, though.

Were there any black heroes? I want to know. So I look at the local library. War books—most have small print and only a few photos. There are dozens just on World War II. I don't see any black heroes in the photos. I ask Daddy. He suggests that I check the reference section at the big library in Chicago, since some heroes are never written about in regular war books.

The main branch of the Chicago Public Library is just a few minutes' walk from the last stop on the commuter train line that follows Lake Michigan from our town to Randolph Street in the Loop. I arrive at opening time one Saturday morning. It has columns, high steps, austere walls inside, mosaic floors. I think this place will have the answers: confirm that there were many valiant black soldiers in World War II. The uniformed janitor, a muscular black man older than Daddy, smiles and nods at me as I arrive at the landing. And I nod hello back before I enter the research reading room.

The work spaces in the reading room are draped in a resonant silence more lush than the tall velvet curtains that veil half the light reflecting off the nearby lake and muffle the city sounds. I can almost hear people's minds explore, analyze, cipher, learn. The young white man at the counter smiles at me. I wonder if he wants something, if he likes me. "I am looking for information about soldiers in World War II."

"Check the card catalog, over there." He tilts his silky straight brown hair in its direction. "Under World War."

"Thank you."

This librarian clears his throat. "Is there any particular topic you're interested in?"

He does like me. "Yes, I want to find out something about the black soldiers who fought."

"Oh." He looks down. "I've never seen anything about that."

Neither have I. "My father was a soldier in World War II." There must be something.

He smiles as if he knows I've got my work cut out for me. "Good luck." He turns to take some books that just arrived on a dolly. "Let me know if you need anything else."

I check the Dewey decimal system card catalog for war, World War II, black, Negro, colored, and cross-reference Negro and World War II. (I actually see a listing for pickaninny.) There are two selections, one of them published by Tuskegee Institute. I fill out the request slips with the appropriate sequence of letters and numbers and return to my new brown-haired friend. "Could I see these, please?"

"Oh, you found something." He looks at the slips. "These are both reference books, so you can't take them out."

"That's okay. I can read them here."

He gives me a number.

A few minutes later, I see my number on the scoreboard-like display above the counter. I rush to the librarian.

He gives me one book. "The Tuskegee one is missing. I'm sorry."

I hurry to consume the newfound information, the truth. I find the reference to Negro troops in the index. I flip to the page and read a general's comment on the Negroes under his command. He asserted in black and white, "The Negro soldiers, though they were often Negro college graduates, could never truly develop the skills for combat even though we gave them additional hours of training. So we were forced to put them in positions more in line with their traditional trades: quartermaster, cook, driver, and unskilled laborer."

I am embarrassed and disappointed. The men this general described were not soldiers, they were just modern-day slaves serving white soldiers. Why didn't Daddy tell me that? Did

Daddy, one of the college grads and an army captain, end up washing dishes or digging ditches, or was this general just prejudiced from the start? Had the general decided that his Negro troops couldn't cut it even before they enlisted? What test was there to predict adequate courage for front-line duty? How would he know if we could fight if he never gave us the chance?

I tell the librarian, "This book is not enough. Is there anything else?"

"You can check the periodicals." He glances over his shoulder, and his hair swirls over his left ear. "They're over there in bound volumes."

I spend the remaining morning hours checking these tomes, larger than the biggest Bible and harder to read than the fine print of heavy Supreme Court documents, with little luck.

The Chicago Public Library has nothing on black soldiers except a few articles in *Ebony* magazine. There, I find photos of the retired soldiers, but not of black soldiers on the battlefield. Why are black soldiers overlooked? Or kept secret? "I want more," I tell the once trustworthy librarian. "I need details, reports on valiant heroes, serious documentation." I feel as though historians don't care about black soldiers, and if they don't care, then why should we? If only Negro soldiers remember, how can I know for sure? People can say anything, but the facts should be written down!

"Well, I'm not hiding anything from you." The librarian doesn't like me anymore. "Maybe you should contact the Veterans of Foreign Wars."

"Thanks, I will." I stroll out empty-handed and angry that librarians don't know more. The Veterans of Foreign Wars ask me to specify the unit in which the black soldiers served. I just want to know about every black hero. I ask Daddy what battalion he was in. I tell that to the veterans. They suggest contacting the Office of Military Personnel Records. They send me a record about Daddy. It tells me his date and place of birth, college attended, and date of his bachelor's degree. It confirms that he graduated with majors in math and teaching and that he served in India and Burma from 1939 to 1944. I already knew all that. I want to know about black heroes who fought: in Europe, where the real war happened, or in Japan. I call the Veterans of Foreign Affairs again. This time they suggest the National Archives. National Archives wants to know more about my interests. I write back, black heroes in World War II, fighting the Nazis. They answer: CLASSIFIED.

I focus on my regular school work. This research involves too much red tape. I see more war movies on Saturday afternoons and at home on television. I am forced to empirically conclude that there were no black heroes in World War II. Not in the movies, not on file.

I win a scholarship to study French over the summer. In France. I am proud and excited. There were two tests and an interview. (The white interviewer asked me three times whether or not I came from Haiti. I guess he thought that a black American student couldn't have learned French so well without unusual circumstances, like speaking French at home. Well, he can call my parents if he doesn't believe me.) Only thirty high school students were chosen from across the entire state. Two are black: Janet, from our rival high school, and me. We leave for Brittany in June. My first trip alone, without Mama, Daddy, and Sister or the Boy Scouts. My first trip out of North America, to Europe. My first trip for the entire summer.

Everyone is happy for me. Sharon's mother gives me a travel clock. Lonnie's mother gives me a folding umbrella. Spider gives me some rubbers (not for my feet, either). Charlane calls and wishes me good luck over the telephone. She's not at our school anymore. I guess Sharon told her. Tanya's mother asks me to stop by after dinner to pick up my bon voyage gift. (I bet Tanya gave her French lessons because she says it with a French accent.) I go over. She asks me to go downstairs and get the gift since it is too heavy for her to carry upstairs and her husband is at work. I go downstairs, wondering what travel gift could be so big or heavy. Tanya is following me. She will help carry the gift upstairs. When I reach the bottom step, all my classmates jump out of nowhere: "Surprise." I am shocked. I don't know what to do. Tanya gives me a kiss. In front of everyone. I can't even say thank you for at least twenty minutes. This would never have happened if I had gone to the military academy.

I am thinking in French now. I have a French family with three brothers around my age. Perfect. My French mother, Madame DeForet, has a part-time job and raises vegetables in her back-yard. Monsieur DeForet died in World War II. The oldest of my French brothers, Guy, is studying to be a mechanic. He has a motor scooter. He took me for a ride. He also borrows a friend's car sometimes. We drove through the countryside on Sunday. He is cute. But he didn't cheat when we wrestled. I did. I guess he's not interested in boy games anymore, or maybe French boys have other games.

I eat breakfast, lunch, and dinner with my "family." Breakfast consists of café au lait, bread and butter, and jam. It took me a few days but I don't miss cereal and eggs and salt pork on Sunday morning anymore. Everyone gets two hours' lunch break to go home, cook, eat, and take a nap. Nobody at home will believe me when I tell them. Everyone thinks only the lazy Mexicans take siesta. Lunch is bigger than dinner. Mme. DeForet serves each dish separately, right after she cooks or tosses it. First soup, then meat and a vegetable (like *steak-frites,* a thinly sliced steak fried in butter, and french fries, or chicken and *haricots verts,* which are green beans but they taste different from the ones at home), then salad, fruit, cheese, and coffee. Long thin French bread is on the table throughout the meal. And Guy and his two younger brothers drink a mix of half wine and half water at lunch and dinner. Everyone in my program had to get parental permission to drink wine. Daddy doesn't want me to, so I drink bottled water.

For fancy meals, Mme. DeForet invites one or two of her neighbors. Then she serves little glasses of colorful drinks before dinner, *aperitifs,* and strong-smelling brown liquor after the meal, *digestifs.* Before, during, and after meals, I struggle to discuss a variety of topics in French: French politics (they have seven parties!), the assassination of President Kennedy (whom the French loved), and the years of war between France and Britain over northern France (where we are sitting this very moment), to mention a few. The DeForets and their guests are all very patient with my improving fluency. (And all the time, I am questioning them about the way the French live: I have only to watch and see the differences; see that people can live honorably, comfortably, and well under a disparate set of rules.) One guest, the doctor from across the street, tells me, "You are the first *noir* [black man] to live on this block. Welcome."

"Thank you."

"I have great respect," he continues, "for the darker people. When I was in Algeria, doing my alternative military service shortly after World War II, I made many good friends with the local people. Very industrious and very faithful to Allah, their God."

"I want to go to Africa some day. We had an exchange student from Nigeria staying at our house while he was at college. He walked very erect, proud, and was smarter than most of the people in my neighborhood."

"I think," the doctor continued, "that U.S. politics hinder many *noirs* in your country."

I don't want to get into trouble, but I confide in him because he is a doctor and has sworn never to repeat what I say; because his hair is gray around the temples; because he smokes Gauloise cigarettes and because light dances in his eyes when he speaks and smiles.

"A lot of people are very mean to us at home. They say we're not as good as white people."

Monsieur le docteur expresses his disappointment in his American counterparts. "But, they are wrong! We will have to introduce you to them. You are quite the European."

"Merci, monsieur le docteur." I would rather be European, as he is, than white, like so many Americans.

When I'm not at the DeForets' home living like a Frenchman, I am with my summer classmates, afraid that I might slip into speaking English and be sent back home in disgrace. We have lots of classes: five hours a day. Our focus is on spoken French, but we spend one hour writing and studying French literature and provincial history.

We also take field trips together. After we arrive at the Paris airport, we spend a day in the city touring the historic sites: Notre Dame, Le Louvre, La Tour Eiffel, and so much more. Since coming to Bretagne (that's French for Brittany, the northwest province of France on the English Channel), we have visited an island where there are no motor vehicles, Isle dc Brehat; a folklore festival in Quimper, a large historically and commercially important town on Bretagne's Atlantic coast; and the university in Rennes, Bretagne's largest city. Today we leave on our longest field trip. We are going to spend two and a half days touring Normandie (in English, it's spelled Normandy), the province east of Bretagne. We have a tour bus and plenty of picnic food. The French love to picnic. There are many beautiful and quiet places in northern France where it's okay to stop and have a picnic even if it's not an official rest stop like the ones we have in the United States. Mme. DeForet taught me how to make French sandwiches on long bread with a hard crust.

The tour bus chugs along the coast. I sit in the wide back seat with my home-town friend, Barry Levine, looking for relics left over from World War II, twenty years ago. The road is narrow. No bomb craters. The trees are green. No petrified corpses. No bombed-out buildings. The coast is rugged. There is a bunker! It looks solid all the way through. No windows at all. The tour guide tells us, "The Nazis built these all along the coast."

We see another one. "Why don't you take them down?" Barry asks the tour guide in his very good French.

She answers, "The French government has tried everything, but they can't even blow them up. They're too substantial."

There is a town in front of us. The buildings come right up to the street. The bus slows to a crawl. It can barely fit between the houses. It has to stop and back up and start again in order to turn to the central square, where it parks. The tour guide leads us out of the bus, saying, "This town was liberated on D day." I'm not sure I remember what that means.

By the time I get out of the bus, I see several people around Janet. I walk over to see what's going on. They surround me, babbling thank-yous and gratitude nonstop. "Welcome, welcome," they tell me. "Thank you for returning." I don't understand.

I look around for an explanation. The white students are watching, their faces blank and perplexed. No villagers thank them. The tour guide shrugs when I look at her, questions covering my brow. Then I ask a much older man (eighty years old or more) standing near me, *"Pourquoi faites-vous cela?"*

"Because our little village is so near the Nazi bunker. The Nazis bothered us all the time. On June 6, 1944, D day, the day of liberation, the soldiers who arrived—Americans—were all *noirs:* black soldiers. Like the demoiselle and you. I was here, already too old to be a soldier. Black men saved our village and our lives. Thank you." He takes my hand and shakes it vigorously while kissing my left cheek, right cheek, and left cheek again.

"Il n'y a pas de quoi." I shake his hand again. I can't do anything else. There really were some black heros. They saved lives and they were brave. I shake so many hands, saying you're welcome, you're welcome, over and over again to their repeated thank-yous. Black soldiers helped people here in France. I feel so bad about doubting Daddy.

The bus honks like a foghorn. The older man shakes my hand once more and gives me a hug before stepping back to watch me leave. I return to the bus with the others. I feel so proud to be the son of a black soldier, to be the generation that came from black soldiers who saved French towns and lives.

The tour guide points out old battlegrounds and recites, "Gold Beach, Juno Beach." I absorb everything about the war that I can. And my thoughts wander, too: to Daddy. To his attempts to teach me. To the military. Its attempts to keep black soldiers from fighting for the only country they knew. To the films that don't show the whole truth. And the historians who don't seem to care whether or not I learn about my extraordinary and courageous *black* forebears as long as I memorize the exploits of *white* imperialists, religious zealots, colonizers, revolutionaries, and land (not to mention slave) owners, not to mention slave fathers.

She tells us even more when we stop to have lunch on the picnic grounds of the American cemetery. "Omaha Beach, Juno Beach, Gold Beach. English names because the British, Canadians, and Americans planned and carried out the attack. The largest amphibian operation in military history. Hundreds— no, thousands—of soldiers landed with the sole intention of ending the Nazi hold on northern France and liberating the Normans."

I try to imagine the troops landing on June 6, 1944. I see many black soldiers among them, enlisted and commissioned men of every hue.

The guide concludes, "So many men were killed on D day that your government couldn't afford to return all the bodies to *les Etats-Unis*. The American Cemetery is made of perfectly spaced rows of stone markers. The name of each soldier is chiseled into a star of David or a cross."

I notice that the markers make horizontal, vertical, or diagonal lines, depending how you look at them. I read the names on the crosses. There are Adamses and Jordans and Moores and Williamses, but I can't tell if they are from the families I know. Black people with those names.

"*Bonjour.*" I greet my family at the airport. "You're in America now," Sister blurts out. "Speak English." She's just angry because she didn't go to Europe.

"I had the best summer ever."

"And don't pretend you have a French accent." Mother scolds me to make sure I don't get too big-headed.

I really am too old for this. "I haven't spoken English all summer, Mother. I'm not faking," I correct her.

"Welcome, home, Chief," Daddy gets out his greeting, cutting off Mother before she has time to fill her opened mouth with a retort. He really puts her in her place.

"Thanks, Daddy." For more than the welcome.

"Did you learn a lot?" He shows Mama and Sister what counts.

"Yes. I made some new friends and I got the second-highest score on the tests at the end of the summer." I think I got the highest mark, but the American administrators didn't want to give that honor to a black, just like American historians don't want to recognize our Negro troops.

"Congratulations."

"And . . . Daddy . . . I saw the Norman battlefields. I met some survivors. They told me there were lots of black soldiers."

Daddy smiles at me as we get into the car for the drive home.

I decide to have a man-to-man talk with him as soon as we get home. I want to know why our service record is classified in the U.S. but easy to find in France. I want to apologize for doubting him. I want to know more about the black soldiers in Burma. "I'm glad to be home."

Sister scowls, Mother smiles, and Daddy looks into my eyes through the rear-view mirror letting me know: He believes me; he is proud of me; he loves me. And I reflect the same back to him.

Sarah Bracey White

When Sarah Bracey White was growing up in Sumter, South Carolina, in the 1950s and 1960s, she could not enter the local public library and could not learn to swim in the town's pool. "By law," she says, "I had to drink from *colored only* water fountains, sit in the balcony of the local movie theater, and purchase my train ticket out of town at a back window of the white ticket agent's office."

In this story about her first major departure from the south, Sarah takes us on a journey to a girls' camp in Vermont where she was to be a cook's helper for the summer.

After she left the south, Sarah says she believed at first that all white people were the enemy. The events that she describes in this story began a process of opening her mind to the possibility that not all white people were alike. "In my middle age," she says, "an interracial affair made me look beneath the color of a man's skin into his heart. His skin color didn't match my own, but the emotions of his heart did. I married him and we live very happily."

Currently a writer and an arts consultant, Sarah lives with her husband in Valhalla, New York.

FREEDOM SUMMER

In May of 1963, days after my graduation from the segregated Negro high school in Sumter, South Carolina, I received a letter from my favorite aunt, who lived up north in Philadelphia. The envelope contained a sheet of blue-lined notebook paper, a train ticket, a twenty-dollar bill, and a shiny brochure.

Dear Sarah,

I got you a summer job! My friend Claudia Lee from around the corner is the cook at a fancy white girls' camp up in Vermont. She says you can be her helper. The job pays $300 plus train fare, room and board. Wish I coulda had a chance like this when I was your age. I had to pick cotton or take care of white folks' babies. I'm sending you a little spending money for the trip here. See you soon.

Love,
Aunt Susie

P.S. This is a real opportunity!

I sure didn't feel that cooking for some white girls was an opportunity! Times were changing for Negroes (that's what we called ourselves then). For me, opportunity was joining the Student Nonviolent Coordinating Committee's lunch-counter sit-ins or marching with Dr. Martin Luther King.

I was only seventeen, but I had a heart full of reasons to hate white people and their restrictive laws: I loved to read, but couldn't use the town library; I paid full admission price to the Sumter movie theater, even though my only access was via a side alley that led to seats in the balcony. My mother's death a few months earlier had increased my bitterness. During one of her frequent asthma attacks, I took her to the Negro wing of the local hospital, where she was injected with numerous drugs and admitted—"only for observation," an intern had assured me. "Asthma doesn't kill you." However, the next morning, a white nurse relayed the news that earlier, they had found my mother dead. "How could you have found her dead?" I screamed. "You were supposed to be observing her! Why'd you let her die? You wouldn't have let her die if she'd been white."

The nurse clenched her mouth in a hard line. "That's unfair," she said.

"You're the ones who're unfair!" I said through quivering lips, then turned and ran from the hospital. I remembered a time before when I had railed about the unequal treatment of Negroes. My mother had slapped me and, while the tears welled up in my eyes, said, "I did that for your own good—to teach you to control your tongue. Talking like that causes trouble with white folks, and I've already had my share of that."

My older sisters had explained what she meant: Our long-absent father had once challenged the fairness of paying colored teachers less than white teachers, and joined the National Association for the Advancement of Colored People to seek equal pay. He was fired from his principal's job and blacklisted from teaching. Our family lost everything, and he started drinking heavily, then drifted away.

I wanted to continue my father's fight, but Mama was dead, and no matter how much I mourned her death, I had to get on with my life and college was my only way out of South Carolina. I reread my aunt's letter and ground my teeth in frustration. I didn't want a job as a cook's helper. I deserved a job befitting a college girl. I had an acceptance letter from Morgan State University in Baltimore, Maryland. However, the letter made no mention of a scholarship, and my National Defense Student Loan would barely cover tuition, room, and board. I decided to accept the camp job. How bad could it be?

As my train headed toward my Philadelphia rendezvous with Mrs. Lee, I leafed through the brochure my aunt had sent. From its glossy pages, Camp Beenadeewin emerged as a mountain sanctuary—a place that would inspire parents to gladly pay the extravagant sum of six hundred dollars for their daughters to attend a three-week session "amidst the marvels of nature." Horseback riding, archery, arts and crafts, drama, and swimming in the camp's very own lake. Swimming appealed to me most. Negroes weren't allowed in Sumter's public pool, and Mama's stories about the water moccasins had kept me away from the muddy pond at the edge of town; so I'd never learned to swim. But I wanted to learn, and vowed to do so before the summer was over. A voice in the back of my mind intruded on my daydream by asking whether white people in Vermont were different from those in Sumter. I used an old civics lesson to quiet the voice: Northerners had been opposed to slavery.

Aunt Susie was waiting when I stepped off the train in Philadelphia. "You look more and more like your mother," she said as she touched my cheek. "I'm glad I got a chance to see you before you left for camp."

I leaned into her embrace and inhaled My Sin perfume. Mama had worn it too. My chest tightened and my eyes burned, but I held back the tears and kept my resolve to show my aunt that I was now a grown-up. We made our way from the noisy platform into the cavernous station, where scores of travelers— Negro and white—milled around the ticket counter or sat patiently on curved-back pine benches.

Aunt Susie waved at a buxom, caramel-colored woman. "That's Mrs. Lee," she said.

When we reached her side, the woman extended a plump hand. "Hello, Sarah. I'm glad you're going with us. I don't often get college girls to work in the kitchen."

Thrilled to be called a college girl, I beamed as I returned her gentle handshake. "I'll do my best."

"That's all I ask," she said. "No more, no less." She smiled warmly and I smiled back. She sounded just like my teachers at school.

One by one, five more Negro girls arrived and were introduced by Mrs. Lee as the rest of the kitchen help. A brown-eyed, sandy-haired boy of about eighteen arrived as our train was announced. "My name is Charles," he said, and offered to carry one of my suitcases.

When we reached our track, I kissed Aunt Susie and boarded the train. From a window seat, I waved to her. She blew me a kiss and mouthed the words, "God be with you." It seemed like God had abandoned me. I was filled with a mixture of conflicting emotions. The train whistle blew and we pulled away. I busied myself by arranging my suitcases. I couldn't look back. If I did, I knew I'd cry.

"White River Junction, next stop, White River Junction," the conductor announced, swaying from side to side as he navigated the aisle.

"That's our stop," Mrs. Lee said.

I was the last to step from the train onto the wooden platform, which stood like an unfinished bridge in a cool, green clearing. Mrs. Lee and the others had already started down the steep staircase at the end. Birdcalls drifted from the forest that loomed over the one-room station house a few yards away. A hand-lettered sign on its padlocked door read WHITE RIVER JUNCTION STATION HOUSE. Compared to this place, Sumter was a bustling metropolis. The train snorted and pulled away just as a white man beckoned us toward his wood-paneled station wagon.

"Hello, Mr. Henry, how are you?" Mrs. Lee said to the gangly old man who got out and reached for her suitcases.

"Fine, thank you," he replied, while deftly loading the suitcases onto the wagon's overhead rack. "Throw the big stuff up here," he said gruffly, "and I'll tie it down."

The nine of us squeezed inside the station wagon and embarked on the last leg of our journey. Sumter County had few hills and I was unprepared for the gargantuan mountains covered with thick, green forests. Several of the girls dozed, but I stayed alert, feasting on my new environment. I was enthralled by picture-book farmhouses nestled in deep valleys, clouds that looked like smoke rings around distant mountain tops, cows posed on sloping pastures, where rounded boulders sprouted like oversized watermelons. Vermont really was different!

Suddenly, Mr. Henry's voice startled me. "Look to your right and you'll see Camp Beenadeewin." Carved into the valley below, among the trees surrounding a looking-glass lake, was a series of clearings dotted with wooden cabins. Soon we turned onto a road bordered by stately evergreens, then onto one that skirted a lake. My heart leaped at the sight of that shimmering blue water: It was the place where I'd finally learn to swim.

The sun had just dipped to the horizon and filled the sky with a rosy glow when Mr. Henry stopped the car near a wooden building that resembled a grange hall. "Well, folks," he said, "this is it, Camp Beenadeewin—your home away from home for the next seven weeks."

A silver-haired man and a plump, blond woman hurried toward us and embraced Mrs. Lee. After speaking softly to her for a few moments, the woman turned to us. "Welcome to Camp Beenadeewin. I am Mrs. Victoria Winston and this is Mr. Clay Winston. We have owned Camp Beenadeewin for more than thirty years. I'm sure you'll grow to love it as much as Mr. Winston and I do. We are happy you've come to help us care for our lovely campers and counselors. Mrs. Lee has quite a culinary reputation with our girls. I'm sure all of you will help her maintain it."

She then took her husband's arm, and they strolled off.

"Is anybody besides me hungry?" asked Mrs. Lee.

We all raised our hands, as if we were still in school.

"Good," Mrs. Lee said. "While you get settled, I'll whip up something to eat. How's bacon, scrambled eggs, and pancakes with good old Vermont maple syrup?"

We sent up a chorus of yeses.

"Barbara," Mrs. Lee said to one of the girls in our group, "You've been here before—show everybody where things are. Then bring them over to the kitchen."

At the supply house, Mr. Henry issued each of us a set of

sheets and two scratchy blankets. Barbara then led the girls to a two-room cabin with three cots in one room and a pair of bunk beds in the other. Chinks in the split-pine wallboards allowed the setting sun's rays to filter through and settle in ominous shadows across the room. I had a sinking feeling. Everything seemed old and shabby. I wondered if the white girls' cabins were any better than ours. "Where's the bathroom?" I asked.

Barbara walked to a screened window and pointed to a wooden outhouse a short distance away from our cabin. It looked just like the one in my grandmother's backyard. "They don't have indoor plumbing here?" I asked incredulously. Barbara shook her head and pointed to a roofless wooden enclosure. "That's where we shower."

After finishing my first meal and returning to the cabin, I made my bed and climbed into it fully clothed. I pulled both blankets around me, but they weren't enough to warm the chill that invaded my bones. I lay there shivering, knowing that I had made a mistake. I cried quietly, hoping none of the other girls could hear me. I wished I were still home and wondered how I would survive for seven whole weeks.

Mrs. Lee said her homemade cookies were a big favorite with the campers, so before the girls arrived, we had to make enough to last through both sessions of camp. Day after day, we chopped, measured, and mixed ingredients, then rolled, cut, dropped, and baked cookies. The air was filled with the aroma of oatmeal-raisin, sugar, cinnamon, and molasses crisp cookies. Mrs. Lee was a patient but demanding boss, and Charles and I labored under her demands. She had designated Charles as her *chef's assistant*, but he and I worked side by side, learning our way around the big old kitchen, where bowls were the size of drums and the gleaming stainless-steel mixer stood as tall as I did. Each night, I fell into an exhausted, dreamless sleep.

On our fifth day, the white campers began to arrive. Car doors slammed repeatedly, giggles and screams of joyful reunion echoed all around. Charles and I were peeling potatoes and onions for dinner, but I frequently went to the dining-hall door and peered out at the happy chaos. Chauffeurs in dark suits and visored caps unloaded suitcases from the trunks of big black limousines with license plates from places like Pennsylvania, New York, Connecticut, and Massachusetts.

Some campers were accompanied by young, well-dressed mothers who looked like they had never lifted anything heavier than a cup of tea. My mother had wanted a life like I imagined they lived—a pampered life as the wife of a successful man. She thought she'd found such a life with my father. It probably would have been, too, if he hadn't run afoul of the white establishment.

"These girls actually seem happy to be coming to a place like this," I said to Charles. "I can't imagine anybody paying six hundred dollars to spend three weeks in a raggedy place like this."

Charles chuckled. "All year long, these girls live in mansions—with maids and butlers. They think this place is exciting. Gives them a chance to be on their own and *commune with nature,* like the brochure says." He guffawed. I laughed too, as I recalled my last trip to the outhouse, where I found a raccoon curled up on the floor.

"I hate it here," I said, sobering up. "Mrs. Lee says we can't go in the lake, or ride the horses or anything. It's as bad as being in South Carolina. I thought it was different up north."

Charles dumped a ten-pound bag of onions into one tub of

the big steel sink and turned on the cold water. "It is. You don't have to worry about having your head bashed in for looking a white person in the eye. And you get paid for your labor."

I grunted, picked up an onion, and began to peel off its thin brown layers, grateful that I could cry without anyone asking why. Maybe we were getting paid, but it sure wasn't any better than life in South Carolina.

Camp shifted into full swing and our days were filled with preparing, serving, and cleaning up after meals. Before coming to Beenadeewin, I had never done domestic work, so I found it strange to serve these young white girls. Mrs. Lee said I was to address each camper and counselor, whatever her age, as *Miss.* I said the word only when she was within hearing. None of the campers called me anything except "girl," and they said that only when they wanted more of something. "*Girl,* you! Bring me some more milk." "*Girl,* bring me some more butter." "Some more gravy, *girl.*" God, how I hated that tone.

When I asked Mrs. Lee why we couldn't ride the horses or swim in the lake, she had smiled sadly and said, "We're the help, and up here, the help doesn't mingle with the campers." Up north, it seemed segregation was a matter of class as well as skin color.

Even though it wasn't my job to serve the tables, I helped out wherever I was needed. At first, some campers stared curiously (didn't their rich parents tell them it was impolite to stare?); others pointed and whispered; a few treated me as if I were their personal servant. Occasionally, one muttered "thank you" when I proffered fresh water, napkins, or refilled dishes.

Always, I felt them examining me, as if I were a strange laboratory animal. Couldn't they see that I was just like them? I wanted to tell them that in a few months I would be in college studying to become a French translator at the United Nations. I wanted to show them the medal I won for writing the best news story in any high school paper (Negro or white) in the whole state of South Carolina. I wanted to tell them that I had been elected to the National Honor Society and show them the tiny gold-and-black pin I'd been awarded. Instead, I buttered slices of toast as they dropped off the revolving toaster rack, pressed them into the plate of cinnamon sugar, and pretended it didn't matter what they thought of me.

However, even though I hated the way they studied me, I was shamelessly curious about them. Never before had I been in such close proximity to so many white girls my own age. Day by day, eavesdropping grew easier as they got used to my "brown" presence. No one worries about a pine tree hearing secrets, and I became about as significant as a pine tree. Listening to their conversations, I learned that white skin brought no solace from problems; that money did not prevent sadness and heartache; that white girls were cruel to each other (I had always assumed that whites were only cruel to Negroes); that most white girls want to be blond and would die for the perfect tan. The last discovery gave me a lot to think about. Why, since they didn't even like brown-skinned people, would they want to have skin like mine?

Six days a week, I followed the same schedule: up by 5:30 A.M. and straight into the kitchen. After breakfast was served, I had a two-hour break before starting lunch; after lunch, another two-hour break before dinner. We made everything the campers ate, and it was backbreaking work to prepare such large quantities of food, day after day. My only pleasure was eating.

During a lull in breakfast one morning, Mrs. Lee pointed out a corner table where the counselors ate. Most of them seemed to be my age or a little older. "They're all college girls, like you," she said. "Mrs. Winston thinks college girls set a good example for the young campers."

"They're not college girls like me," I answered. "They're white. And I'll bet they're making more money than I am, for a lot less work."

Mrs. Lee shrugged. "That's how life is."

I couldn't understand why adults just accepted everything. Just because that's the way it's always been doesn't mean that's the way it has to be. I knew that when I got to be an adult, I would do whatever I could to change things.

Every Sunday, after the kitchen crew served breakfast and lunch, and prepared box suppers for the campers, Mr. Henry took us sightseeing. After a few Sundays of becoming "the sights" for the locals, I grew reluctant to join the tour. But there was nothing else to do, so I'd go, forcing myself to ignore the stares, pretending that I was a tourist on vacation. The only trip I looked forward to was the one to Montpelier, the state capital, where I expected to see others who shared my skin color. When we didn't, I surmised that we were the only Negroes in Vermont. No wonder everyone stared at us.

We took a guided tour through the atrium of the state capitol building, where I noticed seashells embedded in the marble floor. The guide said they were prehistoric fossils, left behind when glaciers carved their way across the land. I wondered what I could leave behind as proof that I had been in Vermont, proof for the next Negroes that someone like them had been here before.

The guide talked about the spirit of hard work and self-denial that marked Vermonters, and I began to understand the austerity at Camp Beenadeewin. Back home, Negroes strove to gain the material things that Vermonters could easily have but shunned. To them, matters of principle were more important. Matters of principle were important to me too. I had hated it when clerks at Belk Stroman Department Store left my mother unserved while they waited on all the white folks, even those who arrived after us. I'd hated standing in the rear of a bus while empty seats abounded in the front—seats reserved for whites only. Those things branded me as inferior, though I knew I wasn't, and I wanted to change them. I was ashamed that I was in Vermont, instead of at home, crusading to make southerners change their ways.

After meals, while the other girls who worked in the kitchen cleaned up and washed dishes, Charles and I usually sat at a picnic table and talked. He'd never been south of Philadelphia, and I told him about life below the Mason-Dixon line. He couldn't understand why Negroes stayed in the south, since whites treated them so badly there. I repeated the explanation my mother had offered when I urged her to leave Sumter: "You can love a place and want to stay there, even though it's not perfect."

"That's crazy," Charles said. I smiled, remembering when I had voiced that exact sentiment to my mother.

Mid-July, four weeks after our arrival at Camp Beenadeewin, the first set of campers left and I was free until the second set arrived two days later. I had declined to join the Sunday tour and was alone in the cabin. The afternoon air was hot and still. Sweat beaded up all over me and I was miserably uncomfortable. I decided to go for a walk near the lake, even though I'd been warned that it was off-limits to kitchen help.

The well-worn path to the lake took me through a stand of pine trees, where brown needles cushioned the cool pathway. I considered staying there in the shade, but the persistent gnats and summer flies made me press on. When the path neared the lake, it widened and descended a sharp bank. I stopped, over-powered by the lake's beauty and size. I shaded my eyes against the afternoon sun. The lake extended as far as I could see. Tall trees cloaked in feathery foliage protectively surrounded it. To my right, several rowboats were tied to a wooden dock. To my left, the pathway disappeared into the lake. I swatted a mos-quito on my arm and scratched at the resulting sting. It was minor, compared to the deep sting that tortured my heart. I wanted to cry.

What gave these white people the right to keep me from going into this lake? They didn't make it. God did. And He made it for everybody. Surely there was room for me to enjoy its coolness. I removed my sandals, then walked down the bank. At the water's edge, I stopped. What if someone saw me? The thought of getting caught chilled my bravery. I looked around, but saw no one.

Still, I was afraid. My heart beat faster and I could almost hear Mama's voice. "Sarah, don't make trouble. Put on your shoes and go back to that cabin right now!" I ignored the voice and waded in. The sun was hot against my top half while my feet and legs were icy cold. It was a tantalizing feeling. I squished the mud on the bottom between my toes and a cloud swirled around my feet.

I listened for sounds, but all I heard were chickadees chirping and squirrels rustling through the trees. I lifted my skirt and waded farther out. The water was now midway to my thighs. I shivered with delight, tucked my skirt in my waistband, and bent to splash water on my mosquito-bitten forearm. Suddenly, I was angry. Angry at all the campers, at all the white people in Vermont. Angry at their selfishness, at the unfairness of life, which showed me its bounty but denied me access. Angry at myself for my helplessness and fear.

I began to cry and strike at the water with my palms. I wanted to punish these people. But how? Then it came to me. Since they thought I was going to contaminate their beautiful lake, I would. Slowly and deliberately, I waded back to the water's edge, lowered my cotton panties, squatted down and peed. I watched my urine flow into the lake and felt a sense of satisfaction. I had made my own mark on that vast, beautiful place.

After a while, I collected my sandals and headed back to my cabin. As I approached the stand of pine trees, a young woman with a long blond ponytail stepped out from behind a tree and blocked my path. "Why did you do that?" she asked.

I stared into her big blue eyes and defiantly answered, "Because I wanted to." I tried to pass her, to reach the safety of the cabin, but she thrust out a freckled arm and stopped me. "Let me pass," I said.

"If I tell Mrs. Winston, you'll be in big trouble," she answered.

"You can tell whoever you want. I don't care," I said. But I did care. My heart was doing flip-flops and my blood was pounding in my ears. What would Mrs. Lee say? And Aunt

Susie? I had let them down. Would I be sent home in disgrace? Would I lose all the money I had endured such hardship to earn? A sense of doom settled around my heart.

"If you don't care, why do you look so scared?" the girl asked.

I thought I saw amusement in her eyes. That made me so angry it overpowered my fear. "You startled me," I said, mustering the calmest voice I could. "I didn't think anyone was around."

"There's always somebody around this place when you do something you're not supposed to do," she said.

Suddenly, this mocking girl embodied all the white people who stood between me and what I wanted to do. I shouted at her, "What gives anybody the right to say I'm not supposed to come down to this lake? Or swim in it?"

She laughed. "What you were doing wasn't swimming."

I folded my arms and raised my chin. I wouldn't let her see my fear. "Are you going to let me pass or what?"

"Don't you want to know if I'm going to report you?"

"I don't care what you do," I answered haughtily, though I couldn't banish the tremble I felt in my voice.

"That's not true. You wouldn't be working here if you didn't need the money. If I tell Mrs. Winston, you'll be in big trouble."

"So are you gonna tell her?"

Suddenly, the girl collapsed into giggles. "Everybody pees in the lake. They just don't make a pilgrimage to do it."

I didn't laugh with her. Maybe she thought this was a joke, but I didn't.

"I've seen you in the dining hall," she said, regaining her composure, "watching us. You're always so serious. Don't worry, I won't tell. It'll be our little secret."

"Don't expect me to thank you," I answered, ungraciously.

"Why are you so angry? I'm trying to be nice to you."

"Why am I angry?" I repeated, surprised by the indignation in my voice. "Wouldn't you be angry if they brought you here and kept you penned up like an animal? Everything at this camp is off-limits to me, except the kitchen!"

The girl stared at me, but said nothing. She looked appropriately dismayed. That pleased me and diluted my anger. "I'm not as angry as I should be," I said. "If I were, I would have burned this whole place down, instead of peeing in the lake."

"But that would hurt you too," she said.

Her words sounded sincere, but I was suspicious. "Why do you care?"

"Has it ever occurred to you that all white people don't dislike you?"

"No, it hasn't," I said.

"I don't dislike you," she said softly.

Uncomfortable with her words and the emotion in her voice, I wanted to run back to the safety of my cabin. "Does that mean you're going to let me by?" I asked. She stepped aside and gestured for me to pass. I could feel her eyes following me. After a few steps, I turned back and mumbled, "Thank you." I sprinted back to my cabin, flung myself on my cot, and lay there trembling. Mama had always said you couldn't trust white folks. "They'll lie to you with a smile on their lips," she had said. Was she right? Would this white girl betray me?

The next morning while we prepared breakfast, I told Charles what had happened at the lake.

He guffawed loudly. "I can't imagine prim little you lifting up your dress and peeing in Lake Beenadeewin," he said, then added in a singsong voice, "What would your Mama say to that?"

I narrowed my eyes and stuck my tongue out at him.

"Hey, I like the idea. Sorta like the way dogs mark their territory. Maybe I'll go do it too."

"This isn't funny, Charles. I'm scared she's going to tell somebody and get me in a whole lot of trouble."

He shrugged. "Well, the die's cast—so to speak," he said, grinning. "You'll just have to wait and see what she does."

Later, as I stacked bread on the toaster racks, I looked across the serving counter into the same blue eyes I had seen the previous day. My heart flip-flopped.

"Good morning," she said. "May I have two slices of cinnamon toast?"

I placed the toast on a plate and slid it across to her.

"My name's Sharon," she said. "What's yours?"

"Sarah," I replied, without looking at her.

"Stop looking so scared, Sarah. I told you your secret's safe with me." She flashed me a smile, then returned to the counselor's table.

Was I really safe? Maybe Mama hadn't been right about all white people.

"Sarah, go stir the Maypo before it sticks to the bottom of the pot," Mrs. Lee called to me. "The next round of campers will be coming in soon."

A day later, between lunch and dinner, as I sat at our picnic table waiting for Charles, I heard twigs cracking and looked up to see Sharon approaching. What did she want?

"Sarah," she said, "can I talk to you?"

"About what?" I asked suspiciously.

"Nothing in particular. Just talk."

I shrugged and looked around, hoping Charles would come out and rescue me from this awkward encounter.

"Is it okay if I sit down?" she asked.

I shrugged again. "It's not my picnic table," I said grudgingly, not wanting to encourage her.

Sharon straddled the bench on the other side. "Where are you from?"

"South Carolina."

She laughed. "So that explains your funny accent."

"What funny accent?" I said defensively, wishing Charles would show up.

"You talk different from Mrs. Lee and the other girls in the kitchen."

"They're from Philadelphia."

"The guy too?"

"Charles? Yeah, he's from Philadelphia, too."

"My college roommate is from there. She calls it Philly. You'd like her."

"Is she a Negro?" I asked, implying that that would be the only reason I might like her roommate.

If Sharon got my meaning, she didn't let on. "No, she's not. But you'd like her anyway."

"You don't know what I'd like," I said curtly. "You don't know anything about me."

Sharon gave that amused smile that really irritated me. "I know enough about you to know you'd like her. She's got your spunk. Always in trouble for saying what she thinks. I wish I could be like that."

"Like what?" I asked. "In trouble, or saying what you think?"

"You don't have to take offense at everything I say," Sharon said testily. "It was meant as a compliment."

As I looked at the angry pout her lips formed, I realized that Sharon was treating me like an ordinary human being, the way I wanted white people to treat me, but I was acting like an angry animal.

"I'm sorry," I said. "My mother always told me my mouth would be the death of me. Every year I make a resolution to talk less, but I never keep it more than a few days."

"I don't think you talk much at all—though sometimes you do say mean things." She flashed a mock stern expression that made furrows between her eyebrows. Then she softened. "My resolution is always to talk more, especially about things that matter. I don't do that either."

"I'm curious about something," I said. "Why didn't you tell anyone what you saw me do at the lake?"

Sharon's face grew serious. "I didn't see anything so very wrong with what you did. If they kept me out of the lake, I'd want to do the same thing. Somebody ought to tell Mrs. Winston that what she's doing is wrong. Things are changing in the world today."

What was this girl saying? Was she planning a protest march up here? I thought wryly. "I don't think this is the time for people to start keeping resolutions," I said. "Not if they want to keep their jobs."

From the corner of my eye, I spotted Charles standing at the edge of the dining hall and waved for him to come over. "Sharon, this is Charles. Charles, this is Sharon. I told you about her."

"What did she tell you about me?" Sharon asked as she extended her hand to Charles.

To my surprise, Charles took her hand in his, bent forward, and brushed her fingertips with his lips. "Just that you walk softly and carry a big stick," he said.

"She's only half right," Sharon said.

"Which half?" he asked.

Sharon grinned. "You'll have to find out for yourself."

Uncomfortable with their banter, I interrupted. "Isn't it time for us to get back to work, Charles?"

He nodded. "That's why I came to get you, but I was distracted."

Sharon giggled. "I've got to get back to work too. Maybe we can do this again." I hope not, I said to myself. "What was that all about, Charles?" I asked as soon as we reached the kitchen.

"Drama."

"Drama?"

"Yeah, drama. She's the drama teacher."

"How do you know?"

"I did a little snooping after you told me she saw you at the lake."

"And what's hand kissing got to do with drama?"

"Why, Sarah, do I detect jealousy in your voice?"

"I'm not jealous!"

"You don't need to be. You're my friend and I wanted to help you. I figured if I could get on her good side, maybe I could keep her from telling anybody. Since she teaches drama, she must like acting. I saw Cary Grant do that hand-kissing bit in a movie."

"I don't think I have to worry about her telling anybody," I said. "But you'd better worry about kissing white girls' hands. Where I come from, Negro boys don't do that. Not if they want to grow up to be men."

"We're not down south, Sarah."

"Doesn't matter. Things are the same all over."

"No, they're not, " he said. "That's why the Freedom Riders are going south."

"What do you mean you never talked to a white person before me?" Sharon asked, her voice heavy with disbelief.

"I've talked to them," I answered, "but only when I was buying something in a store. Never like this, except once."

"What did you talk about then?"

"Rip."

"Who's Rip?" she asked.

I hesitated. I hadn't even told Charles about Rip. "Rip was my dog," I finally said. "I named him after Rip van Winkle because he slept a lot when I first got him. One day when I came home from school, I couldn't find him. I cried and cried. About a month later, I saw him in a lady's yard, not far from our house. When I told her he was my dog, she said if I wanted him back, I had to pay for his vet's bill and the food she'd fed him.

"My mother said she didn't have money for that, so I told her to get the sheriff to make the lady give him back. She told me that the sheriff was white, just like the lady, and since it was only our word against hers that Rip was my dog, the sheriff would side with the white lady."

Sharon stared solemnly at me, tears shining in her eyes. "Did you get him back?"

"No."

"Is that why you hate white people?"

"I don't hate white people," I said, then added, "At least, not all of them."

"That was a rotten thing for that woman to do," Sharon said. "I'd hate her too. What did she look like? I want to picture her while I hate her now."

I tried to remember what the woman looked like. All I could recall was that she was white. "I can't remember," I admitted.

"I'd never forget the face of the person who stole my dog," she said. "Not ever."

Sharon was right. As much as I hated that woman, I shouldn't have forgotten what she looked like. She was a cruel person, but only one person, not a whole race of people. I had been wrong to substitute her skin color for her crime.

"Tomorrow the campers leave," Sharon said, as we sat at the picnic table our last afternoon together.

"And we're leaving the day after that," I said. "I can hardly wait."

"Haven't you gotten to like Camp Beenadeewin, even a teeny little bit?" she asked.

I looked up at the trees that towered around the compound. Thanks to Sharon, I could identify them as sugar maples, white birch, eastern hemlock, and chestnut. Still, I longed for oak, pecan, and chinaberry trees . . . even the mulberry tree, which each summer litters the ground beneath its fuzzy green leaves with fat, purple berries that stain everything they touch. Trees that held memories for me. Trees that I would always recognize, whatever the season. "It's been an experience," I said finally. "I learned a lot, and I met you."

"Will you tell your friends about me?" she asked.

"I don't know," I said. "Will you tell your friends about me?"

"I've already written my roommate about you. She wrote back that she's thinking about becoming a Freedom Rider."

A white girl risking her life to get equal rights for Negroes? Would wonders never cease? It had taken a trip to Vermont for me to discover what white people *could* be like. I looked closely at Sharon, trying to memorize her face. I wanted to remember it, so that she would not blend into the faceless mass of white people who inhabited my past. Mostly, I would remember her blue eyes and the way they changed color when she was sad or angry, and her eyelashes—so pale they were almost silver. But I also would remember the way she pressed her lips tightly together when she was tense or amused and trying not to laugh, and the way her cheeks reddened when she blushed. And I would remember that, like me, she bit her nails, which we both resolved to stop.

Mrs. Winston waved as Mr. Henry started the engine. "Goodbye, girls. Thank you for all your hard work. I hope you'll come back next summer."

Not if I can help it, I said to myself. When we reached the road that circled the lake, I spotted Sharon walking alone. When we passed her, she turned toward the car, our eyes met, and she waved. I waved back.

"You know that girl?" Mrs. Lee asked.

"A little," I answered, "just a little." But not nearly enough, I thought. Sharon had made me reconsider a lot of things my mother had taught me—things Mama had thought necessary for my survival. But so much was changing in my world. Since I wanted to change the way white people thought about me, maybe I needed to change the way I thought about them. As the station wagon pulled on to the evergreen-lined road out of camp, I looked back with mixed feelings. I would never *love* Camp Beenadeewin the way Sharon did, but I had learned a lot of things during my stay there. Things that would affect my life forever.

Kenneth Carroll

Kenneth Carroll is approaching forty now, living in Washington, D.C., and is married with two children: a teenage boy and a baby girl. "He is an activist and a witness, in the tradition of James Baldwin and Richard Wright," he says. His work has been published in several poetry anthologies and in the *Washington Post,* and he runs the D.C. Writers Corps program, which sends writers into at-risk communities.

Asked about what helped to form his thoughts and feelings about race relations, Kenneth said, "My mother and grandmother's constant affirmation of the beauty of black folks—especially *dark* black folks—made it possible for me to neither fear nor hate whites."

The story that follows is about "learning to love yourself by defiantly appreciating who you are," Kenneth says. "The future of good race relations is dependent on our ability to struggle through our fear."

SUNDAY KINDA LOVE

"Love, love, love makes you do foolish things," sang Martha Reeves, preaching her Motownian philosophy from my uncle's eight-track car stereo whenever he wheeled his '66 Impala down Cramer Street. It was June of 1967, a year before the riots, and I was a puberty-sick twelve-year-old about to understand exactly what Martha meant.

Cramer Street had a sleepy, small-town feeling, even though it was tucked between two bustling avenues in the heart of D.C. The narrow, one-way street stitched us together like thread, making all its residents physically and emotionally closer. But there was trouble to be had on the quaint corners of Cramer Street, if you wanted it. After dark, the "big boys" shot craps, drank brews, and blew hemp in the doorway of O'Neal's general store. Young girls were rumored to lose their virginity in bunches behind the elementary school, and Mrs. Jean Bideaux ran a numbers operation and voodoo parlor out of her house. But the trouble for me began with "yellow" Tiffany Collins and "black" Burdette Lawson.

A late-June sun was rolling down that Sunday afternoon, and the street rippled with the sound of children hurling themselves noisily through the new summer. I was lying against the

146

wall of O'Neal's store, out of breath and wounded. Burdette, a licorice-stick girl with short hair and a shorter temper, could outrun and outfight me any day of the week, but antagonizing her was one of my favorite pastimes. She had just run me down after I had snatched the head off her black doll baby. Her mother, Mrs. Lawson, would only buy her black dolls, and Burdette, strangely, seemed to enjoy them.

Burdette's dark brown, always Vaselined, skinny legs could stretch from the first pew right into "deacon's row." I heard her long legs slicing the air behind me, forcing me to push my P.F. Flyers (which, according to the ads, could make you "run faster and jump higher") into overdrive. They were no match for Burdette's Woolworth's patent leathers. She caught me near the end of the block, reeling me in as though I had a hook attached to my back.

I screamed up the block, "Forget you, Burdette, wit your black self." I was as dark as she was, perhaps darker, but somewhere it had been made clear that black was bad. Black was worse than being poor or stupid. You could get money or become smarter, but you were always going to be black. Burdette stuck her tongue out and patted her behind at me, her legs shining like new copper as she walked confidently back up the block.

I angrily limped up the street to my house, kicking open the gate and mumbling curses into the warm air. Grandma came to the door dressed in her good clothes and carrying a cake. "Boy," she said, "what you been doing out here? I thought you were dressed and ready to go with us to Aunt Haddie's house."

She looked into my face and clucked her tongue. "All right, who you been fighting now?"

I answered by looking across the street at Burdette Lawson.
"Lord, child, why can't you leave that girl alone?" Grandma
asked, taking out her handkerchief and wiping the sweat and
dirt from my face. I was surprised she didn't understand why I
had to bother the girls. She seemed to understand everything
else. I sure as hell didn't know.

"Lord, here come James to give us a ride and you dirty,
sweaty, and mean. I'm a leave you here, boy, but you know my
rules," said Grandma, pointing her finger at me.

"Yes'm," I mumbled, understanding that knowing Grandma's
rules didn't mean she wasn't going to explain them to you again.

"Don't cook nothing, don't let nobody in the house, and
don't touch them Bessie Smith records," said Grandma, carving
her stern words into the summer air with her index finger.

Uncle James, dressed to the max, as always, in a lime-colored striped shirt and double-knit lime-colored slacks, rubbed
my head. "Girls again, huh, sport? Don't worry, it'll be all right
after while," he said. But I wasn't convinced. Uncle James navigated the big car down the narrow street, smiling like a colored
prince.

I discovered Bessie Smith via my grandfather's record collection, and she had become my first love. Her voice, all sad
and mean, mirrored my feelings as I struggled through that
strange ailment called puberty. I was contemplating what song I
would play first when Tiffany Collins came prancing slowly past
my porch. A high-yellow thirteen-year-old who went to parties
at night, didn't play with the other girls, always wore a dress,
and had good hair, Tiffany was the fantasy of all the boys on
Cramer Street. But she rarely spoke to us, parading her French-
braid, civil-servant-parents, private-school self up and down the

street like she was queen of the block. So you can imagine my surprise when Tiffany boldly opened the gate and sat next to me on the porch. "Can I have some cold water?" she asked.

"What?" I stammered, stunned into stupidity by her presence.

"Water, boy, cold water . . . please."

Why you can't get water at your house? I asked loudly in my head, but the words remained there. I turned to walk in the house and Tiffany followed. She stood at the icebox sipping the cup of water and smiling at me. Tiffany was always smiling. My stomach fluttered as a drop of water ran down her chin and landed on her smooth thigh. She laughed, watching my startled eyes bounce from her thigh back up to her smiling face. "A fast yella-gal" was the term Grandma and the other women on Morton Street used to describe Tiffany. Knowing that Burdette was the fastest girl in our area code, I wondered if grown folks knew as much as they claimed.

Dumping the almost full glass of water in the sink, Tiffany walked into the living room. "Yaw got a nice stereo," she said, sensually stroking Uncle James's hi-fi. She smiled and turned on the stereo. "Let's play some records."

No longer operating under my own will, I reached blindly for a record.

When the music started to play, Tiffany rolled her eyes at me.

"Boy, what in the hell are you playing?"

"Bessie Smith's 'Flood Blues,'" I said.

"That's old people's music," she said, snatching the needle off the record. It made that scratching sound that caused Uncle James to clench his jaws and cuss. She put on his Smokey Robinson record and slid her arms around my shoulders. "Let's dance," she said, moving her hips, slow and easy, against my stiff body, while Smokey crooned, "Oooh baby, baby." Tiffany's voice teased my ear like a whisper. She smelled like one of Uncle James's girlfriends, a distinct departure from the Sulfur 8, Bergamont, and Ivory soap smell of the other girls. She kissed me, her cool lips and hot breath causing the mild fluttering in my stomach to turn into major turbulence. Peering deep into my eyes, she whispered/sang, "I always liked you—you like me?"

I assumed her question was rhetorical, or the foreword to some cruel joke, until she said, "Let's go upstairs."

I might have been in love and a little dizzy from the lack of blood circulating in my brain, but I wasn't insane. I managed to mumble a faint "no" near the record's end.

"Don't you want to do it?" asked Tiffany.

"Do what?"

"It," she replied impatiently.

Then I knew what Grandma had meant by "fast." Tiffany wanted to do "it." The "it" that kids whispered about in the alley. The famed "it" that turned peewees into big boys. The "it" that was reserved for parents and nasty people. Tiffany Collins wanted to do "it" in my Grandma's house on a Sunday. She was Speedy Gonzalez, the Road Runner, Speed Racer, Mario Andretti, and Bob Hayes all rolled into one, I thought as I followed her sheepishly upstairs.

My jaw dropped anchor at my feet, and I stared, mouth agape, while she lay on my bed and raised her dress. "Hurry up before your grandmother comes back," warned Tiffany. Hypnotized by hormones and desire, I walked in a trancelike state, toward her prone body. "Take your pants off and get on top of me," she commanded, aware of my uninitiated condition. I dropped my pants and hoped that I had worn my good drawers. I braced my arms and tried to match the rhythm of Tiffany's gyrating hips beneath me. The single bed, which had belonged to my father when he was a boy, squeaked and creaked with each movement of our bodies. I was forced to concede, as Tiffany painted my face with moist kisses, that sex was slightly better than Bessie Smith. The fluttering in my stomach spread up my thighs and down my back. My body jerked in convulsions of pleasure, signaling the arrival of my first orgasm—with a girl. I was in love like an all-day sucker. I pulled my lips away from Tiffany and looked down at her face. She wasn't smiling.

The second sign of trouble was Tiffany's eyes. I could see her pupils expanding, trying to take in the horror that filled them. Before I could look behind me, I felt a sting like a thousand hot-tipped needles piercing my backside. Defying all laws of physics, I jumped from a prone position straight up in the air. I spun around to find Grandma staring at me with a look of sheer malice on her face. Her left eye jumped and her top lip trembled like it was about to detach from her face. Tiffany sat up in bed, too horrified to move or make a sound. Grandma flipped me over and proceeded to whip me as though I had shot President Kennedy. Between my yelps of pain I could hear Grandma beating me in perfect rhythm to her speech. Years before the advent of hip-hop, Grandma was already rapping to the beat. "Up-here-with-this-fast-girl-on-the-Lord's-day-and-play-ing-Bes-sie-Smith-re-cords-when-I-told-your-nar-row-be-hind-not-to-touch-them-re-cords," sang Grandma. I don't remember exactly how long she beat me, but you could have recorded two disco versions of my ass-whupping.

I thought Tiffany had left somewhere between the first lash and the one-hundredth, but I heard Grandma say, "Now it's your turn."

No, she not goin' beat my first, and only, girlfriend, I thought. I was already rehearsing future conversations with my therapist in my head. Tiffany tried to rush past Grandma and out the door. I coulda told her that wasn't goin' work. Grandma weighed every bit of two hundred pounds. She slung Tiffany's petite body across her lap and whacked her a couple of times. Tiffany screamed like a white woman in a Hitchcock flick. I was sure someone would call the police in response to her bloodcur-dling shrieks echoing in the street. When Grandma finished, she instructed both of us to sit up and fix our clothes. Tears and snot ran down Tiffany's reddened face. Grandma gave us an extended talk about fornication and damnation, complete with copious quotes from the Scriptures, before dragging the kicking and screaming Tiffany home.

Later she sat on the front porch, talking to our neighbors, Mrs. Wilson and Burdette's mama. I listened from the window above the porch. "Yeah, I called Claire soon as I saw her fast tail go in that door," said Mrs. Wilson. Orwell's Big Brother ain't got nothing on the old folks in my neighborhood. They see all and tell all.

"I'm not trying to say that little girl ain't fast," said Burdette's mama. "But, Claire, all these boys be after that little yellow girl cause this society tells them that black is bad and anything white or near white is something to have. That's why her mama don't allow her play with the other girls; she think her light skin make her something special. Your boy probably don't even understand what he was doing with that girl."

"Lord, Vernell," said Mrs. Wilson. "Why you got to put that old mean nigger stuff in everythang? That gal and that boy went in that house and played them slow records and headed up them stairs like they was grown—he know what he was doing all right."

"Well, I know what I'm goin' be doing," said Grandma. "Keeping this leather strap on him. I know he beginning to smell himself, but I don't play that nasty stuff."

"If I was you, Claire, I'd have James talk to that boy," said Mrs. Wilson. "I'd nip this thing in the bud before he end up like Joanne's boy—a father at fifteen."

The women then went on to talk about Joanne's boy, whoever he was, and left me alone. After they left, Grandma sent Uncle James upstairs to talk to me. Despite his protestations, he had failed to convince her that being on time for a date was more important than talking to me. Uncle James walked quickly into my room and sat down on the bed. He was dressed in what he described as his "sporting gear," and he smelled like Hai Karate aftershave. His iridescent slacks matched his jacket, and his polyester shirt looked like regurgitation from a drunken rainbow.

"Look here, sport, Mama want me to talk to you about girls," said Uncle James, barely concealing his amusement. "Just 'cause you like a girl don't mean you gotta lose your mind, dig it? I mean, check it, sport: Mama's house, on a Sunday, dry humping in a room with only one exit—be for real, baby."

Uncle James kept looking at his watch, coolly flinging his arm out to expose the gold-plated band. "Never let a woman drive your car, have keys to your pad, or play your Charlie Parker records," he said, profiling as he cocked his green felt hat in the mirror. He took his hat off and turned to me. "And whatever you do—don't get caught again."

Peeping out into the hallway and putting his arm around my shoulder, he said, "But I gotta admit, you got good taste." He flashed a gold-toothed smile and adjusted his pinkie ring. "Yeah, got me a couple of fine redbone honeys in northeast, a high yellow in southwest, and an ofay in Georgetown—gimme five, slick."

I slapped the smooth, manicured hand of Uncle James as he rose and shook his shirt at the sleeves. He put a toothpick in his mouth and adjusted his gold watch. "You ah big boy now, sport," he said, copping a pose like the Eleganza models in *Sepia* magazine.

"Ah big boy," I mumbled quietly, stroking the words with my lips like they were some grand trophy delivered by my uncle.

"I know that's right," James said, pimp-strutting from my room.

"Ah big boy," I mumbled again. Uncle James and Tiffany had confirmed my ascension, and despite what Grandma wanted, nothing would be the same again.

Our church, Mount Hope Baptist, was around the corner and within shouting distance of our kitchen. My punishment was to be the church's unpaid janitor, where I was forced to listen to the most boring, self-righteous sermon on the evils of flesh and women since Saint Paul. The sermon was delivered by the irascible Reverend Turner, whose high-pitched whining voice cracked good china and saved lost souls every Sunday.

But after a week of janitoring and his grating voice, Grandma freed me, and my friend Pug was waiting at the gate for my return. "Look over there," he said, pointing to Burdette Lawson and the girls playing dolls on her stoop. Burdette, for some strange reason, seemed almost happy to see me, a sly smile turning up the corners of her lips.

"You seen Tiffany?" I whispered to Pug. A good ass-whupping and a week's worth of Reverend Turner had not stopped me from dreaming of her almost every night.

"You goin' do it with her again?" Pug asked.

"Of course," I countered. "She's my girlfriend."

Pug shook his head. Everything had changed. I was one of the big boys now—too hip for jive games, black Burdette, and even Pug. I had a high-yellow girlfriend like my cool Uncle James. "I seen her going toward the school . . . ." said Pug sadly, as if I were about to commit suicide.

I broke away without letting him finish his sentence. All the girls, except for Burdette, clutched their dolls tightly as I recreated Uncle James's ritual strut, swaggering evidence of my new "big boy" status. My "love jones" was definitely coming down, as Uncle James would say.

Tiffany wasn't on the playground, so I walked behind the school, where the older kids hung out. I turned the corner of the building in time to find out why Jerry Butler called love "a hurting thing." My new love, the girl who I did "it" with a week ago, was leaning in the doorway doing "it" with Eddie Harris. Tiffany was holding up her dress, and Eddie's pants were down around his ankles.

I ran toward them, screaming out Eddie's name and reaching for his throat. "Leave my girlfriend alone!" I screamed, choking Eddie with both hands.

"I ain't your girlfriend," Tiffany screamed, trying to pull my hands away from his throat.

"What you mean?" I asked.

"My mother said you're too black to be my boyfriend," said Tiffany.

I let my hands fall in surrender from around Eddie's neck and walked slowly away from the doorway. Tears ran in torrents down my cheeks, sending Cramer Street floating in watery colors in front of my eyes. I looked back and saw Eddie coughing and struggling to pull his pants up.

It was two weeks before Grandma forced me back out in the cruel, loveless environs of Cramer Street again. I had gotten deep into Bessie Smith, understanding for the first time what she was feeling when she sang them blues.

Not much had changed on Cramer Street—it was just hotter. Ol' Pug was there to give me the rundown on things since my self-imposed exile. He said that Tiffany's parents had sent her to North Carolina to live with relatives after catching her doing "it" with Carlos Watson. (Carlos was yellow too. Tiffany was consistent.) I was glad I wouldn't have to see her anymore, though her face still haunted my pubescent dreams, just as her last words still haunted my ego.

I found myself searching old *Ebony* and *Sepia* magazines for skin-lightening products. "For an even tone use Porcellana fading creme," the bold print read. I tried to avoid the sun as much as possible, concerned that getting any darker would severely hamper my future love life. *Tarzan, Little Black Sambo,* and *National Geographic* were to be avoided. Despite such cool black people as Uncle James, Tiffany had made it clear that being too black was not hip. And even Uncle James had expressed that high yellows, redbones, and white girls were what hip guys wanted. Didn't take too long to figure out that I wasn't hip no more. Like Bessie, I was just black and broken-hearted.

Later that summer, as Pug and I headed toward the swimming pool, Burdette Lawson jumped out of the bushes into our path. Pug took off like a light, disappearing around the corner. Nearly a month of lamenting Tiffany had made me almost forget completely about Burdette.

"What you want?" I asked, prepared to fight her.

"Why you do 'it' with Tiffany?" she asked.

"None of your business, that's why," I angrily responded.

"I thought you was my boyfriend," she said.

I leaned back, recoiling from her suggestion, the words escaping my mouth like errant missiles before I could stop them. "You ain't my girlfriend—you too black." In the same instant in which I released them, I wanted to reach out and snatch them back, to disarm them before they wounded Burdette the way they had wounded me. But they hung, just above our heads, in the humid July air like anvil-heavy storm clouds.

"Hmmph," Burdette said, her hands on her narrow hips. "You black too. Besides, my mama say, the blacker the berry the sweeter the juice."

My words, so seemingly terrifying, now evaporated, exposing a blazing sun that rested flush in Burdette's face. She squinted, her smooth dark skin simultaneously reflecting and soaking up its rays. She pursed her lips, rolling her eyes at me and bouncing on her double-Dutch hips while she waited for my response. Her thick eyebrows shined, almost sparkled, above her brown eyes. Her long legs stretched to form perfect black satin appendages.

"Maybe you are kinda beautiful," I almost blurted out, but I held the words inside my head, suspicious of my new and sudden admiration.

"Black don't make you ugly," Burdette said defiantly, as if trying to help me understand my feelings. "You black and pretty to me."

Moving closer, Burdette leaned down and kissed me full on the lips. The kiss was awkward and quick, but her lips were soft and their fullness made my lips tingle for a while after she kissed me. Burdette blushed, failing to conceal her wide smile beneath her thin hand, and walked quickly away. She looked back over her shoulder and stuck her tongue out at me. I was in love again.

Me and Burdette "went together" after that, though we never came close to doing "it." We kissed often, or as often as we could while evading my ubiquitous grandmother and the ever-present Mrs. Lawson. I developed a fondness for full lips and a strange taste for Vaseline and learned that in the Lawson household black was beautiful but ash was a sin.

I continued to get in plenty of fights, mostly over boys calling Burdette black, though she told me not to sweat it. I still wasn't as culturally hip as she was, but slowly I began to like all the shades of black people who filled my life. I stayed away from television and movies and listened instead to music, discovering Uncle James's collection of Aretha Franklin and Esther Phillips records.

At church I suffered beneath the new stained-glass window depicting a white Jesus holding a white sheep, while a black sheep trailed in the background. I was bothered by the depiction, but I thought Mrs. Lawson had gone too far when she said that Jesus was black.

Burdette quit me after a few weeks (I don't remember why),

but she ended up "going with" Pug. (They're married today, though Pug swears he didn't steal her from me.) I found another "fine brown honey," as Uncle James called them, and got caught kissing in the church basement. I spent most of the rest of the summer on punishment.

A week before school started, the Black Panthers came to the school yard with African drums heralding their arrival. "Yaw need to go hear what they're saying," Mrs. Lawson advised. We raced down Cramer Street to the school yard. Burdette was first; Pug was a distant third. We cupped our hands over our sweating brows to get a better look at the dancers and drummers, who seemed oblivious to the broiling heat. A black man with a giant Afro hairdo screamed, leading the cheering crowd in a militant, fist-raising chant of "BLACK IS BEAUTIFUL!" Even the crap shooters and hemp smokers joined in, removing their toothpicks from their mouths and waving their hair scarfs in the air.

"BLACK IS BEAUTIFUL," the crowd chanted over and over again, the echoes colliding in front of O'Neal's store, beckoning people out to their porches and stoops to listen.

Burdette locked a skinny arm to her hip and leaned toward me. "Black is beautiful," she said. "Who don't know that?"

"Yeah," I laughed, "I been knowing that 'bout a month already."

Pug joined our hip laughter as we headed back up Cramer Street into a blazing sun.

Ronald K. Fitten

"**W**riting has saved me! It is my God," says Ron Fitten of the process that continually yields new perspectives on the world around him. As a young man coming out of the projects in Detroit, the only employment he could find was a mind-numbing, body-destroying job as a steelworker, but his belief in the vision of Dr. Martin Luther King, Jr., allowed him to quit that job and to trust that there would be something beyond the daily torture of working in the foundry. Now in his early forties and living in Seattle with his wife and two daughters, Ron is a reporter for the *Seattle Times* and gets up at five each morning to work on his fiction and his memoirs.

The most important thing he has learned, Ron says, is the importance of going on, no matter how many difficulties and disappointments one is faced with. Quoting Dr. King, he says, "Powerful living always involves overcoming one's situation or circumstances."

Surely his terrifying experiences in the 1967 Detroit riot, which he describes in this story, were an incredible challenge for a young boy to make sense of. Fortunately, as an adult, he was able to transmute the resulting feelings of powerlessness, fear, and hatred into a powerfully moving story.

FIRST LESSON IN RAGE:
FASCINATION TURNED TO HATE
IN 1967 DETROIT RIOT

There was an irreducible gap between my teachers and my experience—a gap between my education and my experience. Children are the only people you cannot fool.

—James Baldwin, in a speech
at Wayne State University

My mother was afraid.

Her oldest son, the second of her six children, already had been arrested and taken to the Wayne County jail, where he sat in one of many buses filled with hundreds of other teenage black males accused of looting and stealing during the second day of the 1967 Detroit riot.

This was the third day, and my mother feared for his life. And our lives. And the life of my father, who had left earlier that morning in search of his son.

All around us the landmarks of our childhood—Eddie's corner store, the Big Dipper supermarket, and the storage company across the street from our elementary school—were looted or in flames.

White or Middle Eastern merchants owned all these shops and others. In my neighborhood, "Negroes" rarely thought about ownership—just survival.

Outside, the sound of gunshots crashed against the roar of fire engines, the screams of anger from our neighbors and friends, the helicopters hovering above our rooftop, and National Guardsmen shouting to each other.

There was chaos.

There also was a new rumor: The city was going to shut off the water supply. My mother ran upstairs and turned on the faucets. Water gushed into the basin and bathtub and rose to the top, where it almost overflowed.

My mother wiped sweat from her brow with her right hand, then rushed downstairs into the kitchen, with me close on her heels.

She told me and my brother and sisters not to look out the window, not to open the doors, not to lift the shades, or make any noise. She told us to huddle in the basement and lie still.

Outside, there was no stillness. Only violence and burning and looting and arrests.

Some of those arrested, like my brother, were teenagers. Others were out-of-work factory employees, family men angered over what they believed was society's failure to open the doors of opportunity to black men and women.

I was too young, at age eleven, to understand all these feelings.

While I had experienced several incidents in school that

left me numb and made me wonder about my skin color and our life in the housing projects, I was still too naive and afraid to explore those issues.

So I suppressed them.

Even as my mother raced from one faucet to the next, I did not share her alarm. Neither was I alarmed by the sight of neighbors looting, stealing hamburgers and kitchen chairs, or the sight of Bay-Bay Williams hurrying down the sidewalk, a sofa on his back.

For me, there was only fascination.

I couldn't believe the men who were running, shouting, giving orders to others, taking charge in a way I never thought possible. Many of these men, I had suspected, were incapable of action of any kind. All day they would talk about how they'd been laid off from the automobile factories and how they needed a steady job. These talks would last for hours at a time. Sometimes, my father sat and talked with them.

But now they were rushing around in a frenzy. They were shouting and screaming, denouncing the white man and the system and the automobile companies that provided them with a living one moment and a layoff notice the next.

I had seen fear before.

I saw it in my father's eyes whenever he was laid off work. I saw it in the wide eyes of almost every man and woman whenever the Big Four, burly white police officers with a reputation for brutality and cruelty, drove up and down the streets of the projects.

But I'd never really seen the fear turn to rage until that Sunday afternoon, when the fury of men like my father and his friends, and my friends' fathers, exploded into one of the nation's bloodiest riots.

I did not share this rage, even as I was engulfed by it.

For me, rage was something I felt coming from others. It was something I observed. As the rioting continued, I sensed it was something frightening and powerful, powerful enough to make the adults in my neighborhood loot Eddie's store, where my friends and I turned in pop bottles for licorice and candy, and burn down the Big Dipper, where we carried people's groceries to their cars for nickels and dimes.

For the first two days, I did not understand this rage. I did not feel the anger that many of the people in the projects expressed about white people and the system.

At our family discussions on Sundays at the dinner table, which often resulted in the six children shouting, screaming, and disagreeing about every conceivable subject, the issue of white people, as far as my parents were concerned, was quite simple: Some were good and some were bad, just like us.

They drilled that into our minds.

So it was with some dismay that I— and my brothers and sisters, and indeed other children in my neighborhood who'd been taught similarly—listened to the ranting and raving about the white man and the system.

Yet the power of this rage, of people looting and burning and shouting, did not escape us. This rage flared with a fury and turned some of us into rioters and looters just like the adults around us.

On that day, the third of what ultimately would be eight days of the Detroit riot, I was not among the group of looters and rioters. I was only a fascinated observer.

That would change.

"Go downstairs," my mother ordered me, shortly after she had filled a pot with warm water. "Go downstairs."

My sisters and brother already had obeyed her, but I hedged. I did not understand why she was so alarmed, and I did not like the idea of being herded into the basement when, it appeared to me, so many exciting things were happening around us.

My mother squatted down and reached inside the bottom kitchen cabinet for another pot, and I took a few short steps out of the kitchen into the living room.

"Ron, go downstairs," my mother repeated, pulling the pot out of the cabinet.

Suddenly, there were gunshots. Several shots in a row. And screaming and shouting—and the sound of people scattering.

I ran to the front door, opened it, cracked the screen door, and peered outside. I saw five, maybe six, National Guardsmen milling around the sidewalk. They were standing at the end of our next-door neighbor's front lawn, about twenty-five yards from me. They looked like aliens, like people from a foreign land, with riot masks covering their faces, bulky suits covering their bodies, and rifles in hand.

I opened the door wider.

"Shut that door, Ron!" yelled my mother, who rarely, if ever shouted.

I stared at the Guardsmen, who suddenly turned and looked. At me. They charged. Startled by the urgency of their onrush, I paused, darted inside, and slammed the door.

I felt something that I'd never felt before—bone-chilling fear. It was a fear so strong that I could not move. I couldn't gather myself. I couldn't cry out to my mother or brother or sisters. I couldn't think. All I felt was this fear of these men rushing toward me, a fear of their charging footsteps heading toward the place I knew as home, toward the only place that had always provided me with safety.

As I stood there, dumbfounded, I looked back at the screen door and saw the masks—one, two, three of them—outside. I heard the muffled voices and my fear intensified.

I heard what I thought was the screen door open, and then I heard my mother, her voice both a plea and demand, shout: "Please, please don't hurt my baby," and I felt her slight body engulf me. I felt her heartbeat against mine, and I felt her tears fall onto my face.

I looked up at the screen door. The men wearing the masks and carrying the rifles were gone.

I heard their footsteps as they rushed away. Suddenly I felt something inside me that I'd never felt before: utter powerlessness. I wondered what gave them the right to invade our home. When I looked at my mother's tear-filled face, I felt something else—something the adults in the projects had felt for years: rage.

It was a strange, terrible combination of fear and anger and frenzied will to survive. It produced what I now know is hatred.

I hated those men.

Though I did not see their faces, I knew that underneath those masks these aliens—who tore away my safety and terrorized my mother and made her cry and made me feel so cowardly and helpless—were white men.

The riots were never the same for me after that. I lost the fascination with the looting and burning and gunshots. I wanted it to end. I wanted the masked men to leave my neighborhood. I wanted our home—our little project apartment—to be safe again.

It never was.

My perceptions of my community, my friends, my family, black people and white people, everything, changed.

In some ways, shortly thereafter, I turned away from the social and moral foundation my parents had carefully constructed, and turned to those who shared other views and expressed those views in other ways. I had been a good student. But after that incident, I lost my enthusiasm for learning and almost lost my faith in the system.

The experience radicalized me.

I have not been the same since. Over the years, after much reflection and much support, I managed to reconcile that experience with the present-day reality of my life and the lives of the people I love and who, I believe, love me.

Yet even as I write these words, I understand that the incident ruptured my soul and that, in some ways, it will never heal.

That's why I wept when I heard about the Rodney King verdict and the rioting resulting from it.

I suspected then, as I do now, that somewhere in the heart of the nation's second-largest city—unknown to the media and to rioters and looters and National Guardsmen—there were other children who might have experienced for the first time the same rage I felt that day in Detroit.

I also know that they will have to carry that rage with them, just as I did, for the rest of their lives.

Tracy Price Thompson

Tracy Price Thompson, a retired officer with the Army Corps of Engineers and a Desert Storm veteran, lives in the Bronx, New York, with her husband and four children. In this story, she takes us back to 1968, when as a first-grader, she became one of the first black children to attend a previously all-white school in the Bensonhurst neighborhood of Brooklyn, New York. With humor and an eye for telling detail, she shows us what it was like for a little girl to try to make it to school every day with white children taunting and chasing her and their parents egging them on.

Despite the daily dangers she was exposed to, with the help of her family, Tracy overcame the difficulties of being a black girl in a white world. "My parents had pioneering spirits," she says, "and they saw the future value of a quality education. They instilled pride, faith, hope, and strength in me." Today, she says, she strives to give as much love and respect to her husband and children as her parents gave to her.

BENSONHURST:
BLACK AND THEN BLUE

The steel-colored stairs looked steep and insurmountable from my vantage point. The flat gray paint gave them an institutional look that was popular during that era. Gazing up at the crowd at the top, I bravely began my journey.

Facing the formidable flight of stairs, I was flanked on either side by my parents. Each of them clasped one of my hands within the folds of their own: strong and sure. This single flight of stairs was the bridge to my future. Like trampolines, my parents provided the catapulting momentum that my six-year-old frame required to propel itself upward. Since I was small for my age, my knees nearly met my chin with each lunge.

I glanced into the stoic face of my father and noticed how straight his back was, how high he held his head. Subconsciously, I adjusted my posture and bearing to match his. Turning to my mother, I smiled brightly, my six-year-old teeth all jumbled up in a mouth too small to contain them. My mother smiled back.

The year was 1968. The neighborhood was Bensonhurst, Brooklyn. I was black when I arrived and blue when I left. The crowd milling in front of the doors at the top of the stairs was chanting something. I didn't understand their words, nor did they interest me. It was the world that lay just beyond the doors that attracted me. I was soooo excited! Today was my first day of school! Not that preschool stuff—which Mama said was just glorified day care—this was *real* school, the same kind that my siblings attended. I had finally joined their ranks; I was about to become a bona fide first-grader.

As we reached the top of the stairs, the people parted as if Moses had just parted the Red Sea, creating a narrow passage. They were still chanting as we passed, and I noticed that they were carrying signs with letters and words on them. Part of their chant included numbers. It sounded as if they were counting, "Two, four, six, eight . . ." Didn't these grown-ups know that you always begin counting with the number one? And what happened to numbers three and five? I wasn't even in first grade yet, and *I* knew better than that.

My parents marched me into the building and into a huge room with a million kids swarming around. Their voices were humming like hornets all around my head, making it hard for me to concentrate. Something was strange, but in the midst of my excitement and the children's noise, I was unable to grasp my feelings and pin them down.

I looked around the room. There was a stage with a red-curtained border, and there were more chairs than I'd ever seen. Mama said they were seats, not chairs, and that this room was called an auditorium.

I looked down at my new green dress with the red apples and yellow sun embroidered on the front. Green was Daddy's favorite color; thus, green was my favorite color. I thought I looked very cute. My socks were a perfect match for the red apples, and my shoes were shiny buckle-up Mary Janes. They were authentic Buster Browns. You could tell if your shoes were real Buster Browns because, just like I'd seen on television, Buster's dog, Tige, would be inside 'cause that's where he lived.

I didn't have a dog, although I wanted one, and a pony too. Mama said if we had a dog it would definitely have to live in my shoes. There was hardly room enough for the six of us in our apartment.

My parents led me through the auditorium to the area where I was supposed to wait for my teacher. When Mama told me to have a seat, I smoothed the back of my dress and held it against my legs before sitting, just as she had shown me. This was to keep your dress from wrinkling up in the back. Wrinkles made you look trifling.

Mama and Daddy prepared to leave me. I could tell they expected me to cry and fall out like those other kids did in the stores downtown, but I didn't. I was a big girl now, a first-grader, and I knew how to behave myself.

We had already had "the talk," my parents and I. The talk in which they told me everything I needed to know about going to school. I was told to be sure and mind my manners, to politely raise my hand if I wanted to answer a question, to pay close attention to the teacher's instructions, and follow all directions the best I could. "Please" and "thank you" were mandatory in our lives at home, so they didn't mention them—politeness went without saying. Mama reminded me to wash my hands after using the bathroom and before eating lunch, and Daddy reminded me to get on school bus number forty-four at the end of the day.

Mama kissed me and told me she loved me, and Daddy kissed me, echoing Mama's love, and told me to have a good day. I wondered why they looked more nervous than I felt. And then they were gone.

Finding myself in the midst of strangers, I looked at my shoes and then at my fingernails and then at my shoes again. Finally I got up my courage and looked all around me. No one was watching me—all the kids were oblivious to my presence—which gave me a chance to safely study them.

None of the kids that I played with in my neighborhood even remotely resembled *these* kids. *Nobody* here looked like me.

I felt funny again, but I didn't know why. As I studied them, a few kids began to look back at me. Their eyes were question marks—not unfriendly, but not friendly either. It was almost as if, after their initial gaze, I became invisible. Nobody came over to talk to me, and I began to slide downward in my seat, making myself even smaller than I already was.

Chancing a peek toward the front of the auditorium, I nearly jumped out of my skin. There, seated in the third row but turned around and looking at me, was a boy whose eyes mirrored mine. He wasn't just any ol' boy; he too had been reduced to being an invisible person. Becoming visible again, at least to one another, we stared into each other's faces, as happy as could be to see familiar features.

Although we couldn't adequately verbalize it, we'd both instinctively known that we looked like two kernels of golden yellow corn sticking out in a can full of bright green peas.

As if in slow motion and by a preconceived mutual agreement, we rose from our respective seats and made a beeline toward each other. Dodging and maneuvering through the visible children, we, the invisible, were magnetically drawn together.

When we reached each other we stood mutely looking, eyes and hearts taking in each other's nappy hair, thick lips, and dark chocolate skin.

"Hi, I'm David," he finally said.

I replied, as I'd been taught, "Nice to meet you, David. I'm Tracy."

We found two seats together and tried to make our corny selves resemble peas. By the time our first-grade teacher came to collect her thirty-two students, it was apparent that there would be only David and me who shared the bond of invisibility.

For the entire first week, my parents drove me to school. Each morning my father, who stood only five feet, two inches in his shoes, clutched one of my hands, squared his strong shoulders, braced his broad back, and, along with Mama, marched me resolutely through the chanting crowd of adults at the top of the stairs. It was a long car ride to Bensonhurst, but, as an eagle protects his nest, Daddy's single-minded determination for me to get a good education was paramount.

During the second week, I was allowed to ride the school bus both to and from school. Mama stopped grilling me about my every experience, and I began to settle into the rhythm of first grade.

Imagine the look on my parents' faces when, during dinner on the second day of my third week of school, their baby girl said she wanted to recite a poem she'd learned in school. I had everyone's attention. Even my brother, whose attraction to food was phenomenal, put his fork down to hear me out. I cleared my throat, eager to impress, hoping I wouldn't make a mistake, and began in a sweet, clear voice:

Niggers and flies,
I do despise;
The more I see niggers,
The more I like flies!

My brother, Bland, twelve years old, began to snicker in glee. I was happy that he liked my poem, and I flashed him a smile.

Daddy's fork jumped out of his hand and he arched his back, nearly dislodging himself from his chair at the head of the table. His mouth was working, but nothing came out except a small piece of lettuce, and white salad dressing was on his lips. I wanted to tell him to please use his napkin and wipe his mouth the way he'd taught me, but his body shook and jerked in what Mama called an epileptic fit.

I thought poor Daddy would choke to death, and so did my sister Michelle. She ran over and began to punch him vigorously on his back, the same way she punched me when Mama wasn't looking.

Mama, ignoring Daddy's choking spasms, my brother's snickering, and my oldest sister's elbows on the table, stared at me as if I'd just slapped my grandma. Her eyes narrowed into slits—just like an alley cat—a sure sign that I was in trouble. I'd been so careful to memorize the poem exactly right, and they all acted as if somebody had died.

"Where the heck did you learn something like that?" Mama demanded.

Daddy was not sitting still, but making short whooing sounds that put me in mind of a sick pigeon. There were tears in his eyes as he gave a powerful, final cough, and took a sip of his drink.

Just then, I saw Michelle cock her arm back and swing it all the way down to Mississippi, come back up through Tennessee, cover the entire state of Kentucky, cut clear across West Virginia, and finally land in New York. Her fist hit Daddy's back with a solid whump.

The force rocked Daddy's torso forward, and red Kool Aid went flying out of his mouth and across the table, soaking my plate. He coughed and sputtered for air. Daddy looked oxygen-deprived.

Michelle looked satisfied.

"Put your head between your knees, Daddy!" my brother suggested happily.

Mama was still burning holes in me with her eyes, waiting for an answer.

"In school," I replied in a timid whisper. Mama was no joke when her eyes got all little and slanted like that. My sister once said that whenever Mama's eyes shrunk down at you like that you could best believe that you were about to "catch hell."

I wasn't sure how you caught hell if you were still alive, but I wasn't trying to find out either. Hell was for sinners, and I was a good girl.

Her face a mere two inches from my own, Mama asked, "Tracy, who in tarnation taught you that *trash?*" She was so close to me that I smelled the meat loaf on her breath.

It smelled like a whupping.

I explained that during recess we were lining up in size order and, as the teachers weren't paying close attention, we began to talk among ourselves. I'd overheard the boys behind me reciting poetry. Eager to fit in with my new classmates, I turned around and asked them to teach me that cute poem. It had sounded pretty darn snappy to my innocent ears.

Well, they'd taught me, laughing each time I recited it. Like the apt pupil I was, I quickly got it down pat. I didn't understand what the big deal was; it was just a poem.

Daddy, recovering from his fit with tears streaming from his eyes, told me that I hadn't done anything wrong, but he didn't ever want to hear that poem recited in his house again. Inquisitive by nature, I asked why. He said that it was uncouth to say the word "nigger." I wanted to ask what a nigger was, but Mama's eyes had hell in them, so I shut my mouth and went back to my meat loaf.

It was red and cold.

My parents excused themselves from the table without finishing their dinner. Daddy's eyes read "tomcat" and seemed to promise Michelle that he was going to *deal* with her. Then he and Mama went into their bedroom and closed the door.

My brother, the brainiac, said they were having a "conference" and somebody at my school was going to be "one sorry motor scooter."

The poem was never again mentioned in my house.

During what was called "the integration of the New York City public school system" in the mid-1960s and early 1970s, I was what was termed a "bus child." I was taken out of my predominantly black and Hispanic neighborhood and bused to Bensonhurst, an all-white, mostly Italian, community where blacks like me were on the same level as six-day-old trash.

Although I was born and raised in one of the toughest neighborhoods in Brooklyn, it took Bensonhurst to teach me the meaning of real, unadulterated, straight-up, piss-in-your-pants *fear*. I was eleven years old the first time I felt my life was in imminent danger:

Beat 'em black and beat 'em blue!
Catch a nigger, why don't you?
Kick him, cut him, stomp him too!
If he hollers, use your shoe,
I beat one and you can too!

There were many afternoons when we were chased to the train station by mobs of angry, screaming, violent whites. We'd scurry like cockroaches, our terrified eyes wide open, visualizing our impending demise. Our knees pumped desperately, our chests heaved, and we panted like dogs. Our eyes frantically searched for help that never came.

The white men and boys ran after us, hurling bottles, rocks, sticks, and whatever else they could get their hands on. Brandishing tire irons, chains, and baseball bats, they were clearly eager to bash our tender black skulls. The school provided no security during our dangerous trek to the train station, and the natives were free to harass us, spit on us, throw bottles, sic dogs on us, and even kill us. Yes, kill us. There were a few unfortunate blacks whose lives were ended by the boys and men of Bensonhurst, Yusef Hawkins being but one of them. If I had a dollar for every time I was called nigger as a child in Bensonhurst, I'd be rich.

The negative effects of being removed from my people and my culture and being placed, at a very young age, in a hostile environment soon became evident in my life. I'd walked into that school excited, motivated, full of promise, and proud to be a first-grader. I left Bensonhurst with my lip poked out and my fists balled up.

I developed an invisible antenna, tuned to pick up whatever I perceived to be the slightest trace of racism. Deeply suspicious and defensive, I believed that most white people judged me as inferior, uneducated, and ignorant. This judgment was based merely on my skin color; as a result, I used the same measuring stick when judging them. I became ever-cautious, paranoid, even, and if I perceived that a white person was secretly ridiculing me, I was ready to prove to him or her, with my fists, who was the better person.

I was angry. I saw a redneck lurking around every corner. I became super-sensitive to little things. I took it personally when people made racist or ethnic jokes, and I began to itch for a fight with a white. I could think of no other way to make them respect me and my people other than by brute force. White adults taught their children to be intolerant, violent, and racist, and their children were quick studies.

So was I.

Graduation day at my elementary school in Bensonhurst was a warm afternoon in late June. I still felt like that kernel of corn, desperately trying to become a pea. My original blackness was now eclipsed with blue. All decked out in a cap and gown, I sang the words to "Pomp and Circumstance" with my fists balled up — just in case these crazy white folks wanted to *start* something.

When I was twenty-six years old—by then a wife, mother, and a soldier—I called Mama and asked her about a fleeting memory I had of a crowd standing at the top of the stairs on my first day of school. I asked her what those people had been doing at the top of the stairs and what had they been saying.

She explained that those supposedly respectable, white-collar professional adults had been protesting, exercising their

Constitutional rights in the hopes of denying me and my kind ours. The signs they brandished had read, "KEEP OUR SCHOOLS PURE," and "NO NIGGERS ALLOWED." The chant they'd been shouting was, "TWO, FOUR, SIX, EIGHT . . . WE DON'T WANNA IN-TE-GRATE!"

Dianne E. Dixon

A civil rights attorney, Dianne Dixon lives in a brownstone in Bedford-Stuyvesant, the area of Brooklyn, New York, where she was born in the late 1950s.

"My writing informs who I am as much as my gender, my race, and my profession," she says. "My experiences during sixteen years as a black female civil rights attorney permeate my writing, and my work tends to spotlight themes of social justice and personal responsibility."

Dianne says that her experiences with race relations have been "overwhelmingly negative. I developed a deep distrust of white people from being mistreated by my teachers and fellow classmates when I attended a predominantly white school for the first time." Perhaps partially as a consequence of the discrimination that Dianne recounts in her story, she is a strong advocate of affirmative action. But she is careful to define it accurately. "Too many people are of the belief that affirmative action means that those less qualified will be given jobs, promoted, or admitted into schools based solely on their race or gender, giving rise to the concept of 'reverse discrimination.' But, this is not what affirmative action is about. Rather, affirmative action simply authorizes an employer or educator to consider race as *one* factor in making decisions on hiring or admissions."

An accomplished attorney and writer, Dianne is also a writing teacher and the assistant director of the John Oliver Killens Writers' Workshop. She currently teaches legal writing at New York University and is working on her first novel, *How Sweet the Sound*.

THE LESSON

Often when I sit down to write, I am transported momentarily back to the sixth grade. It was 1969. One year earlier, Dr. Martin Luther King, Jr., had been murdered, and fifteen years before that, the United States Supreme Court had delivered the landmark *Brown v. Board of Education of Topcka* decision. Throughout the country, people were protesting against racism while black children were being attacked on school buses for having the audacity to attend white schools.

In Bedford-Stuyvesant, Brooklyn, where I lived, racism was something that I had only seen on TV or heard about in my parents' stories of growing up in the south. I had graduated from an all-black elementary school two blocks from my home, where the majority of my teachers were black and their expectations that I and my classmates would succeed had been both obvious and uplifting. In the school where I attended sixth grade, everything changed.

It seemed like my mother had called every school official in the city to make sure I got into that school. I overheard her explain to my aunt, "Dianne is a bright girl. That school is the nearest one to us with a program for gifted kids. I know it's a long ride on the bus, and I know she will have to get up real early to get there on time. But they have smaller classes and newer equipment—and why shouldn't our kids get the best that's out there?" So, with little fanfare, I boarded the city bus alone every day and rode for fifty minutes to a predominantly white school, in an all white neighborhood, with all-white teachers. Mr. Perlman was one of those teachers, and I still remember the lessons he taught me.

"Well, Miss Dixon, I had hoped that you would do better than this," Mr. Perlman sneered as he handed me back my writing assignment. The bright red F on the first page of my paper was so large that I was sure everyone in the class had seen it. An F. An F! I had never gotten an F before. I shoved my paper inside my notebook and tried not to look around to see who was watching me. I knew, of course, that Nancy Cicero had seen the F. How could she miss it? She was sitting right next to me.

"Good job, Nancy!" Mr. Perlman made a point of saying as he handed Nancy back her paper with a normal-sized B+ on it.

"Thank you, Mr. Perlman," she said. And then, turning to me, she said, "I didn't think I was going to do well on this paper at all. I didn't write it until the night before we had to hand it in. What did you get, Dianne?"

"A headache," I answered, turning my head to look out the window.

"Those of you who received a D or lower, please see me

after the bell rings," Mr. Perlman announced, looking directly at me.

"Well, I guess you'll have to stick around, won't you, Dianne?" Nancy laughed.

"Drop dead, Nancy," I shot back.

I waited to see who the other kids with bad grades would be, gathering around Mr. Perlman's desk. But only one kid remained with me. It was Nat, the only other black kid in my class. I didn't know what I would have done had I not had him to talk to. The kids in the other classes—even the few black ones—hated us for being in the gifted program. And the kids in our gifted class acted like we didn't exist. It was because of Nat that I tried to ignore my Sunday night headaches and the nose-bleeds that I so often got on Monday mornings. And it was because of him that I tried never to be absent from school. I couldn't do that to Nat, and I knew he wouldn't do it to me. We both had perfect attendance records.

After class I asked Mr. Perlman what I had done wrong on the assignment.

"Well, for one thing, you didn't write on the topic I assigned the class. Do you remember what it was supposed to be?"

"Yeah, I remember," I said. "You told us to write an essay about an event in our lives that changed the way others viewed us."

"And what did you write about?"

I told him what he already knew, that I had written about the double-Dutch contest between me and my friend Charlene the preceding summer.

He became agitated. "You see? You see what I mean? Now what has *that* got to do with the assignment I gave? You write about a rope jumping contest which, I might add, you didn't even win."

"No, I didn't win it," I agreed, "but I was new on the block and when I stood up to Charlene's rope-jumping challenge everybody stopped thinking of me as an outsider."

My explanation had not moved Mr. Perlman. He just sucked his teeth and rolled his tiny blue eyes at me. "Listen, Dianne, if you intend to pass this class, you are going to have to do the assignments properly. And that goes for you, too, Nathaniel. Your grammar is pathetic, surpassed only by your atrocious spelling."

Nat said nothing. He just stared at Mr. Perlman, but I could see he was mad.

"I want the two of you to read chapters seven through nine in your writing textbooks and answer the questions at the end of each chapter. Maybe by reading some information on essay writing, you'll get it. Now, tomorrow I'm going to ask a few of the students to read their essays to the class to illustrate the proper way the assignment should have been done. Be sure to listen carefully. In fact, I'll be doing this for the rest of the school year, so you'll get to hear lots of good writing."

Nat and I tried to ignore the fact that Mr. Perlman was really telling us that he thought we could never write anything good enough to read to the class, and that all we could ever hope to do well was listen. In the hall, as we walked to our lockers, Nat exploded. He hated Mr. Perlman for always picking on us. He seemed to enjoy telling people on the sly how Nat and I didn't belong in the gifted program. The fact that both of us had been in gifted classes our entire school lives and that we performed well above average on every test put in front of us seemed to escape him.

The next day, instead of waiting until the end of class, Mr. Perlman asked for the homework assignment he had given Nat and me as soon as everybody had taken their seats. With everyone watching, we had to walk up to Mr. Perlman's desk and hand in our work. We both knew that Mr. Perlman wanted to embarrass us, but I refused to give him the satisfaction. I held my head up high, put a smile on my face, and handed him the homework, saying, "Here, Mr. Perlman. It really helped. Thanks." Watching his face turn red made my smile genuine.

Before Nat and I could return to our seats, Mr. Perlman told the class that he was giving another writing assignment. "I want to see those creative juices flowing," he said. "There is no particular topic on which you must write, which should make the assignment easier for some of you," he said, looking directly at me. All papers are due on Monday, so you have the entire weekend to create your masterpiece. Are there any questions?"

When no hands went up, Mr. Perlman began the day's exercise. But I didn't listen to anything he was saying. I was excited about the opportunity to show Mr. Perlman how I could write. Since no specific topic was required, nothing I wrote could be wrong. Here was my chance, and Nat's too, to prove to Mr. Perlman and the class that we belonged there. Maybe then Mr. Perlman would treat us like the other kids.

After school I asked Nat what he was going to write about. He wrinkled his face and shrugged his shoulders like he was trying really hard to come up with an answer. Then he smiled. "I don't know, Dianne, but maybe I'll write a murder mystery with Mr. Perlman as the corpse."

I shook my head. I really wanted to come up with a good

topic. Nat was somewhat less enthusiastic. "You know, whatever we do, Mr. Perlman is going to hate it."

But I insisted that this time had to be different. "This time we can write anything. If we just double-check our grammar and spelling—"

"—Why do *we* have to dot every I and cross every T?" Nat interrupted me.

He had a point, but I was certain that if we did a good job on the paper Mr. Perlman would not have any excuse to treat us differently from the rest of the class.

Nat just looked at me and said nothing.

By the time I reached home I had my topic. I had seen twin girls on the bus. They made me wonder what it would be like to have a twin, and so I decided to write about twin sisters. I shouted a hello to my mother and ran to my room to change my clothes and begin writing. At first, all I could do was stare at the paper and chew my pencil eraser. I knew I wanted to write something about twin sisters, but what exactly? At dinner that night I stared at my plate, mad at myself for not having come up with an adventure for my twins.

I barely heard my father speaking to me. "Dianne, that food on your plate did not do a thing to you, so why are you giving it such a dirty look?"

"I'm not that hungry, Dad."

He looked at my mother for explanation, but she offered none. "Are you feeling okay, Dianne?"

"Yeah, I'm okay. I'm just thinking about something," I said.

"Uh-huh. Well, try eating some of those black-eyed peas on your plate. Don't you know that black-eyed peas are good for thinking?" He teased me further. "Yeah, black-eyed peas—not fish—is the real brain food."

"Black-eyed peas, huh, Daddy?"

"That's right. I heard tell that George Washington Carver himself used to eat a bowl of black-eyed peas every day. That's how come he was able to make his discoveries about the peanut and the sweet potato. A lot of people don't know that."

"I bet they don't," I said, laughing and scooping up a forkful of the new brain food. Then it hit me. Why not make my twins geniuses like George Washington Carver? Why not have them discover something, as he did? I quickly finished my dinner, making sure to eat my black-eyed peas, and rushed back to my room. This time, when I sat down to write, the words began to flow. I wrote for hours, until I was so sleepy I had to go to bed.

I spent Sunday, after church, cleaning up my grammar and spelling. I wasn't going to let Mr. Perlman use that excuse to keep from giving me an A.

Monday morning, Nat was waiting for me in front of the school building when I got off the bus. We exchanged stories, sitting on the steps. His story was good, and what impressed me even more was that Nat said it was true. He had written about his grandparents, who were threatened by the Ku Klux Klan after refusing to sell their land in South Carolina to a white farmer who wanted it, but they were able to defend themselves and keep their land.

I asked Nat what he thought of my story. When he told me that he really liked it, I thought we both had Mr. Perlman this time.

We hurried into the building to beat the late bell. That was probably the first time that I had actually looked forward to Mr.

Perlman's class. But by the time the bell rang, I began to have some doubts. I kept thinking of different ways I could have written my story. We barely had a chance to take our seats before Mr. Perlman demanded our assignments. He announced that he would return them that Friday. Great! All I had to do was make it to Friday.

The week just dragged. Nat kept telling me not to worry, that we were sure to do well. But nothing he said could make the sickly feeling in my stomach go away. The more I tried to put the story out of my mind, the more I thought about nothing else. Every day I tried to read the expression on Mr. Perlman's face for some clue about whether he had read and liked my story. Was he smiling at me or was that a sneer? It was hard to tell with his thin lips. Finally, Friday came.

Nat made a point of telling me that we were going to get our papers back that day. I rolled my eyes at him. Like I needed him to remind me about Friday. I asked him what grade he thought we would get on our papers. He frowned for a moment and then laughed. "Knowing Mr. Perlman, I bet he didn't like me putting down the Ku Klux Klan. And in your story the black girls are smart, which he probably didn't like either, so we'll both only get C's. But, hey, a C is better than an F."

I didn't laugh.

When the bell rang, my heart jumped. This was it. I stared at Mr. Perlman's face as I entered the classroom. Was he happy, upset, aggravated, excited? I couldn't tell. I took my seat next to Nancy Cicero and waited for the verdict.

"Settle down, please, everyone." I have your papers to return, and I must say there were some interesting stories from some of you. Of course, others showed no improvement at all."

Was he looking at me when he said that?

He walked around the classroom handing back the papers and making his usual comments. "Well done, Rebecca. George, watch your spelling. Nice job, Nancy."

Nancy smiled and laid her story on her desk to make sure I saw her B.

Mr. Perlman gave Nat back his story without saying a word. Nat looked at his paper and shrugged. Then he looked at me, holding up the title page to show me the C+ scribbled across the top. We both knew that Nat deserved better. There was not one red mark for grammar or spelling corrections, so why the C+? I shook my head and frowned. Things didn't look good for me, and I began to get angry.

When Mr. Perlman walked to the front of the classroom to announce the names of the students who would read their work to the class, I was surprised. He hadn't given me back my paper yet. I wondered how it could be so bad that he wouldn't even return it, but then I remembered that he had given me back my other assignment with the huge red F on it without blinking an eye. So where was my paper now? When he called out my name, I sat frozen. He had included me with the students who would read their papers to the class.

Nancy Cicero's mouth dropped open. She seemed to be more in shock than I was.

I watched as, one by one, the four other kids whose names had been called before mine read their stories. I watched them, but I couldn't listen to them read. I was too excited.

I was going to read my story to the class! He wanted *me* to read my story to the class! I was glad that I had put so much work into the writing.

Mr. Perlman stood, holding out my paper to me. "All right, Miss Dixon, we will hear from you now."

I smiled at him as I took it from his hands. I noticed that there was no grade on it, but I didn't think much about that. I looked up at the class, smiling so hard my cheeks hurt. I looked at Nat. He raised his fist halfway and mouthed the words "Way to go, Dianne!" to me. I was enjoying this.

I began reading my story to the class. It was about my genius twins. I had given them telepathic powers, but only between each other. They had discovered a cure for cancer from their experiments with black-eyed peas. One of the girls was kidnapped by the owners of a large drug company, who tried to force her to hand over the cancer cure. They wanted to develop an expensive pharmaceutical from the natural black-eyed peas cure so that they could make a lot of money. But the girls outsmarted the kidnappers. They sent telepathic messages to each other so that the police had no trouble finding the kidnappers' hideout. At the end of the story, I had the twins broadcast their experiments on the news so that everyone would know what the cure was and no drug company would be able to cheat people out of it.

When I finished reading my story, I looked up to see the expressions on the other kids' faces. They were smiling. And then they did something that I never would have expected. They began to clap. They were actually clapping for my story! All except Nancy Cicero, of course.

I looked at Nat and watched him put two fingers in his mouth and whistle, loud. Then I turned my head to look at Mr. Perlman. I wanted to see the face that I usually tried to avoid. I wanted to see what those thin lips looked like when they formed a smile. He stood glaring at me with his hands on his hips and his head tilted to one side. He was squinting his tiny blue eyes, and his lips were pinched tightly together. He cleared his throat and then he spoke.

"Well, well, well, Dianne. That was quite some story. Yes, a very good story in fact. And, as you can see, the whole class enjoyed it. They even clapped for you. So perhaps you will tell us who the author is so that we can give him or her proper credit."

At first I couldn't stop blinking my eyes, as though opening and closing them could somehow change what I had just heard. I was sure I had misunderstood.

"You heard me. We're all waiting. Whose book did you copy that story from? I know *you* couldn't have written that yourself."

I began to shake. I felt cold. My stomach churned and I half hoped I would vomit . . . yeah, vomit right in Mr. Perlman's face.

I was holding my story in my hand at my side, and slowly I began to crumple it between my fingers, rolling it against my thigh until all six pages were nothing more than a huge ball in my clenched fist.

I looked around the classroom. I could tell from my classmates' expressions that they all believed I had copied my story out of a book. Nancy Cicero was looking smug, as if to say, "I knew you couldn't have written it."

I looked at Nat. He was mad. He was clutching the edge of his desk and staring at Mr. Perlman. I turned back to Mr. Perlman and let out all my feelings of anger and frustration.

"I wrote this story myself," I said through clenched teeth, softly at first. I was not even sure I had spoken.

Mr. Perlman smiled. "Excuse me, Dianne, you said something?"

"I said I wrote this story myself!" I was yelling. I couldn't hold it in. I struggled to keep from crying in shame and embarrassment. I refused to give him that.

"That's right, Mr. Perlman . . . me, I wrote this. I know why that's so hard for *you* to believe, but that's your problem. I bet if I showed you all the drafts and rewriting I went through to get to this story, you still wouldn't be satisfied, would you Mr. Perlman? Do you want to ask my mother who wrote this, huh? Would you like to ask both my parents about this? I'll tell them to come here and see you. In fact, I want them to come. I think it's time they talked to you—and maybe the principal too—about the way you treat me and Nat. Is that what you want?"

The room was silent. Mr. Perlman's mouth hung open, but he recovered quickly.

"There's no need to speak with your parents or anybody else's. Evidently the homework assignment I gave you and Nathaniel to do after the last writing assignment paid off. You see that, class? It is possible to improve your writing by paying attention to the . . . ah . . . instructions in your texts. If Dianne can improve her writing, anyone can. Thank you, Dianne. You may take your seat now."

I didn't move.

Mr. Perlman glared at me, folding his arms across his chest.

"I said you may sit down, Dianne. We've heard quite enough from you for one day."

I didn't move.

"What are you waiting for, a handwritten invitation?" Mr. Perlman appeared nervous.

"No," I said. "I'm waiting for my grade. You didn't give me a grade for my story."

I walked over to him and shoved the ball of paper into his hands. He just looked at it at first, and then he looked at me. Slowly, he unwrapped the ball, smoothing out the pages. He walked over to his desk to pick up a pen. He reached out his hand for the red one and then stopped. He glanced back at me and then at the class, pausing for only a moment to look at Nat. He quickly picked up his blue ballpoint pen and scribbled across the top of my paper. Then he shoved the pages back into my hand, a sneer forming at the corners of his mouth.

I took back the pages and walked slowly to my seat. Sitting down next to Nancy, I spread my story out on my desk. I looked at the mark, not quite sure what to feel, until I caught her expression. Then I smiled as I watched her quickly turn her head so as not to see the A- just above the title.

I can still see her now . . . Mr. Perlman too. And I have often wondered how much of my experience in that sixth-grade class has shaped the person I have become. I suppose some credit must be due to Mr. Perlman for my decision to become a civil rights lawyer, a published writer of both fiction and nonfiction, and a teacher of legal writing. Perhaps, then, I have learned that even the most negative of circumstances can yield positive consequences. But he deserves much more "credit" than that, for I have also learned to be deeply suspicious of an entire group of people, based solely on their skin color. In the end, that is a lesson no eleven-year-old, or anyone else for that matter, should ever have to learn.

Dawn D. Bennett-Alexander

The mother of three daughters, (all of whom have stories published in this anthology), Dawn D. Bennett-Alexander is a law professor and writer who lives in Athens, Georgia.

As she describes in her story, she was given an unusual window through which to view the world when she was two years old, the point at which her family moved into a previously all-white neighborhood in Washington, D.C. Contrary to what she might have been expected to feel about being the only African-American child in her neighborhood, she remembers thinking that she and her family were as good as, if not superior to, their white neighbors.

Dawn's willingness to share her sometimes controversial thoughts and feelings, and her occasional use of anatomical slang, make this story one that is likely to provoke strong feelings. "As a writer I see myself as someone who shares personal, often painful, experiences as a way of helping others," she says. "I value honesty, integrity, openness, and willingness to grow."

(R)EVOLUTION OF BLACK AND WHITE

"I'm not going to suck your cock anymore!" "Fine, I'm not eating your pussy, either!"

"Cock?" Why would someone suck on a chicken? And eating a cat? Yucky! What in the world were they talking about?

Our white next-door neighbors were at it again. They were running down the pathway between our houses, screaming at the top of their voices for all to hear. The man grabbed the woman by the hair and dragged her to the ground. She screamed bloody murder, and he beat his fists against her head.

Not many black people may recollect the first time they saw someone white. I do. I was four years old, and she was the woman we bought our new house from two years before. At age six, I knew enough to know that before I saw this white woman who sold us our new home, and before we moved into it, surrounded by white neighbors rather than black ones, I had never before seen things such as I was witnessing. Such things never happened with our old black neighbors. These new kinds of folks, white ones, were *very* strange.

Actually, when I was three, a woman named Inza came to our old house in trouble, and my parents helped her out by letting her be our housekeeper. She seemed to cry and whine a lot, but I figured it was because she was white and so different from everyone else. Since she lived with us and had to adapt to our culture, she didn't really seem too terribly different. It was a while before I realized most maids weren't white. But Inza had left us when we moved to the new house, and these new neighbors were a different matter altogether.

My dad had moved us into an all-white area of Washington, D.C., at the corner of Thirteenth and East Capitol Street, against the wishes of the real estate agent whom he approached about buying the house and the unctuous white banker, both of whom advised my dad to "stay with his own."

Moving to the new area had been a challenge of a type I don't think my parents expected. The whites, who were supposedly better than we were, did not keep their yards up, ate weird food like hominy and canned spaghetti every night, had no phones (and constantly used ours), and had screaming fights like the one I had witnessed. We had never seen such things before in our black neighborhood.

I didn't understand. Why were they better than we were? This new neighborhood was just around the corner from the old one, but there was a world of difference. I longed for the security, familiarity, and tranquillity of my old neighborhood and for people who looked like me and didn't act strangely.

The Irbys, to our left, had a house full of kids, including two teenage daughters, Patsy and Ruby, who practically lived at our house with my older sisters of the same ages. We had a phone, and our house didn't have drunk, abusive parents. At least once a day (and usually more often than that), one of the Irby girls would motion one of my sisters to pretend she had a phone call so she could get out of the house. I gathered that it was okay for them to come use our phone, but they could not visit black neighbors just to socialize.

The Irby boys were my age. I only remember them for their attempts to get me into the closet at their house and play "show me yours and I'll show you mine." Their wormy-looking, tiny little pale penises looked like the grubs my mother dug up in the garden in the springtime. Ugh! I would always run away without holding up my end of the bargain. You'd have thought they'd eventually get it. No such luck. Eventually I did. I realized they were as interested (or more interested) in showing off their penises than in seeing my private parts. The best thing about that closet was that I saw my first set of kittens birthed there. That was far more memorable than the penis show.

Mr. Irby was a bus driver for the city and was of interest to me only because he brought home books of bus transfers, which we kids would play with. When Mr. Irby was home, he was always yelling at Mrs. Irby or the kids for something or other. They all seemed afraid of him. Mrs. Irby was a nonentity, whose only purpose I could see was to serve up dishes of nasty looking white hominy balls and spaghetti from cans and bear the brunt of Mr. Irby's unspecific ire.

None of the Irbys did what we considered to be the normal things of life. They didn't go to church, take care of their house, eat decent meals, or have a family routine that we could ascertain. The teenage sisters seemed happiest when they were at our house baking up a batch of cookies or a cake—something they never did at home.

Before long, the Irbys were gone. They had moved away, to parts unknown, because "their" neighborhood was now "going down," i.e., my family had moved in. As far as I was concerned, these people were pure trash, regardless of their color, yet because they were white, they considered themselves to be better than my family—so much so that they were willing to pull up stakes and move away. Despite the snub, I didn't mind their moving because it meant I didn't have to keep looking at tiny little white weenies.

The house to our right was a wonderful old mansion, complete with huge white columns in the front and a little house for servants attached to the back. The servants' quarters had long ago fallen into disrepair and was by then used mostly as a dumping ground for tools and discarded furniture. Placed as it was above the garage, in the shade of a wonderful huge mimosa tree, it was perfect for little kids to explore, and we did. The mansion had been divided into huge apartments, and all of the tenants were white except an interracial couple composed of a black female and a white male.

JoAnn Wolfrey, a skinny, scraggly-looking white girl with limp dishwater-brown hair, was my age, lived in the second-floor front apartment, and was my best friend. Even then, I understood that she held that position solely because of proximity. She was fine for me to play with at home, where there were no kids from school, few girls my age, and none very close to my house, but I was embarrassed by her at school. She had a speech impediment, a trashy, neglected appearance, and was commonly thought to be mentally slow. Her parents, Fred and Ruby, were hugely fat, red-faced chain smokers who were either sitting at the front window smoking and drinking or drunkenly beating each other up while screaming so that the entire neighborhood could hear.

Her parents clearly embarrassed JoAnn, who was often at the end of her father's drunken foot, so she found comfort in having our social circle confined to the two of us, so much so that she never gave me a hard time about ignoring her at school. It was as if she understood I should be embarrassed to be seen with her. I felt badly about doing it, especially since she voiced no opposition, but the price to pay with my school friends was too heavy to have it any other way.

My mother took a job as a crossing guard at my school. As a result, she was not at home for lunch. This was in the days when kids came home from school for lunch, and so my mother contracted with JoAnn's mother to feed me each day. JoAnn and I walked the two blocks home, ate, then walked back to school, sometimes sneaking a cigarette on the way. Until, that is, we burned off JoAnn's eyelashes without even noticing. Her mother noticed, got JoAnn to fess up, and JoAnn ratted on me. Much to my delight, my mother refused to believe I would do such a thing.

One day I told Ma I was tired of having potted meat for lunch. Ma raced over to Ruby's and demanded to know what Ruby was feeding me for lunch. My parents had been paying her to provide me with nutritious lunches, only to find out that I had been fed a steady diet of potted meat with crackers, alternating with undercooked red beans. I actually thought they were supposed to be crunchy. It hadn't occurred to me that Ruby was being paid to feed me. Ma cussed Ruby out for pocketing the money without feeding me correctly, and immediately made other arrangements for my lunch.

It had gotten to the point where I prayed for rain so I could wear my raincoat with pockets. I'd stuff my potted meat into the pockets and empty them out under the mailbox across the street on the way back to school. It was not until this brouhaha that I found out that Ruby had been watching me do this from the window. She knew I didn't eat the potted meat, but continued to serve it anyway because it was the cheapest thing to buy (aside from the beans) and enabled her to keep more of the money. To this day, I can't stand the sight of potted meat. What *is* that stuff, anyway?

Our basement apartment neighbors in the mansion had a six-year-old daughter named Terry Lynn Myers. They were from "Faaayv'l Norfkilliiiinah," they'd say, as we snickered. Terry Lynn is the one from whom I learned the dreaded N word. One day I went over to ask if she could come out and play. Her grandmother told me that Terry Lynn couldn't play with niggers. I had no idea what it meant, but I was sure from Ma's reaction that it was bad. My mother told me to go back and ask again and to tell the grandmother not to call me a nigger again. I went back and it happened again.

Before I could get it out good, Ma was next door dragging Terry Lynn's mother out of her basement apartment. Ma didn't want to beat the old grandmother, so she grabbed the mother. Ma was tall, thin, and big-boned like her mother before her. She had herself grown up in North Carolina, had known the hard life of a migrant farmworker as a young girl, and was all too familiar with the ways of the south. Ma was damned if she was going to take the same crap from a trashy white neighbor as she had been forced to take from the sleazy white landowner whose crops she needed to pick. In a flash, Terry Lynn's mother was on the ground, Ma was straddled across her with the woman's head in her hands, and was hitting it against the cement in time with her admonitions. "Didn't, whack, I, whack, tell, whack, you, whack, not, whack, to, whack, call, whack, my, whack, daughter, whack, a, whack, nigger, whack, again, whack?!" Terry Lynn's poor little skinny mama was screaming at the top of her lungs.

Yes, there were people around, including Terry Lynn's father, but they were not about to interfere with Ma, who was clearly on a roll. When Ma was finished making her point, she got up and went home, saying only that when she told someone to do something, she meant it, and when they didn't listen, the consequences weren't her fault. Needless to say, the Myers family moved soon after. I heard they were going back to "Faaayv'l Norfkilliiiinah." I guess they figured that the "niggers" knew how to act there.

The whole time I was growing up, in junior high and high school, the only white person in my entire school was inevitably one of my next-door neighbors (my graduating class alone had six hundred students). After JoAnn's family moved, a little boy named Robbie moved in. We were fast friends, but again, it was embarrassing at school. I'm not sure if I was embarrassed because they were white and everyone else was black, or because they lived next door to me, and somehow that made me less cool than everyone else. I do know that there were clear racial lines drawn, and I did not like being forced to cross them.

Thirty years later, my old neighborhood changed back to predominantly white. At some point in the 1970s, white folks decided they loved the spacious houses with wood floors, high ceilings, and original woodwork. (Of course, I'm sure it had nothing to do with the fuel crisis, which put them in a bind when they had to drive into town from the suburbs, to which they had fled twenty years before.) So to accommodate their wishes, taxes were raised, making it difficult, if not impossible, for blacks to stay in our neighborhood. They left in droves, as the whites, anxious to get back to town, quickly bought the blacks out and renovated the houses, raising the prices and making it nearly impossible for most blacks to move into the area.

All our old neighbors are gone. My dad managed to pay off the house and hang on, but he is now in the painful throes of advanced Alzheimer's and was recently put in a nursing home. The house is still in the family, the property taxes have skyrocketed, and, once again, our next-door neighbors are white, as are all the rest of the homeowners on the street.

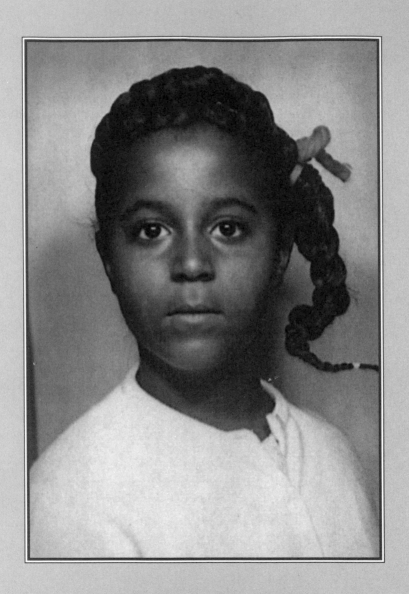

E-K. Daufin

E-K. Daufin is a writer who teaches at a university in Alabama. She has had a varied career: newspaper reporter, freelance journalist, part-time maid, bookstore clerk, secretary, antiracism consultant, and psychic. Her stories and poems have been published in more than a dozen magazines and journals.

One of several writers in this anthology to focus on the psychological impact of childhood hair rituals, E-K. Daufin tells us how she finally liberated herself from other people's expectations of her and her hair. She says of her story, "I wish I could give out copies of this story in tracts like the ones evangelists give out about Jesus. I wish I could say to well-meaning but ignorant people, 'Read this before you say *anything* to me about my hair or black folks' hair or white folks' hair. Read this before you make any assumptions about me because of my hair. . . .'"

WHAT I DREADED

I dreaded many things before I dreaded my hair. I dreaded scratching my head during the night—an absent-minded gesture, in a sleep-filled dreamland, was enough to bring serious repercussions. Where I had scratched, the white cream would seep through the protective layer of grease and burn fury in my scalp.

Yet this cream relaxer that turned my head into my own personal inferno was better than the hot comb. Mother began to press my hair because, as family legend would have it, I was born with "real nigger hair." That is the kind of hair that was said to be "God-cropped," and probably wouldn't grow more than a smidgen. God-cropped girls were doomed to not even have the bodhi-tree bush of Angela Davis. These sad souls were condemned to wear the pitifully pressed, weedy wisps of nappy-haired girls.

In the days of the hot comb, Mother set me in the high chair and opened a three-row package of Oreo cookies on the tray in front of me. "My nerves can not stand that child screamin'," she used to say. Taught to compulsively eat not long after I learned to walk, the otherwise forbidden treats became a distracting cornucopia.

Sugar-sedated, I lost the fear of the steaming cast-iron comb and the smoking melted grease. My mother carefully tested the hot-toothed monster, pulling it from the blue propane flame and rubbing it quickly against three thicknesses of white paper towels. If the paper came away only beige from burning, she would swiftly pull the comb through a thin layer of my damp, well-oiled hair. Years later, she would place my hair between the barrel and clamp of a forge-hot curling iron.

Hair-care experts say that you're not supposed to press hair with a hot comb, or even with the new electric curling irons, unless the hair is absolutely dry. Pressing damp hair practically fries it. But it also gives it a straighter look—the desired result. That's why it's said that vain black women who had no flair for domesticity had "nothin' cookin'" at their houses but hair." From these fallen Afro-dites came that lingering, telltale smell of fried hair mixed with perfume.

Few black women use a hot comb to press their hair anymore. Most black women use chemical relaxers to straighten their hair, *if* they were not born with "good hair." That's how straight, potentially long hair is still depressingly referred to in the African-American community. Thanks to modern science, there is no longer a need to first coat the entire head with grease before spreading and working a lye mixture into the hair. If you've seen the early scenes in Spike Lee's *Malcolm X*, when Malcolm, né Little, gets his hair conked in a barbershop, you have some idea of what that process looks like.

But even the modern, milder, no-lye relaxers usually require the kinky-haired maiden to bear the searing pain of a scalp on fire long enough for the most resistant parts of our hair (near the nape of the neck, referred to as "the kitchen") to "take." The nappy-headed, would-be queen is usually coaxed, coddled, or coerced into enduring the burning pain as long as possible in hopes that her hair will be as straight as possible.

Relaxing my hair was always a gamble. We had to toy with the odds of how much straightness would win over what portion of my scalp would be covered with scabs for a couple of weeks. Sometimes, in the gamble, luck was a lady, and I'd come out looking like the black women you see in the magazines. Sometimes the dice crapped out on me, and my hair was not much straighter than it was before the ordeal. But I'd still have scabs to show for it, and my mother would have lost the fifteen dollars for a home kit or the eighty-five dollars for a salon job.

After each cosmetic humiliation—professional or home-made—I only had two or three weeks to nurse a pink, freshly healed scalp before I would bloody it again—a lifelong menstruation of the tresses. In retrospect, I see that I greeted each straightening of my hair with the same kind of shame and secrecy with which I had been taught to regard the monthly blood that flowed from the lips of my vulva, which was, ironically, covered with hidden *straight* hair.

When and where I grew up, hair straightening was a matter of survival for a female African-American adolescent in an integrated world. My life was confined by, and in some ways defined by, the necessity of perpetuating the farce that my hair was "good," i.e., long and soft like that of the white girls or the luckier black girls who had more "Indian blood" to thin the gene for thick hair that refused to blow lithely in the wind.

Therefore, there was no swimming in my youth because it would have made my hair "turn back." The chlorine's foul mating with the chemical relaxers left the relaxers impotent against the naturally resilient, rising kink. There was no participation in sports without hell to pay at home. Salty sweat invites the ever-ready kinky roots to spring forth.

In my twenties, I still stealthily rubbed white cream into my hair, always careful to shred the boxes so that no one would identify them in the trash. From the time I was fifteen, I traced my hairline with petroleum jelly before I used the relaxers so that I would not have the fresh, pink outline of a chemical burn that would have revealed the secret behind my mask—that I did not have good, straight, acceptable hair.

As world-class survivors, black women know how to find what joy there may be in any pain we have to endure. Some of my most intense feelings of sisterhood and cultural belonging were bred during the whole Saturdays I spent in clandestine basement beauty shops in Baltimore.

The cosmetologist was always late. In the early morning coolness, some of us would lean on the wrought-iron fence that surrounded the four steps that descended to the beauty shop. Others would balance their broad brown butts on the cool, clean marble steps outside of a neighbor's front door. Three generations of women would get their hair done on the same day. Usually my grandmother would go first, out of deference, and out of everyone's desire to drown her sharp tongue's bitter words in the drone of the hair dryer as soon as possible. Next was my mother, who would watch me with keen eyes to make sure I didn't scratch before it was my turn to be crowned with white cream in the red vinyl throne.

By the time my turn came, everyone was already tired and cranky. Nothing less than stoicism was permitted during the yanking, burning, and sitting with migraine-making tight rollers under the hot blast of a preheated dryer. Pins pressed into my cranium. Fat brown flesh stuck like a Band-Aid to the pink plastic seat. I felt a fearsome freedom when I was finally "brushed out" and released to the cool evening air.

Also dwelling in this torture chamber were: luscious neighborhood gossip; sexy young black women whispering witty compliments in my ear; a child-bragging contest that *my* mother always won. It was a world where women reigned supreme in the stories they told about their fine fucking or frequent infidelities. It was a sorority in which straightening our hair bound us like the interlaced parts of my braids.

Still, even though I enjoyed the sweet sisterhood born in black beauty parlors, I began to see the high price I paid for it. Black women are some of the poorest people in the world, yet we spend large portions of our incomes to torch our scalps or whip our hair into a greased frenzy of Jheri-Curled cyclones. When I relaxed my hair, I had it cut as cheaply as possible at the beauty school, and, for the most part, I bought the chemical relaxers at the drugstore rather than paying to go to a salon. Even so, in the two years I have let my hair grow naturally, I have saved nearly fourteen hundred dollars in hair care products and services that I no longer have to buy.

Now, shampooing and twisting the hair near my scalp with a little oil and beeswax each week is all it takes to maintain my dreads. This process saves me about ten hours a week in grooming time, compared to the time it took to maintain my straight-at-the-root and curled-at-the-end processed hair. That's 1,040 extra hours over two years—forty-three and one-third days.

That leaves me time to write in my journal, sleep a little longer, get to work a little earlier. Hell, for some people that's time enough for another part-time job.

We are led to believe that straightening our hair is *not* expensive self-torture but a small price to pay in order to be man-attracting, professional-looking black women. I wanted to be those things too, but as I entered my adulthood I began to dread the price the white cream commanded for its payoff of sexiness and acceptability. I dreaded the silent self-hatred I kept buried in a basket of unlaundered rationalizations while I proclaimed the gospel of self-love at my workshops and ceremonies. (I am a lecturer and ordained minister.) I grew tired of dreading myself so much that I didn't even know what my head was like off the white-cream jones of soft length.

So, instead of continuing to dread myself, I dreaded my hair. I cut off the thin, chemically altered wisps. With a minimum of histrionics, I bravely threw away my comb and straightener, which I had always kept with my emergency supplies. Hey, if fire, flood, or earthquake hit, I was going to make sure that I wouldn't be caught dead in any nasty, nappy roots.

At first I thought my hair was taking revenge upon me for three decades of oppression. For the first two months it looked as though it wasn't going to lock. Even the gentlest washing seemed to tear the twisted strands asunder. The new growth was softer than I had expected. Perhaps I thought a Brillo-textured, Patti LaBelle-esque spike would naturally erupt from my untamed follicles. My fears were unfounded. The jagged lightning strokes of my single strands eventually bound together to form sensational, soon-to-be-styleable dreads.

Once the dreads began to grow, I began to dread my encounters with well-intentioned white women who, upon seeing me, would:

—ask me how they could make their hair look like mine,

—rush up to me, a stranger, grasp my small, black dreads in tight, pink fists, and exclaim how much they *love* my hair,

—try to commiserate with me about how tangled their curled straight hair gets and say "I know *just* how you feel," or

—tell me how lucky I am to have hair that will twist into braid-like sculptures and bemoan all the trouble *they* have to go through with their straight hair.

When I try to explain to them what straightening my hair cost me in self-love, dollars, cents, and time, they'd ho-ho and say, "Isn't it funny that black women want to straighten their hair and white women want to curl theirs?" Rarely did they give me a chance to tell them that it is not an even equation. At any rate, I used to have to straighten *and* curl my hair—not every couple of months but, in some way, every day.

Now, when white women ask me how they can make their hair look like mine, I tell them they can't. Few of them have hair kinky enough to form dreads. My kinky hair, and the hard-won pride with which I now wear it, they can not take from me or adapt it to their own uses. When well-meaning strangers reach for my hair, I do my best to intercept their grasp and explain that my locks draw in divine energy, and no, they can not touch them. When my white sisters try to tell me about how my hair *really is* just like theirs, or start going on about how *lucky* I am to have my kind of hair, I don't argue anymore.

I just smile and agree. I *am* really lucky . . . lucky to have won back the beauty of my nappy hair. Now I sport shoulder-length locks, twirled with beeswax and left to pull into my psyche Mother Earth's delicate, Jah-love vibration through an uncharred scalp. My sacred antennae become me. Dreaded, I dread my natural self no more.

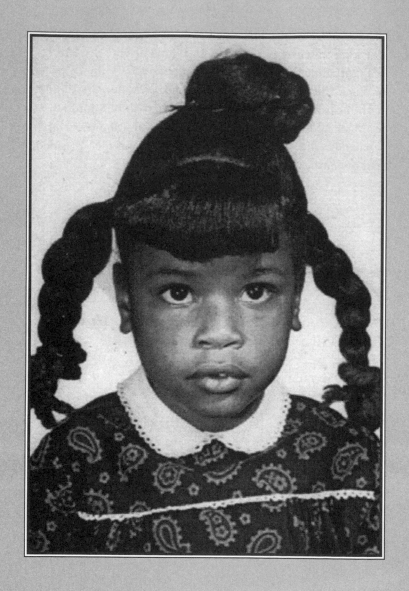

Yvonne "Princess" Jackson

A professor of English and creative writing, Yvonne A. Jackson lives in Birmingham, Alabama, where she was born in the 1960s. She has had several stories and poems published in national publications, and she was awarded the Alabama State Council on the Arts Individual Artist Fellowship for 1996-1997.

Yvonne says that her intent as a writer is to give voice to people who usually don't have voice in print, "the struggling and working black poor." Having grown up in poverty, she says she knew that her family was always under the threat of total annihilation. "There was never enough money for any of those things called 'necessities.' We were poor and, though I didn't understand the precise connection, I knew it was because we were black, and I was equally sure that white people were not poor."

In her story, Yvonne describes her childhood response to

the extreme poverty she grew up in. With a striking, poetic choice of words and images, she conveys how she mothered her own hungry and exhausted mother, taking on adult responsibilities long before her childhood was over.

RUNOVER

The bellies of small black Alabama girls are something else again.

When I was six, my sister, Peaches, ran over mine with her bike and, though I felt tires bearing in, I did not yield. She was trying to learn to ride by coasting down the steep hill of our mortician neighbor's driveway. She was rolling faster and faster. I had been spinning myself drunk and had crumpled to the ground and lay on the driveway watching the cloud ponies circle on the sky carousel. When I could focus again, Peaches was bearing down on me, screaming, her legs veed out from the spinning pedals. I waited to be scared in half, But the bicycle's front tire popped over my body, and the rear tire too, as though I were but a smooth brown stone. There was no pain, nothing of the burn that being run over should be.

When I sat up, tearless and whole, everyone was amazed. Peaches made me pull my shirt over my head so she could get a better look, and she leaned in close, knifing the pudgy mortician's kids with her elbows for breathing their hot breath in her ears. When she was satisfied, she stepped back and let them see the clay of my unmarked belly. They reached first with the tips of their fingers, then grabbed with the full cups of their grubby hands to hold my visceral, messianic secrets. "Stop! That tickles."

Peaches shoved me with the flat of her hand. "Lay down," she said. "I was going too fast. Let's make sure."

This seemed like a good idea to the chubby mortician's kids, who grabbed me on either side, by wrist and shoulder. "Lay down." They would have pushed me down and held me, but just then we heard the rattle of Mama's old Chevy, Nellie Bell, rounding the curve. Peaches sliced her chin left and right. The mortician's kids let go of me and turned to watch Mama as she pulled into the gravel drive. "Good evening," they chanted, like they were in Sunday morning worship. I skipped, to the beat of their chant, over to Mama.

Mama cupped my chin to her hip. "You awright, Princess?"

"Unh-hunh," I nodded.

Mama looked over to Peaches. "I told y'all I didn't want you outside when I'm gone."

Peaches reminded her it was *Wizard of Oz* night, the one time in the year when the mortician's wife allowed us to darken the doorway of her split-level brick house to sprawl barefoot, spread-eagled, and ashy-legged on the floor of her plaid den to watch Princess Dorothy find the golden road, instead of standing outside to receive the small oatmeal cookies she passed through the top half of her split back door while her kids sat down to their lunch of cream of broccoli soup, ham and cheese sandwiches, and corn curls. "She say she don't mind watching us," Peaches told Ma. "Come on, Princess," she said to me.

I spent the rest of the afternoon on the front step of our duplex, rocking my Suzy doll baby and trying to style her hard, synthetic hair into ponytails like Peaches and I wore, all the time keeping an eye on Peaches and the pudgy mortician's kids, who kept waving to me to come back over. Once, Peaches came over and, leaning close and hooking my waist in a sisterly vise, whispered, "I'll let you play with my yo-yo." I shook my head and Peaches stood up. Kneeing me in the chest and head, "Oops," she stomped into the house. When she came back she had her Suzy doll baby, which used to be identical to mine.

"I'll let you play with *my doll.*" She nodded toward the mess of startled twigs on my Suzy doll baby's head. This was to remind me how much more lush *her* Suzy doll baby's hair was, since she hadn't done like me and tried to straighten the "life-like Afro hair" with Mama's hot comb. The hair had fallen out in handfuls so that my Suzy doll baby's over-straight spears of rubber-banded hair made her look like the girls in the Mickens family down the street, who Ma always said, closing her eyes and shaking her head, just didn't have growing hair.

I looked over at her doll baby, snuggled down in her cradling arms. Peaches's Suzy doll baby still had soft hair that could be combed out into a tall Afro or, if you picked your part lines carefully, divided into puffy ponytails. But Peaches hadn't been under the bike tires.

It hadn't hurt exactly, but for the slightest moment I'd felt two things at once—my insides locking up as they did right before vomiting and as they did right before last Christmas, when Peaches pointed to the stash of flimsy plastic toys in the back of Mama's chifforobe and said, "Told you." I didn't tell Peaches, but I was sure if she ran her bike over me again, some precious line that tied me to that place might be torn, and I would no longer know my name or who I belonged to.

Peaches punched me in the bulb of my shoulder. "Be that way then, red gal," she said. "I'm not gone play with you no more." She hip-walked over to rejoin the mortician's kids, banging her Suzy doll baby against her thigh as she went. When she was back on their driveway and out of earshot, she posed Suzy on her bike handlebars, turned and mouthed a single word, "Sissy."

Mama was opening and closing the kitchen cabinet doors when I went in. She worked her way left to right and back again as though she expected the contents of the cabinets to change. "They say food or study, I cain't have both. Father, you do make your children to stumble," she said. She was tired. On the counter were two small white potatoes and a can of string beans.

"Mama?"

She looked down at me. "You're always underfoot. Get out of here. Be a child. Something."

I didn't go out. I pretended to be invisible. As quiet and close as a person can get. I watched Mama peel and boil the potatoes and add the green beans.

At dinnertime everybody went in, our awe and bodies intact, sure in some way that the bellies of small black Alabama girls were made of marble—dense, sweetly veined blacktop, where tires ran their most smooth, unhindered by friction or any laws of nature.

Peaches wanted to know how come there wasn't no corn-bread or Kool Aid. Mama sat there watching us, Peaches practically inhaling her food and eyeing my plate. "You gone eat that?"

I sat there with my hand on my belly, wondering about what had happened. How come I didn't split in two—did I have a future as the magician's lady what gets sawed in half on the TV in the mortician's plaid den?

"Princess? Baby?" Mama leaned toward me, touching the back of her hand to my face.

"I'm not hungry."

"You sure?"

"Unh-hunh."

She pulled my plate to her. Peaches narrowed her eyes. "I thought you said you already ate."

"I could do with a little more," Mama said, scooping half of my plate onto Peaches's plate. My sister stared across at me like she could pin me down with her eyes.

I was almost asleep when I felt a sharp pain in my right thigh. Peaches was holding my flesh between her thumb and forefinger. "You're a liar," she hissed.

Now she feels the need to pinch me. Frequently. At bathtub's edge, rinsing the ink of scalding summer days from the thick hulls of our feet. In the backseat or the back pew. Or just before I fall asleep in the narrow bed we share. When I cry out, she flashes her white smile in the blue night. But the secret is not to be found in the palatte of my thigh—in the blush red, hard purple-black, or rotted green.

I am different. I spend more time at Mama's side, at first to avoid experimentation with flying bicycles and pinchers, but, later, because I prefer it. I help Mama take off her shoes. I heat and pour the water for her Epsom soaks. With one of Mama's old shirts cinched around me for an apron, I peel potatoes and wash collards and mix up cornbread. Wash dishes. On her Father-you-do-make-your-children-to-stumble nights, I sit on her lap with my legs snaked around hers. I pretend she is my doll baby and, talking high and shrill, I scoop up cornbread soaked in pot liquor and dump it into her mouth. Time with her is filled with deliberate ritual. I nestle with her late at night as she fans through the pile of bills. When she turns to me, her face as brown and expressionless as a pancake, I think I see the beginning of a smile.

The kids on the block see the difference. They stand back. They listen to me when disputes arise about who tagged whom. If this person had an O or a U before the last hit in dodgeball.

Mama finally notices too. When telling me to get out from under her—"Go outside, go play, get away from grown folks' business"—no longer works, she lets go a long breath. I feel the tremble of stillness.

Seeing her form swell out from me in the chifforobe mirror, a superhero's cape, I understand what I, wrenched from her earth, am to be. I look for my inheritance. Mama's super black velvet must be in the closet, in her purse, or pillowing her head at night. Maybe it's behind the couch, where earrings, pennies, and lost faith congregate.

Sometimes as Mama tucks me in at night I think I hear the sound of wings unfurling, secret strengths arching upward.

I want to tell her that I know, so I squeeze my fists down to show my muscles. "I'm . . ." But not having the words I need, I settle back against my sister's already still and quiet knees, my limbs growing thick and speechless. I say it again . . . the incomplete thought, "I'm . . . I am . . ." Then I sleep, held close in the arms of fragile sleep.

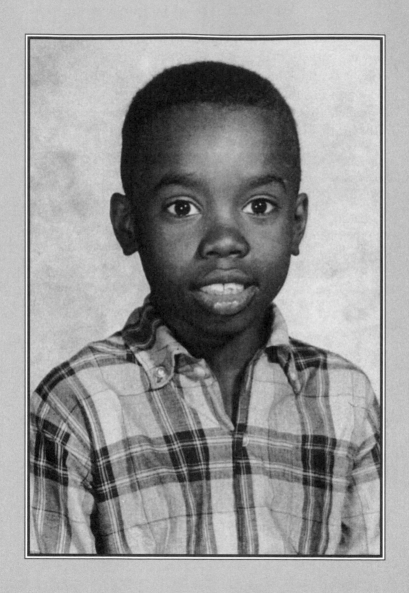

Anthony Ross

Anthony Ross is a prisoner on death row in San Quentin. "Whether or not I live another second," he says, "I have to reach beyond these prison walls and show someone, anyone, that even in the face of the worst circumstances, anything is possible if you have faith in what you're doing and confidence in yourself."

Anthony began writing in 1989. Completely self-taught, he says that as a writer he is constantly developing, constantly trying to take his work to the next level. "I write to connect with others, with the creative energy inside and beyond me, and, ultimately, with myself." In 1995, Anthony's short story "Walker's Requiem" received a PEN award.

In the story that follows, Anthony recounts two horrific experiences with racism that he says caused him to hate white people so much that, for the first time in his life, he considered killing them. "I hope the reader is able to understand how single events and choices can have cosmic effects," he says. "I went on to drop out of school a couple of years later, and I became a gang member. I've been in prison for seventeen years."

LITTLE TIGERS DON'T ROAR

On a May day in Los Angeles, in 1970, when I was eleven years old, two things happened that changed my life.

I had taken to riding the RTD bus down to the Black Panthers' small storefront office on Broadway. The walls of the reception area were covered with posters of Huey Newton sitting in a wicker chair; a rifle, a spear, the eyes of a cat, and "Free Huey" flyers were stacked all around the office. Behind the desk a huge flag hung on the wall with a black panther on it that looked like it was ready to leap.

For a few hours after school each day, I ran errands, passed out flyers, and listened to a beautiful sister with a big Afro rap about some guy named Mao as she read from a little red book she claimed would fix everything. (She sure had me convinced.) Afterward, they would let the kids who'd helped out that day eat all the cookies and doughnuts we wanted.

On the day that Huey Newton was to be released from prison, I took a stand of my own at West Athens Elementary School. My teacher, a fiftyish white woman named Mrs. Paget, had just called me a nigger because I refused to stay in the classroom while she read *Little Black Sambo* aloud to the class. There was something about that story that made me angry, something in the way Mrs. Paget read it that gave me the distinct feeling that Sambo was in the classroom and she fully expected him to come forward holding a big plate of flapjacks.

"Don't be a nigger, Ross," she said as I walked out of the classroom.

It was my first real experience with the issue of race, and her words made me conscious of my blackness in a way that all of the black power and black pride slogans down at the Panther office had not. This was the first of two things that happened that day that changed my life.

When . . . why . . . how . . . did I become a nigger? The questions exploded in my mind. It had never occurred to me that, even though I was one of the best students in her class, to her I still was, at the core, a nigger. The word was hurled with all the force of slavery behind it, and it stung just as deeply as if I'd been hit with a bullwhip.

That afternoon I hooked up with a cat I hung out with named Billy Cadwell. He ran it down to me about Huey being freed. "He's outta jail, man, and there's gonna be some righteous shit going down now!" Billy, who was also eleven, considered us Black Panthers. He'd stolen us each a black tam from the New York Hat Store in downtown Los Angeles, saying, "All we gotta do now is get us some leather coats."

But I knew it meant more than that. I told him, "Naw, man, we gotta meet Mao first," remembering what the sister had said, knowing there was a connection somewhere. "Then we meet Huey and help fix things in the ghetto."

"Right on," Billy said, holding up a clenched fist.

I told Billy I wanted to go down to the Panther office but didn't have money for the bus.

"I'm tapped too, man," he said, pulling out his pockets for emphasis.

After giving our situation some thought, we decided to go try to collect some golf balls for some quick change at the golf course in Gardena, a small suburb on the south end of Los Angeles that was predominately white and Asian with just a smidgen of blacks. I rode all the way there on the handlebars of Billy's Schwinn bike, but when we got there the place was closing.

"Now what we gonna do, Tony?" Billy asked as we stood in front of the golf course contemplating our next move.

"I'll think of something," I said. But I didn't have a clue as to what we were going to do. And that's when the second thing happened that changed my life.

A white kid about our age walked up to us. "Hey, you guys aren't supposed to be here. You better leave." His voice carried that same tone I'd heard in Mrs. Paget's voice. The same tone as the white manager at Ralph's supermarket used when he asked, "You here to buy something?" It was a tone that came down from some high peak I was never supposed to ascend, a tone that pushed without apology.

"Well?" the white kid asked, his bright blue eyes embodying both problem and solution.

I socked him so fast it made Billy flinch. I told the kid to give me all his money. Stunned, he reached into his pocket and took out a few bills. I snatched them, feeling a heightened sense of his whiteness—my blackness. I hopped on the handlebars, and Billy took off like a demon was on our heels.

"Man, you decked that mothafuckin' white boy!" Billy shouted in my ear, laughing.

But I wasn't laughing. I wasn't even thinking about that white kid any longer. I was thinking about whether or not I would go back to school ever again.

We made it to Helen Keller Park, about a mile away. A dark ring of sweat was working its way around Billy's collar. "Tony, you gonna have to go to the office without me," Billy said, holding his stomach and breathing hard.

"Why?" I asked, thinking something might be wrong with his health.

" 'Cause," he grimaced, "I gotta dookie reeeal bad."

We both laughed. "It's cool, man. I'll tell you all about it when I get back."

We gave each other a soul handshake, and then Billy sped off for home, hunched down over the handlebars, feet pumping the pedals at a dizzying speed.

I began walking up Vermont Avenue toward the bus stop, but I didn't get two blocks before I heard the sudden wail of a siren that made me turn around to see a police car speeding toward me with lights flashing. It jumped the curb and came to a halt, inches from my legs. I stepped back, ready to bolt, when two white sheriffs hopped out, guns drawn, screaming at the top of their lungs. "Lay down, asshole! Get on the fucking ground."

I stood frozen, unable to move. "You better lay down, motherfucker!" they screamed. I wanted to—God knows I wanted to—but my brain was short-circuited. I was scared shitless. From somewhere behind me I heard voices pleading for me to lie down. Someone—a woman—begged, "Please, son, don't give them a reason to kill you."

Kill me? The words spun in my mind like an out-of-control

Disney ride. I heard a childlike voice ask, "What'd I do?" I didn't even realize it was my own voice until one of the sheriffs yelled, "You're under arrest for robbery."

The entire scene switched to slow motion. "On the ground, asshole, or I will blow your fucking head off!" he screamed, each word dripping with venom. I knew instinctively that he would kill me.

Taking that kid's money still hadn't registered, but I did finally get my motor skills to work and I lay on the ground. The men rushed over and I felt a knee come down hard on my neck, knocking my face into the pavement and busting my lip. They pulled my arms back, sending a shock wave of pain through my shoulders. One of them handcuffed me, and the other one knocked the tam from my head and whispered, "Another second and I'd blow you away . . . you hear me, nigger?"

I said nothing.

The two of them yanked me up off the ground, and a fresh bolt of pain shot through my shoulders. They hauled me to the police car, where I saw the moon face of the white kid looking tearfully out at me from the backseat. My heart pounded in my chest. This wasn't about the money anymore. It was about an old equation of black and white, about place and status. Again, something instinctive gripped me as I stood there, my black skin seeming to take on some awful substance that separated me from everything, making me conscious of who I was, who I was not—a substance that saddled me with a deep hatred for myself, for whites. I had no idea of what it was like to be black in America, but I knew what it was like being black in Los Angeles.

"This the one?" one of the sheriffs asked the white kid.

I prayed the kid had lost his memory. No such luck—he nodded his head, mumbling, "Uh-huh."

I felt like a gigantic fist had knocked me down, and for a moment I was overcome with the sensation of vertigo. I was falling . . . falling into the racial quicksand with no way out.

The sheriffs got the money from me, gave it to the kid, and told him to go home. They tossed me into the backseat, where I bounced on the handcuffs, immediately tightening them. I asked if they could loosen them, and my question was met with a barrage of obscenities. I was told to shut my fucking mouth or my nigger ass would be put in the trunk.

As we drove away, I saw the sidewalk was lined with people, black people. Their faces showed not the slightest hint of protest or concern. Instead, I saw a mixture of fear and relief. I wished the Panthers were there. I wished Huey was there.

The two sheriffs apparently found delight in my pain, and they intentionally drove over every pothole, bump, and manhole cover they could find en route to the Lennox Sheriff Station. The sheriff on the passenger side would point and say, "Look, look, here comes another one." And then they would burst out laughing when I winced from the cuffs biting into my wrists. For the entire ride, I had to endure the steady onslaught of profanity, threats, and laughter as they described in detail how they were going to kill me and then dump my body in a vacant lot or behind a trash dumpster.

"Just another dead nigger," the sheriff who was driving said.

"Yeah, who's gonna care about that?" asked the sheriff on the passenger side, turning to me.

I sat in my own silence, trying to escape the inescapable. And as if he could read my mind, the sheriff on the passenger side asked, "What you thinking about, nigger, you wanna escape, huh?" He looked over at the driver and yelled, "Stop the car! The nigger is trying to escape."

His partner hit the brakes. My head whiplashed, hitting the back of the front seat. They both drew their guns, pointing them at my head. I shut my eyes, crunched my small frame into the seat, and waited to be shot. But no shot came— just the loud yell of "Boom!" making me jump. I opened my eyes. The two sheriffs were cracking up.

All that I had ever heard about police was confirmed by these two, so once we arrived at the substation and I was pulled from the backseat, I tried to make a run for it. I got almost a full two feet before one of them snatched my shirt collar, swung me around, and sunk his fist in my stomach. I folded up into a ball of pain, trying to suck in gulps of air as they dragged me across the ground toward a brick building.

"What you got there?" someone asked.

"A little monkey," one of the sheriffs answered.

"Come on, we got a nice cage for him," a voice said.

I heard the jingling of keys as they pulled me down a dimly lit hallway with large steel doors on the sides. Someone shouted from behind one of the doors, "Do me like that, you punk pig!"

The men paid no attention to the challenge as they half kicked, half threw me into a small dank cell.

I could see the sheriff with the keys. On the shoulder of his shirt were yellow stripes. "What this one do?" he asked.

"Robbed a little white kid," the sheriff who'd driven us there told him.

"The nigger also tried to run on us, Sergeant," the other sheriff added, smiling.

The sergeant leaned over me and said, "Boy, we gon teach you bout messin wit our kind."

They started hitting and kicking my whole body. Every ounce of emotion I had was being beat out of me. A seething hatred would be the only thing left.

I hadn't realized they had stopped until I heard the steel door slam shut. I glanced up from the floor and saw a pale face peering through a small window in the center of the door. "You better get used to it, nigger. You just better get used to it."

I felt, rather than thought, that this is how things are, but I was angry and I needed to protest. I rose from the floor and started banging on the door, screaming. "Come back, mothafuckahs! I'll kill you! You pigs! Honky mothafuckahs!" I kept it up for about ten minutes—until older and stronger voices from the other cells joined in, drowning me out. I lay on the steel cot, my body bruised, numb. Eventually I fell asleep out of exhaustion . . . and rage.

Sometime later I awoke to the sound of jingling keys and the door opened. I had lost all sense of time, and it seemed as if I had been in the cell for a day or two; actually, it had only been a few hours. In the doorway stood a white man wearing a suit. We stared at each other for a moment, and finally he said, "If you ever come back, I'ma kick your black ass personally."

He took me out into a lighted reception room, where my mother sat on a long wooden bench. I could see she had been crying.

"What them people do to you?" Mamma asked me in the car.

For some reason I didn't tell her. Maybe I thought there was nothing she could do, that it was too late. All I could think about for days afterward was how I wanted to kill a white policeman. In the span of a few hours I had gone from an eleven-year-old who made one mistake to one with enough racial hatred to kill. And, before that day, I had never thought about killing anyone.

That night I told Mamma about Mrs. Paget, and the next morning she marched into the principal's office demanding that something be done. The school took immediate action—they merely transferred me out of Mrs. Paget's class into another one. And she just kept right on teaching and reading that Black Sambo book.

As I grew up, my life became so inextricably bound up in black and white that, no matter where I went, I couldn't avoid seeing things in those terms. I searched for confrontation, perhaps even creating it at times. The race shit was always there, soiling and dominating everything I did. It was an insane way to grow up, an insane way to live. And just as the two white sheriffs had zealously threatened, I was killed that day . . . my boyhood buried beneath the harsh, often violent, reality of race.

Tisa Bryant

T isa Bryant is a writer in her early thir-
ties whose work has been published in a number of magazines
and anthologies. She currently lives in San Francisco, where
she has worked for various AIDS-service and arts/activist organizations.

Set in the mid-seventies, "Zoo Kid" explores race, class,
identity, and assimilation from the perspective of a young girl
who could not fully comprehend the challenges and the bene-
fits of Boston's desegregation.

ZOO KID

Yellow has a greedy mouth.

It eats rocks and dark people. It's the nasty school bus color and my pretend best friend's house I'm colorin' blue. I take Pippi everywhere and my blue crayon too. Mommy ties my hair up in a yellow scarf after she braids it, talkin' 'bout that new school. Says it's a good thing and won't hurt me. I know yellow better than that. I scream. It gets my hands and sometimes my eyes. It's gonna try to go for my brain unless I keep dark colors comin' out my mouth. Keep me comin' out.

I get in trouble at this new school cause I ask people why they stare so much. Specially when I open my mouth. They stare like I'm crazy then go back to colorin' fat yellow suns on their papers, fake yellow moons. Teachers try to play it off, like, it's okay to be feelin' like a spot in the rice, but they starin' too, even the principal. Fake yellow hair. Pippi's got red hair. Red hair's better if it gotta be somethin' like that. Mommy says I'm pare-noid, or maybe they're scared. Best be scared. All they do is stare every day the bus comes to drag us off and dump us at the zoo.

I say zoo cause we was all black and bunched up them first days, watchin' their eyes watch us. They point and step back.

242

Mommy said don't let no one touch me on my head. Then the principal spread us out, one, or if they had to, two to a class, trapped in a space too small to be in. So everybody can get a look. Lookit them black kids. At lunch now all we do is run, see who'll get away. See who can be the wind best. Space. I color it hard with blue till it almost melts.

Davy says that's the trick. Turn dark and get loose. If you gotta jump in the water, then jump in the water, like them tribe peoples his mother told him about. He likes me because he knows I'll do anything to be a storm. See, he's a storm of somethin' black like me and somethin' white like them. Makes his skin mad but pretty.

When Mom goes out, he comes to watch me, and we play tag till he gets mad and snatches me. He always gets mad and goes for the scarves, cause I don't get caught till he gets mad and moves like he's not playin' anymore. Gets me both wrists with one hand and pulls me to my bed. Always uses the yellow scarf, too, all worn soft from knots, my head and hands. He knows I hate that one. I don't make it easy for him to get me. It's just already that way. And that Pippi girl thinks she's the strongest girl in the world. Her yellow house gone blue by me.

These days it's a lot harder to get free. Usta to be easy. I usta not get loose at all so he could come free me, get close. But he likes it better when I try. So do I, 'cause it feels better when I win on my own. He ties me up and starts the watch. Times me. Says, "You don't have much time and if you take too long lookin' at what's got you, it'll be too late." I only get a minute but I get more for really hard knots. I bit one scarf off me one time. Little strings in my teeth like yellow hair. "See," Davy said. "You getting closer to being grown."

He got bused too but he didn't like it and raised hell to go back where he was. He's got a white daddy but he got his mother mouth. Pippi's white but still my pretend best friend. She ain't got a mother. No daddy neither, just like me and Neicy, my real friend. We all know what's up, though. Everybody round here says if you learn to do without you learn better.

Davy teaches me stuff nobody else seems to know. I ain't scared to fight like the rest of them. Mommas, pickets, police make me small. They want to scare you outta fightin' with they belts and yellin', big mouths and dogs. Davy's good for not bein' that way. He wants me to fight. I whip, try to lift the bed off the floor. He's gotta sit on me to undo me if I mess up. I won't stop movin', even then. He presses down hard. Sometimes I like it. He breathes in my face, in my mouth like I need him. At least he tries to help me out, keep me strong.

If I could just bite everything. White people beatin' on the bus. Ugly mouth eatin' at dark people. Squinted-up eyes and red cheeks, their fists punchin' holes in the air. Rocks bust through the windows like bombs. Can't throw them back. Me and Neicy woulda. Never miss. But we all gotta hit the deck. We drill divin' to the floor at METCO in the morning, coverin' up our heads to not get glass cuts.

This one boy Leon jumped out the emergency door and ran off. He was flyin', knockin' them jerks out the way, and there I was, slappin' the window, talkin' bout, "Go Leon! Go!" thinkin', "Shoot, that should be ME." If you gotta jump in the water, then jump in the water. He got free, and HIS mom took him back to his own school. Davy rolled his eyes real mean at me when I told him that, like, "What's wrong with YOU?" If he ever got a beatin' from my mother, he'd know. But he just started the watch and tied the yellow scarf on my one hand in a real tight knot, but tied the other wrist kinda loose, to show me I could get free. And I did. Now there ain't no yellow scarves left, just like my crayons. But my mother ain't Leon's mother.

My mom said METCO is the metropolitan council for edge occasional oppatunity, but they yellow like scared monkeys. Got us on the floor with all them good rocks while them peoples outside actin' up, tellin' us to go back to our own schools. Police at the bus yard makin' sure we okay, or somethin'. My cousin Tanya already got glass in her eye from tryin' to go to Southie school. I could learn to do without all this. Ain't nobody on this bus choose to be here. My mom ain't on this bus. METCO just makes you stay small. That's why I gotta run. Space and a crayon.

They send us to the zoo school like it's better than bein' somewhere big enough to be in. Where nobody stares. Mommy ties my head up in it and says it's good. Says go get the bus and the sun ain't even up, go to the good school. Don't never say why, what's sposed to be so good about it. I liked them teachers I had before. White people swing chains. Ugly yellow bus takes us where they don't want us to go. So what, forget them, she says. You go, I tell her. Smack. Least I said it. Dark dark colors, houses, and dreams. Blue sun, black moon. We don't get home till dark now cuz there's only one bus to this sposed to be good for alla Dorchester, Roxbury, and Mattapan. Don't get home till dark, Mom lookin' out the window for me. Can't walk home from school no more like I usta.

I melt Pippi's house till it looks like mine. She thinks she got it all. She can't get outta that book and be real, but she more real than them kids she plays with. Gotta house and a horse and a monkey too. With her big corn teeth and them braids stickin' out like frozen rope. Ain't got no daddy or mommy. Clothes all mismatched, socks all stretched out and everybody starin' at her. They found out she could pick a horse up over her head and started bein' round her cause she had more magic than them. Try to use her. Just like that. But when they tried to dress her up and change her talk and stuff it didn't work. So she's still a zoo kid. Point and step back. Mommy says maybe I'll meet somebody like Pippi. Get Davy to tie her up and see how real she can be in a minute. How strong. How fast. It's better now that her house ain't fake happy greedy for your feelings no more. She still white though, but most like me most ways so I'll leave her that way, take her where they talk extra nice in your face cause at least she can ignore it, like Mom says I'm sposed to do.

Me and Neicy always run away at lunch, way to the other side of the soccer field, with the rest of the kids from our bus. This boy Darrell I like always says, "Let's run like Leon!" and starts bookin' so fast he kicks himself in the behind. Sometimes I scream when I run and my sound goes far far away but one day I'll catch up with it. One day I'll catch up to it and it'll hear me runnin' for it and remember me and turn and fly right back in my mouth. Sometimes I get scared it won't remember, that it won't come back. So when they come get us, make us come on back in to class, I think on that real hard. And when I open my mouth in math class all heads turn my way. Every day, I just can't wait to leave.

We crack up and sing in the bus home, pretendin' to be all chained up rowin' the slave ship while Miss Shirl the bus monitor walks up and down tellin' us to sit down and be quiet. Like we so wrong. Wrong color. Wrong school. Wrong everything. I scream and laugh, and we sing anyways, tryin' to hit the high note of "Reasons." *Reasons, the reasons that we're here . . .*

Can't find the reasons. Must be gone blue as space.

Aya de León

Aya de León grew up feeling racially displaced and alienated, severed from both her African-American and Puerto Rican roots. Now in her early thirties, she lives in the Oakland Bay area of California, in an artists' compound with other women of color.

"This was a difficult story to write," Aya says, " because it required me to go back to the emotional reality of childhood. I had to remember the isolation and mutual mistrust of black people as well as the devastation of my relationship with my father. In my adult life, I have worked hard to be a good sister in black community, to be emotionally and spiritually grounded, and to be politically clear. But this story from my childhood reflects a time of confusion, disorientation, and buried grief."

The author of several stories and articles, Aya says she sees herself as a political and spiritual writer. "I write about race, class, and gender," she says. "I write about black people and emotional and spiritual transformation." When she is not writing, she works as the coordinator of an alcohol and drug treatment program for teens and as the director of the Mothertongue Institute for Creative Development in Oakland, which provides classes and workshops in the Bay Area and beyond.

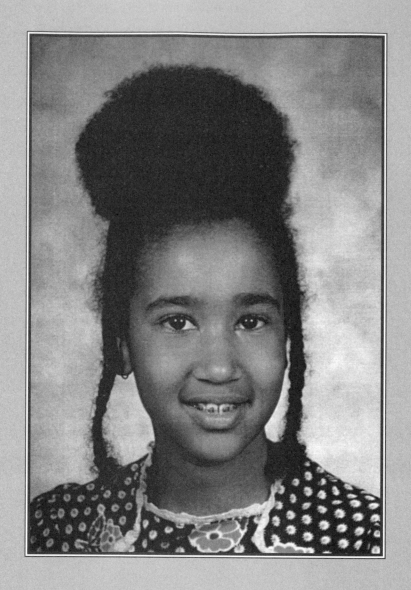

HITTING DANTE

I suspect it was a big, bad sixth-grader who first came up to me talking about my mama. I can imagine the scene: this sixth-grader marching up to me on the Franklin Elementary School playground and getting in my face. And I was thinking, *How does she know my mother? Did she see my mom pick me up after school? Did my mom come down here one time and I didn't know about it?*

Despite a palpitation of terror in my solar plexus, I blinked at her several times and let my eyes slide down to the asphalt. As I focused on the ground, I saw a silver pull tab from a soda can glinting from beneath the toe of my purple high-top Converse All-Star sneakers.

"Did you hear me?" she demanded. "I said 'I saw your mama on the ho' stro' last night.'"

"Tiffany, leave that girl alone!" the yard teacher said. She was a black woman in her forties with brassy red hair.

Eyes on the ground, I stooped to pick up the pull tab. I didn't see Tiffany suck her teeth and stalk off or the yard teacher walk away, shaking her head in pity for me.

I tore off the sharp silver tongue of the pull tab and put the ring on my finger. *I am the princess with a jewel from my father, the king; I am a space explorer and the ring is my walkie-talkie to my ship; I am a gypsy and my ring will ward off all evil.*

It wasn't what the girl said that was so terrible; it was that she said it and *waited.* She stood there, fists on her bony hips, socks accusingly crisp and white, each of her braids so perfectly contained. She was *waiting* for me to respond. I was a black girl, wasn't I? I was supposed to know what a ho' stro' was, or at least get the gist of it and ready up to defend my mama's honor. I was supposed to have a black mama at home—not a blond Puerto Rican mom— who would take me in her arms and say, *Don't cry, my little dumpling. It doesn't matter what that girl said about me. That girl doesn't even know me.*

It would have been different if I had grown up in New York or Miami and there had been some other way to be black. Some *café con leche* way to be black, some *oye, mamita* way to be black. But I grew up in Berkeley, California, and the only way to be black was about greens and cornbread, and I didn't know anything about that. My father was black, was even a blues musician. But he was on the road, sharing African-American culture with the world, leaving me at home to fend for myself.

My Latina mother and white stepfather could comfort me in my troubling run-ins with black kids, but they couldn't translate for me: *That girl is trying to engage you, is testing you, singling you out. There may even be a timid offer of friendship peeking out from under that barbed-wire exterior.*

It is easy to long for New York, or some kind of Puerto Ricanness, but only in Berkeley could I be so soft and get all the way through public school without getting beat up. Except for that one time I hit Dante.

In Berkeley schools in the 1970s, black kids mostly left me alone to play with my two best friends, Anne and Emily, who were white and Asian. While the black girls played hopscotch or jump rope, my friends and I played elaborate serial make-believe games at recess.

Throughout grade school, I watched the black kids with a bewildered fascination. I watched them timidly, for fear of being noticed even in my watching: *What you lookin' at?* Real black kids always had a snappy comeback. They could fight, play kickball, and never let you see them cry. I came to school with a lumpy natural and ashy caramel-colored knees, but real black kids came to school, skin in all shades of brown, shiny with Vaseline. Girls started the day with scalps smarting from sharp combs that parted even rows for braids. Boys had piks peeking out of the back pockets of their Toughskins jeans to keep their Afros round. Real black kids were named Shawnelle, LeMar, and DelTrina. Dante was a real black kid.

Dante had been in my class since fourth grade. He wasn't big and bad like LaVell, whose conked hair stuck straight back and who was always getting sent to the office. Dante was short and wiry with crooked front teeth and a rusty brown Afro that matched his skin. I was bigger than Dante and probably the same brown.

Dante didn't look for trouble, but he was sure to laugh extra loud if someone was getting capped on for having shoes from Kmart. I could never understand what was so funny about that.

Dante and the other black boys in my class always played kickball or dodgeball during lunch and recess. During p.e., the teacher would usually let us do what we wanted, as long as we kept moving. My friends and I would pretend to be archaeologists, hunting the playground's asphalt for Moroccan brown diamonds, which looked suspiciously like fragments of beer bottles.

Sometimes the p.e. teacher would make the whole class play kickball. Once, when Dante was captain, he picked me last. This was usual, but he didn't want to have me on the team at all. He groaned out loud when I was up to kick and Marcus, captain of the other team, clapped his hands together, grinning and yelling, "Easy out! Easy out!"

I would step up timidly to kick, ready to get it over with so Marcus would shut up. Sometimes I made it to first base and even made it home.

After I was up, I ignored the game, doing handstands up against the chain-link fence. When the other team was up, I would brush the gravel from my palms and head outfield. "Way out," Dante would say, because everyone knew I couldn't catch. I practiced cartwheels, and the ball rarely came my way. When it did, I would just duck and cover my head, hearing the red rubber bounce savagely off the ground just behind me.

I ducked from the ball; I shrank from confrontations. What could have possessed me to hit this boy? Dante and I weren't friends, weren't enemies. Not before or after I hit him. It was no big deal to him. He probably tousled with siblings or cousins on a regular basis. But I, the only child in the lost tribe of my family, was breaking new ground with my violence.

What pushed me over the line?

Twenty years later I am searching for an answer. I round up the usual suspects and dismiss them all. I didn't want the teacher's attention—she was out of the room. I didn't have a crush on him. I wasn't showing off. It wasn't self-defense either—I *initiated* the fight with him. The violence is so clear, but my underlying ten-year-old reasons are silent, absent, hidden.

Slowly, a hypothesis crystallizes. I will never be able to prove it, but a new suspect emerges. A new conjecture makes the pieces fit together. I go back and fill in the empty space. I can't vouch for all the details—even some of the names have been changed—but the heart is true.

I woke up at seven forty-five that morning with KFRC, a Top 40 radio station, on my beige plastic radio. It had a dial clock on one side and a beige-and-gold speaker on the other. I listened to Air Supply's "Lost in Love" as I lay under the soft blue cotton comforter with the faux patchwork pattern.

By the time I came downstairs, my stepfather had already gone to work at the restaurant he owned. My mom baked the desserts for his restaurant, and she was sitting at the big wooden kitchen table frosting a lemon tart in a crisscross pattern with meringue.

I noticed six other tarts cooling on the counter and ready to be frosted. I got my breakfast cereal and set the heavy half gallon of milk down next to my bowl.

My mom looked up. "Don't bump the table!" she snapped.

I froze, then went back to preparing my cereal in slow motion, pretending I was bionic, like when they showed Lindsay Wagner running real slow. I kept my eyes on my mom, who tucked a strand of straight, dark blond hair behind her ear as she went back to work. Her hair was naturally a sandy brown that teetered on the edge of blondness. Sometimes she sprayed Sun-In on it to make it blonder.

As I ate my cereal, my eyes traveled idly over the piles of paper on the table: an *Oakland Tribune* from the day before, the previous Sunday's *San Francisco Chronicle*. That's when I saw him. Peeking out from underneath last Sunday's full-color comics that I'd already read, in the pink section, where they had the movie guy with the pointy nose and the hat who jumped out of his chair and clapped for reasons I didn't understand.

It was an ad for Jordan Rivers in concert in San Francisco the weekend before. It was Wednesday. He was my father.

He was smiling impersonally up at me, and I felt an incredible amount of something and nothing at the same time. Like I got all ready to feel something, then changed my mind.

He was here, or had been here, and hadn't called—again. I did not answer a knock at the door to find his towering presence. To me, he was a giant. Big arms, big hands, big feet. He was more of an event than a person. He was a dark pumpernickel brown, with my same small, slanted eyes, but his nose was flatter and his nostrils wider. I was getting to be tall like him, and my feet were already too big for kids' shoes. When he did visit it was usually unexpected, and I was always shy around him. I was likely to say a quiet, startled "Daddy?" before he embraced me with a loud, gravelly "Hey, baby."

I slid the comics all the way over the pink section, over the ad. Then I moved my bowl around in slow circles, making the cereal into a whirlpool.

"I told you not to bump the table, goddamit!" my mom yelled.

I cringed. "Sorry." Not hungry, I took the bowl, fished the soggy cereal into the garbage, and dumped the milk in the sink.

When I looked up at the clock, it was only two minutes till my bus would leave.

"Bye, Mom, I'm late."

She looked up, not really mad, just tired. "Bye, dear."

I didn't have time to kiss her before I grabbed my Day-Glo orange pack and ran down the red wooden steps and up the block for the bus.

I just made it that day, and I slumped into the green vinyl seat, winded and distracted, as the bus pulled off. Dante didn't ride my bus or live in my neighborhood. I didn't know where he lived. Maybe he came to school that day with his own baggage, his own readiness to snap.

Marcus had Jolly Rancher candies that day. I sat in front of him and I could smell the watermelon and green apple flavors. Dante and LaVell noticed too, and kept looking over at him.

We were learning about Japanese-American history. "During World War II, I felt really ashamed to be Japanese," Ms. Yamada was telling the class. "People said, 'Oh, those sneaky Japanese.' I tried to act super-American to let people know I wasn't the enemy."

LaVell raised his hand: "Ms. Yamada, can I go to the bathroom?"

I bet he just wants to get some candy.

"Okay, LaVell. But I want you back in five minutes."

LaVell jumped up from his desk and went to get the cardboard bathroom pass. He sidled up to Marcus on his way out the door, and Marcus passed him a Jolly Rancher. *See, I knew he was faking.*

Ms. Yamada's back was turned as she wrote vocabulary words on the board.

seize

internment

Dante put his hands up for Marcus to throw him a Jolly Rancher. Marcus looked at the teacher, turned to Dante, and shook his head no. Dante sucked his teeth in disappointment. *God, they bug me. Why can't they just pay attention?*

Ms. Yamada turned from the board. "Emily, will you see if there's any chalk on my desk?"

Emily crossed the room. The chalk in Ms. Yamada's hand had become tiny—the size of a jelly bean.

Emily looked on the desktop. "I don't see any."

Ms. Yamada walked over to her desk. "Thanks anyway, Emily."

As Emily went back to her seat and Ms. Yamada rummaged through her desk for chalk, Dante said, "Come on, man," in an urgent whisper. *Shut up, Dante. He's not gonna give you any.*

Ms. Yamada looked up. "You guys should be copying down the vocabulary words." *Yeah. Be quiet and do your work.* She kept opening and closing drawers. Dante lowered his head as if to copy the board, then turned to Marcus. "Come on," he mouthed. *Why are boys so dumb?* Ms. Yamada was kneeling in front of her desk, head obscured. Dante put his hands up again. Marcus considered it, looked at the teacher, and prepared to throw.

"I can't find any chalk," Ms. Yamada said. "Listen you guys, finish copying down those words. I'll be back in one minute."

She left the door open, but the moment she stepped out,

258

Dante popped up from his desk and came over to Marcus with his hand out. *I hope she comes back and catches them.*

"Ugh, I don't like watermelon. You got anything else? Apple! Yeah, yeah! Aw, nigga, gimme more than one!"

"I ain't got that many." *Why don't they just shut up?* I poked my pencil into a groove in the desk and the lead broke.

"Come on, Marcus . . ." Dante whined.

Marcus gave Dante a second piece as I stood up to sharpen my pencil. Dante turned to head back to his desk. We collided.

"Ugh, Aya, watch where you're going!"

And suddenly something in my brain told something in my arm to propel my hand through the space between us. I hit him. I smacked him hard in the shoulder.

I didn't even see his face react, his focus sharpen, his lips contract into a tight circle. I just felt the blow, the thundering shove in my chest, and then the floor as it leapt up to catch me.

Dante stalked back to his desk. No one said anything. I lay dazed for a second on the olive-green carpet. There were staples and tiny fragments of paper caught in the dark loops that the custodian's weekly vacuuming didn't pick up.

As I stood up on unsteady legs and slid back into my desk chair, my numbness disintegrated. I barely had time to put my head down before the tears descended, hot and involuntary.

Ms. Yamada came back with LaVell in tow. LaVell lingered by Marcus's desk on his way to his own.

"Have a seat, LaVell," Ms. Yamada said, her eyes following him until he did so.

She scanned the room from behind her thick, round glasses. We were all in our seats. It didn't occur to her to look at me. I never fought, never got in trouble. I turned my work in on time, got good grades, rarely talked in class when I wasn't supposed to.

She took her new, full-length piece of chalk and finished writing the vocabulary words on the board:

seize

internment

reparations

She did not notice me with my head down. No one told. My only fight got to be my private defeat in the world of my classmates. I cried in embarrassment and pain.

And relief. And gratitude. Tears spilled out from underneath Dante's handprint on my chest. All of the shame that had been patiently waiting could be released. Tears spilled out and across my folded brown arms. I could feel worthless. Tears ran down the beige fake wood surface of my desk. I could feel alone. Tears soaked into my navy-blue T-shirt. Several dripped down onto my thighs and dotted the rust-colored fabric of my corduroy bell-bottoms. I could feel utterly desolate. Tears spilled out because no one had taught me, forced me, to bottle up like real black kids. I could feel lacerated and incomplete.

Tears spilled out until I was empty and could wipe my eyes and nose with the soft cotton fabric of my T-shirt. *Thank God I have something to cry about, instead of my stupid dad who I don't even care about anyway.* Tears spilled out until I could pick my head back up and pay attention to the teacher. By the time I looked up, the edge of the chalk was rounded.

seize—to grab something

internment—to be locked up

reparation—

Dante was engrossed in drawing a picture on the brown paper bag cover of his math book. Marcus was sneaking a Jolly Rancher candy into his mouth. Anne and Emily were copying down what the teacher had written. LaVell was going to get a check mark by his name on the board because he was interrupting the teacher, hissing at Marcus to give him another piece of candy.

I stood up to sharpen my pencil.

Desiree Cooper

Desiree Cooper was born in Itazuke, Japan, where she was a United States military dependent. By the time she turned sixteen, she had lived in Texas, Colorado, New Mexico, Florida, and Virginia.

Desiree's career has been as diverse as her geographical background. She has worked as an attorney, the director of anti-crime and fair-housing programs, a university instructor, a newspaper columnist, and editor in chief of a newspaper. Still in her thirties, and married for fourteen years, she has two children, ages ten and seven.

Desiree has written and published many articles and essays. This poignant and moving account of her childhood discovery of racism is told in the voice of the little girl she was at the time the events she recounts took place. "When my father retired from the air force in 1974," she says, "we moved to Virginia. There I was hit with the reality of civilian life in the south: American apartheid. My world became strictly black and white, and I was forced to choose between the two. The divide was so complete, I rarely associated with white classmates who lived next door."

As a mother, Desiree struggles with how to tell her children about race. "How do you tell your children, so innocent and full of promise, that they will be hated because of the color of their skin?" she asks. "How do you prepare them for the sting of racism?" She says that Dr. Martin Luther King, Jr.'s, dream is a vision that every black mother has for her children. "It is a prayer that no mother should ever have to wipe tears from her children's faces . . . and explain the incomprehensible reality that they will be hated for the crime of being black."

Desiree is careful to acknowledge that "there are many rivers that flow through my blood." One of her grandmothers was white. "To hate whites would mean to hate myself," she says. "I despise racism, but not the white race. I offer my contribution in the spirit of forging greater understanding between the races, not to condemn."

COLOR MY WORLD

Pammie is tall and beautiful, just like my Malibu Barbie. She lives in the nice neighborhood up the hill from my house. Her hair is blond with streaks of oak brown. I used to stare at her hair all the time because, even though it's blond, it's kinky like mine. It's full of frizzy little ringlets that spring back even though she tries to pull her hair tight in a band. The bands match her outfits. She must have a thousand.

But even those pretty bands don't straighten out the waves. She can't do anything about it. Before I knew her, I used to feel sorry for her. Being a white girl with blond hair, but not being able to let it loose or get it wet, like a black girl. Like me.

Back in ninth grade, everyone wanted to sit by Pammie, even though her hair was kinky. She lived in a big house at the top of Bowman's Hill, and her dad was important. I really didn't try to be her friend, because I knew that someone like her wouldn't want to be the friend of the only black girl on the bus. Besides, most of my friends lived on my street at the bottom of the hill.

But then I noticed that Pammie would be looking at me sometimes. And every once in a while, she would strike up a conversation on the bus. Once she told me that she was taking piano lessons and wanted to learn to play "Color My World," just like it sounded on the radio. I told her that I had the sheet music at my house, why not come over and we'd try to learn it? And she said, why not bring it up the hill to her house? That's how we became friends. Learning to play "Color My World."

Her house was huge, but my house smelled and felt more like a real home. You know, like when my friends came over, my mom would always be there to bake cookies and just talk—about school or boys or whatever. But Pammie's mom never came around us when I went to her house. I wasn't even sure if she was at home. She could have been, but I never saw her.

Pammie's room was just a bed and a dresser and no flowers or music or anything. My bedroom had a stereo, and a dresser with all kinds of Baby Soft perfumes on top, and there were pink and yellow flowers on my bedspread. It was like a garden. That's why I always wanted us to play the piano at my house, but Pammie just wanted to stay in her neighborhood.

Her piano was in the basement. We'd sit there on the piano stool, side by side, singing and playing. Pammie was really good at reading the music, and I stunk, but I could memorize pretty well. So Pammie would read and play, and I'd memorize keys. Pretty soon, we were playing together: Pammie would play the right hand, and I'd play the left. We were so close, sitting on that piano stool. So close. I'll bet from behind, we looked sort of the same. Like sisters, even. Two skinny girls with wavy, frizzy ponytails.

But there was stuff Pammie would do to let me know we were only friends when we sat at the piano. Our friendship ended when the music ended. Like I remember one Saturday I was really bored and my mom said, "Why don't you walk up the hill to Pam's house?" That's when it dawned on me that Pammie never called me; she always waited for me to call her. So I started keeping score. After a few days, when I couldn't stand it anymore, I'd call her. She'd be home doing nothing, bored to death, but she hadn't called me to see if I could come over.

And sometimes she'd say stuff and I'd get real mad, real fast, then I'd try to forget about it and we'd just have fun. I should have told her she was making me mad, but I felt that if she were a real friend she would be able to tell when she was upsetting me. Like how could she mention her birthday party or her swimming party at the clubhouse, knowing that it would hurt my feelings that she didn't even invite me?

And the weirdest part was that everyone loved playing with Pammie, but she never brought her friends along when we got together. I would've brought my friends over to her house. But she made me feel that if I brought too many of my friends with me up the hill, it would be like we were taking over or making a big scene or something. But I went along with it because it was nice to play music with Pammie. Anyway, there was only room for two on the piano stool.

Toward the end of the summer, we didn't see each other so much. I got tired of trying to be a good friend. The girls on my street were more fun and had fun moms and fun bedrooms. But none of them could play the piano.

When school started again, I walked up to Pammie at the bus stop, like normal, and just started talking like we were still close. But she wasn't the same. It seemed like she had more to say to Shelly and the other girls. I just said to myself, "Forget it," and kept sitting beside my old friends, who never made me feel like keeping score. I really didn't care.

One day after school, when we got on the bus, Pammie and I ended up sitting together. It felt pretty good to be near her again. Like old times. We started talking and talking, sitting side by side like we used to do on the piano stool. All of a sudden, Shelly turned around in her seat and started telling Pammie about her pets. Shelly's face was all round and puffy, and her hair was all stringy and greasy, and she was just grinning like a big goofball, talking on and on about her stupid cat and her stupid dog. Pammie listened and would say something like, "Really?" or "Dig that!"—just enough to keep Shelly going. She was definitely getting on my nerves, but I just smiled and tried to be nice.

Then Shelly started talking about how her brother let the dog out and had to run all over the neighborhood to get him back into the house before their mom got home. So I said, just to be nice and stuff, "What's your dog's name?"

I swear, the whole bus went quiet, like how right before the fireworks go off, the whole world gets dead silent, waiting for the explosion. Shelly looked at me with that round, rubbery face and dirty hair and said, "Well, my kitty is white, and we call her Fluffy. My doggie is black, and we call her Nigger."

Just like that. Everyone on the bus started laughing. Pammie didn't laugh, but looked right at me, like the whole thing was a test to see what I would do. Shelly was looking at me, too, grinning with her nasty teeth. I was choking on my own tongue, which felt like it was swelling in my mouth. My face was hot and I felt like two people at once: like a little baby screaming because it was hurting, and like an evil person just wanting to punch someone.

I sat there, getting madder and madder, trying not to let

them see me cry. The bus stopped and people got off. Pammie sat next to me, totally quiet, doing nothing.

At my stop at the bottom of Bowman's Hill, I got up before anyone else, leaned over Shelly and screamed, "I don't have to take that from a piece of white trash like you! I'll kick your butt tomorrow if you try to get on this bus without apologizing to me!"

I ran off the bus even though my legs were like rubber. I had never yelled at anyone like that before, and I was nervous and scared. I could hear Shelly whining to Pammie, "Did you hear what she said to me? I didn't mean anything, I swear, I didn't!"

The next day at the bus stop, no one would speak to me. Which I kind of expected because you definitely can't yell at people like that and still be their friends. The only person who spoke to me was Shelly, who gave me an apology, loud and clear, when I blocked her way onto the bus.

Pammie stopped speaking to me too. Except she did tell me in front of everyone that I shouldn't have embarrassed Shelly like that. With that comment, she made me mad for the last time. I finally realized that even though Pammie's hair was kinky like mine, and we could sit so close on a piano stool that it took two of us to make one song, Pammie was a hundred percent white.

I never went to her house again. Now I stay on my own street, with my old friends. Sometimes I sit at my piano and play "Color My World" over and over again by heart.

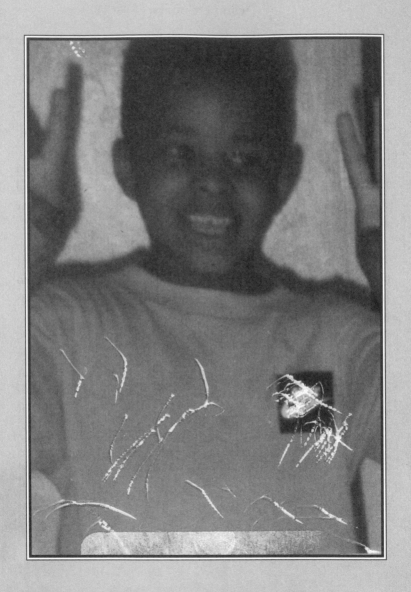

Antoine P. Reddick

In his early forties and living in New Haven, Connecticut, Antoine Reddick says his "first and only story" is a tribute to all the members of his family who died young, struggling with racism, poverty, and crime.

ALL THE BLACK CHILDREN

Sixteen children is a very large family, and I was number ten. I was raised in New Haven, Connecticut, a college town of predominantly middle-class liberal whites, in the 1960s. It was a time of civil unrest: the Vietnam war was headline news and desegregation was being pushed and fought for in the streets all over the country. But these events had no effect on me or my family at that time.

To raise sixteen children costs a lot of money, and it was beyond my mother and father's abilities. Since my father had no kind of useful education and was unskilled, my mother went to the state for help. She had to declare my father as missing or delinquent in his role as a parent. She had no choice, there was no other way to support so many children.

My father became the outcast of the family. Legally, he could not live with us or he would have to pay child support. If he didn't pay, he would go to jail.

I'm not sure when my father became an alcoholic or what the cause of his heavy drinking was, but it started before I was born. As I grew older I hardly saw him except when he would come by to beg money from Mother for drinking. My mother loved my father, but drinking became his life, and we children could not be part of his love and affection anymore. He became a stranger to us.

The result was that my mother was left with a houseful of kids, dependent on welfare. I should have been grateful that we lived in a house. Most black families on welfare lived in a low-income housing project on the other side of town. Even with four bedrooms, though, there was not enough space for us to live comfortably. My sisters had their room, and the older boys theirs, but we smaller children had to find space where we could. Five of us slept in the same bed, which seemed normal to me.

At that time, the nation was caught up in busing black children to desegregated schools. I and a few of my brothers and sisters were bused to a school in the suburbs with all white students. And most of the teachers were white as well. I was the only black kid in the classroom, but I felt equal. I made friends, I played with the white children, and they invited me to their homes.

A Jewish kid named Jeff Novak became a close friend, and I would spend the night at his home. It was hard to believe that such a small family (he, his mother, his father, and his younger brother) could live in such a big house all by themselves. They had two cars and lived in a beautiful neighborhood with clean streets and cut lawns. Jeff's father was a doctor, so we rarely saw him. His mother was a nice woman who would drive us to the movies or to the park. They ate dinner together as a family, which was new to me because at my house food was not plentiful—when it was there at all.

I was accepted by these white people for reasons I did not question, even though my clothes were hand-me-downs or secondhand. They never stopped me from being part of their world.

But when I left their big house and Jeff's mother would drop me off at home in their shiny new car and drive away, the dream would come to a halt. I was back to a world and a life that I began to hate. There were no cars, no toys, no bikes. There was never enough food, money, clothes, or even love. My mother could only focus her attention on the babies she still had to raise. I know she loved us all the best she could, but being a single parent was hard on my mother. With every bit of her endurance she held us together as a family, but the struggle was hopeless.

My older brothers and sister found escape in the streets. There they could forget the poverty and destitution of living in an overcrowded house. The streets were a new way to survive as black children. With no father to guide us and no discipline, as a family we became totally dysfunctional.

Drugs were a big part of the struggle for change in the 1960s. And drugs became the answer to a lot of problems—or so most kids thought. My brothers and sister found their dreams in the drug houses and back alleys, where narcotics ran free and were easy to buy or sell. It would be years before I realized the destructive effect drugs would have on my family and my life. They turned into a fire that spread through my family and dominated our lives.

With the drugs, came crime. As a child, I had no understanding of crime or drugs, but many nights the police visited our house, asking for one or the other of my brothers. Some crime had been committed, and they were involved. It was a strange and scary feeling to be awakened in the middle of the night by big white men with flashlights searching the house from top to bottom, looking for my brothers.

My mother always protected them and denied they were about. After the police left, my mother and sisters would sit and talk in low voices, feeling bewildered and helpless. But the drugs and crime would go on for years to come—shooting drugs in the house, bringing home stolen property, coming and going at all hours of the night and day. My mother was helpless to act. She had five sons who were too old and too big to send to their rooms for discipline. All she could do was pray.

My mother never gave up on us younger children. She pushed us to go to school, and she enrolled us in summer camp programs. Camp was the best time of my childhood. For two weeks I was free of my poverty and free to be a kid. Getting on that bus, heading for the campground, was so thrilling and new. Getting out of the city and into the woods still touches me today as an experience of wonder and joy. Being with other kids, sleeping in cabins, swimming, and sitting around the campfire singing—I felt like a part of something. Camp showed me that the world was not all fear and hate, that it could be a place of peace and a newborn joy. I was not poor or black any longer, I was just a kid with a heart full of excitement and adventure.

But the dream always came to an end when I returned home. Nothing had changed. My family still had to struggle from day to day, for money was everybody's urgency. Economics played such a dominating role in my family's life and mine.

I began to ask why my family never seemed to have the kind of life the white families enjoyed. I loved my family very much and, struggling along with them, I accepted the poverty and the slums in which I lived, but secretly, inside me, I yearned to live like the white children. The color of their skin meant happiness. I wanted to spend my life at summer camp and stay over at the white children's homes and be a part of their world. But it was a world I would never know because my skin was black, and poverty ruled my life. I thought there would never be a chance for me as long as my skin was black.

Slowly I began to notice the difference between being black and poor and living in a crowded rundown house and being white and living in a nice home in a clean neighborhood. In my heart and mind, frustration began to form along with hate for these separate societies.

The awareness of bigotry, discrimination, and segregation came into my life. Crime was the way I struck out at all of this; it became the most destructive force in my life.

I had plenty of teachers to lead me into this life of crime. One who stands out is my brother Eddie, who is five years older than me. I looked up to him as most kids do their big brothers. In my eyes he was a hero who feared nothing, knew everything, and lived the way he chose. He dressed well, had girlfriends, and drove cars. He had a charm about him that drew me in but ended up being totally detrimental to me for the rest of my life.

My brother was a breed apart from the rest of my family. He looked down on my brothers and sisters who did drugs or drank alcohol. He believed himself to be smarter than anyone else, and I believed in him. But what he taught me was a form of deterioration and destruction that slowly chipped away at any chance of my having a morally or ethically decent and honest life.

Today they would call my brother a player or hustler—a smooth-talking, confident liar. He was without love or feelings for anyone but himself, and shame never crossed his mind about the way he used family and friends.

Naive, gullible, and young, I was the perfect person for him to use and abuse. I was elated to join him in his life of crime. I was fourteen years old, wanting excitement and adventure. I could have found it in sports, fishing, camping—or even a good job—if someone would have pointed me in the right direction. The cost of following Eddie's influence was a high price to pay. Twenty-five years later, I'm still payng the cost of learning from him about crime.

At the time, I believed in my brother and I wanted to prove myself to him. He would wake me in the middle of the night to go on these unknown missions—stealing cars, burglarizing, and committing other crimes. The money and property we stole had no great meaning to me; it was the excitement of it that filled my childish mind. One night we were caught and charged with burglary. My brother, being older, was sent to jail, and I was sent to the juvenile center. It would be years before I would ever see my brother again. Since I was a minor, the juvenile court gave me six months in a boys' school thirty miles from home.

I look back on these events wanting to hate my brother for the seeds of destruction he planted in my head. But it goes deeper than my brother—poverty, drugs, unemployment, and discrimination all play a part. My brother's ideas were all wrong and damaging to me as a child, but poverty, frustration, and hate for a society that refused black children equality as human beings were the creators of the crimes we committed.

The boy's school I was sent to was not as bad as I had feared. There were tough kids and street-smart kids, most of them from broken homes or dysfunctional families, white and black, so I didn't feel alone. My mother visited me when she could. The six months passed, and I came home a little older, but still full of doubts about my life and what the future would bring.

I started junior high school and was bused to a racially mixed school in the suburbs. The kids came from all over town and those who were black were as poverty-stricken as I was but, coming from the projects, they were distinctly different in their attitudes. They were loud, aggressive, and very hostile—attitudes stemming from the environment in which they were raised. They had a grudge against the system and society for having to live in neighborhoods of total destitution. You had to be tough to live in the projects, where the gangs, the drug dealers, drunks, and hustlers all struggled to survive. It wasn't hard for me to understand their dislike for the system and white society. It seemed that nobody cared how they lived or who they were. They lived as outcasts from society.

I was fifteen years old when I made a friend, a boy who lived in the projects named Anthony Redford. I'll never forget the day he invited me home with him. He lived in one of the many high-rise buildings that were in total ruin. The halls were filled with trash, the stairwells smelled of urine, and the walls and doors were spray-painted with graffitti. Most of the apartment doors and windows had been kicked or broken into.

The nighttime was a very dangerous time to walk the streets of this neighborhood. To hear gunfire was common, and cars sped up and down the streets. It was very rare to see police enter these buildings. Only for serious kinds of emergencies would they venture into the dark halls. And white people were never seen in the streets, day or night. They were very much afraid of what hid in the alleys and side streets of these poverty-dominated black environments.

The white people who did venture into this world were usually drug addicts. They came from the suburbs and colleges looking to buy drugs. They always came in quickly, with frightened faces and eager, false smiles, knowing the danger if things went bad, which they sometimes did. They became targets for the rip-off artists and stickup men who lived there—men and women who preyed on anyone they could profit from. Shootings, stabbings, and killings were common.

Summer in the projects was the worst time of year. The smell of the sewers and the trash rotting in the heat on the streets was nauseating. There was no happiness for black children growing up in this environment. These streets were where I learned what being black and welfare-dependent was all about. I forgot about the white kids and their big houses and clean neighborhoods. These were my people, and I belonged with them in the struggle for life and what we could grab or force from a society that gave us nothing to build on, nothing to live for.

The impression that the environment of the projects and the people who lived there left inside me was one of sorrow and pain. I spent years in the project neighborhoods trying to understand why black people were placed so low down in society's system.

I turned eighteen years old, but I felt older from hanging with the rough crowd in the projects. School was my only chance to escape from the mounting chaos. When black history was added to my class schedule, it brought dramatic change to my whole outlook.

For the first time in American history, black children were being taught the origin of their ancestors by professional teachers. My class was taught by a black woman named Ms. Magumba. She dressed in African robes and colorful head wraps. She seemed out of place in this formally dressed society, but she fascinated me. I felt she was part of a culture that was truly born of black people and belonged to us. She seemed very proud to be be black, and she said that Africa was a continent as great and wondrous as any nation in the world.

In all the years that I had attended school, nothing touched me more than to learn that black people had been kings and queens of great nations and empires in a world so different from the poverty, crime, and drug-filled streets I walked each day.

I left school my first day that year in bewilderment. It had taken eighteen years for me to learn that there had been and still is a great culture that was part of me and my family. In one word, I finally understood why black men, women, and children struggle to survive. Slavery—it was so hard to accept and understand that black people were bought and sold like cattle and sheep.

It's 1972: Men had walked on the moon, the atom had been split, and science was moving at the speed of light. It seemed unbelievable that just four hundred years earlier, black men, women, and children belonged to white people as property. Slave ships, plantations, and auction blocks were a big part of this nation's history. Black men and women came off the ships in neck chains and leg irons. They were stripped of a culture they would never know again. They were refused education and human rights. I finally saw why the black people of this country had nothing to show but frustration, hatred, and poverty. Black men and women were no more than tools to the whites of that time. Still, four hundred years later, blacks have very little to show for their suffering and the degrading struggle they were forced by the whites to endure.

When school ended for the season, I might have left feeling that what I learned in my black history class was just history—something from the past that could not be changed. But it was not easy to put the subject out of my mind: images of slave ships with black people packed on top of one another, many of them dying from disease and lack of food and fresh water; the whips and chains, and the burning sun beating down on them as they labored endless hours and days in the fields of the plantations.

I'd never thought of myself as a racist or bigot, but it was hard to fight the feeling of hate that slowly grew in me for the white race. I had slept in their houses, played with their children, eaten at their tables, and I was envious of their lives. But I felt tricked and betrayed. These were confusing emotions for me, and that summer I took them into the streets with very destructive results.

The kids I chose to hang out with were a very tough and defiant gang. Crime—getting over on the system—was like a game to them. They talked of the easy money to be made in robbery. A gun was easy to come by in the slums and back alleys of New Haven, and on a hot summer day in July of 1975 I joined a few kids and robbed a store in a white neighborhood.

I was arrested and charged with robbery. I was eighteen years old and locked in a cell with steel bars and no windows. A feeling of total helplessness and misery took hold of me so tight that I wished I were dead. When my mother came to the jail to visit me, I was filled with shame and longing for her to hold me and tell me it would be all right and we could go home. But that would not happen for years. I was given five years in a reformatory for youthful offenders.

There is no experience to match that of having your freedom taken away from you and your life not being yours to control any longer. I felt things could not get any worse, but they did. One day I was called to the prison chaplain's office. He sat me down and looked in my face and told me my mother had called on the phone to ask him to tell me that my brother Butch had died of a drug overdose.

That night I cried for my brother like I'd never cried before. A few days later I was allowed to go to his wake. But I had to be escorted by a prison guard, and I had to wear handcuffs. It was very hard to look at my brother as he lay in his coffin, knowing I would never see him smile or laugh again.

Being sent to prison and the death of my brother ended my childhood. . . .

Anita LaFrance Allen

As a University of Pennsylvania law pro-
fessor and as the holder of a law degree from Harvard and a Ph.D.
from the University of Michigan, Anita LaFrance Allen certainly
can be said to have achieved all the success anyone would have
thought possible for a Fort Benning army brat, as she calls herself,
whose father had joined the military to escape poverty in Atlanta.
Now in her forties, Anita believes that Martin Luther King, Jr.'s
dream has come true for her and her family. "For others it is an
elusive goal," she says, and "the continuance of affirmative action
is critical."

The author of more than sixty published essays and articles,
Anita says this story is special for her because it is a heartfelt account
of the racism she endured in public schools in the south, where she
attended the same previously all-white high school that Newt
Gingrich had attended ten years earlier, in Columbus, Georgia. But
clearly Anita's experience at Baker High was a very different experience from Gingrich's; despite the mandatory quasi-integration of the
student body, the teachers and administration were still white.

THE DIVIDED CAFETERIA

I was born in 1953, just in time for *Brown v. Board of Education of Topeka.* I ought never to have experienced enforced public school segregation, but I did. The Supreme Court's 1954 decision in *Brown* held that racial segregation in public primary and secondary schools violates the Constitution. The Court considered expert testimony arguing that separate schools were inherently unequal. The experts said that compelling black children to attend legally segregated schools made them feel like social inferiors. School segregation lowered African-American children's self-esteem. This self-esteem claim remains controversial, but there could be something to it. After a couple of years in black primary schools, my older sister explained that segregation was necessary on the grounds that blacks, but not whites, have the shameful biological need to defecate and urinate.

Showing no urgent concern for the self-esteem or basic education of African-American children, most southern towns responded slowly to *Brown.* Foot-dragging on public-school integration was common in the south. The seemingly far-reaching *Brown* decision had not demanded that the states dismantle their segregated school systems immediately. The monumental Civil Rights Act of 1964 legislated integration of public accommodations and outlawed discrimination in housing, voting, and education. Yet foot-dragging on public-school segregation continued in many places, prompting the Supreme Court to rule in 1965 that "delays in desegregating school systems are no longer tolerable."

For me and other African-American children, post-*Brown* foot-dragging had practical consequences. Foot-dragging by Anniston, Alabama, meant that in 1958, at the age of five, I took a solo bus-and-car journey each day miles from my home in Fort McClellan, Alabama, to reach a Negro kindergarten somewhere in Anniston. Foot-dragging by Atlanta, Georgia, meant that in 1959, at the age of six, I attended first grade at a Negro elementary school.

As it happens, I received a good education in these two segregated schools. When I left kindergarten, I could already read and write at the level of a second-grader. Luckily, I was not the least bit aware of racial differences at the time. I suffered no conscious blows to my self-esteem and harbored no sense of racial injustice. Those things came later, when I attended a racially integrated public high school.

The now-defunct Baker High School in Columbus, Georgia, counted Newton (Newt) Gingrich as among its most illustrious graduates. Mr. Gingrich graduated in 1960. I also attended Baker High, graduating ten years later than the United States congressman who, in 1995, became the first Republican Speaker of the House of Representatives in decades. Even before he officially assumed the Speaker's office, Gingrich had declared war on what he termed the "Great Society, counterculture, McGovernik" legacy of the 1960s.

The second half of the 1960s brought us comprehensive national civil rights laws banning discrimination on the basis of sex and race, along with antipoverty legislation and constitutional privacy rights. I have been personally acquainted with so many hardworking, poor, underemployed, and child-burdened black people that I view these legal reforms as nothing less than basic moral justice. Yet in the mind of Mr. Gingrich, the 1960s killed morality in America. According to him, after 1965 there was no more "commitment to creating . . . character," no more "work ethic," no "honesty, right, and wrong," no "vigilant . . . defense of liberty." The glib representations of a powerful politician rewrite history only for the people who did not live it.

Speaker Gingrich and I went to Baker for the same reason. We were both army brats, the children of military men stationed at Fort Benning, Georgia. Although Fort Benning operated its own elementary and middle schools, reserved solely for military children, it did not operate a high school. Typical secondary school–age children who lived at Fort Benning traveled in a convoy of olive-green buses to nearby Baker or one of Muscogee County's other public high schools.

In many respects Baker High was the same school in 1960, when Gingrich graduated, as it was in 1970, when I graduated. It was a plain complex of two-story red brick buildings on a scruffy baked lawn. It overlooked Victory Drive, a soldier's playground of cheap motels, hamburger stands, porn shops, girlie shows, and car dealerships. It had a decent academic curriculum and a decent football team.

But in one key respect, Gingrich's Baker High School and mine were very different. When Gingrich graduated, the Columbus schools were segregated. In fact, barely any public facilities or private businesses open to the Columbus public were available to blacks and whites on equal and nondiscriminatory bases. Gingrich's Baker High was what southerners used to call a white school. A white public school rarely knowingly enrolled colored (or, as we were also called, Negro) children.

Like Newt Gingrich, my older sister attended a segregated high school. Years of post-*Brown* foot-dragging in Columbus meant that when she was ready for secondary school in 1963, Fort Benning military authorities had no choice but to transport her to a black school twice as far from home as Baker High would have been. A fourteen-year-old accustomed to racial diversity in military neighborhoods, churches, and schools, my sister was forced to separate herself from her peer group and go to a colored school. If experts cited in *Brown* were correct that legally compelled segregation harms the self-esteem of African-American children, consider the effects of legally compelled resegregation of a military dependent accustomed to racial diversity.

Both my parents came from very poor Atlanta families. My father joined the military in the early 1950s to escape denigrating economic prospects. My parents had attended colored high schools in Atlanta, where they studied from outdated used textbooks cast off from white schools. They believed, with warrant, that the colored high schools in Columbus would have fewer and poorer resources than the white schools. As a consequence, they could not explain why my sister had to go to a Negro school in ways that did not make all three of their school-age children feel sad and inferior.

Under a so-called stair-step plan adopted in 1964, Columbus school authorities had planned to desegregate the student bodies (but not the teachers or staffs) of its public schools one grade at a time over a twelve-year period, beginning with the twelfth grade. A federal lawsuit brought by African-Americans forced school authorities to abandon their dilatory twelve-year plan. Under the watchful eye of the federal courts, Muscogee County administrators moved more quickly to desegregate. By 1967, Columbus had enrolled a significant number of blacks in its previously white schools. Gingrich's Baker became an integrated school.

The first wave of youthful African-American school integrators went to white schools throughout the south in the early 1960s surrounded by police, politicians, and protesters. The photographic images of their brave moments are unforgettable. I was a second-wave black integrator. I attended a white school in the months and years after the white community had ceased to fight school desegregation with shrill protests and brute force. Resistance had gone underground. We second-wave integrators at Baker High required no federal marshals to escort us safely to our classes. But we might have used a good psychologist.

I am reluctant to tell anyone who did not live through the sixties that I attended an integrated high school. An integrated school in this period was usually a formerly white school that had begun to enroll a quota of blacks to comply with—or to avoid—court-ordered desegregation. To say that I attended an integrated school might falsely suggest that I went to a racially diverse high school in which black and white students coexisted on equal footing. The truth of the matter is that I attended a school whose administrators seemed to view integration solely as a matter of permitting black students to enroll in a white school and letting them take their chances.

During the years that I attended Baker, the faculty and staff remained virtually all white. Despite the presence of African-American, Hispanic, Asian-American, and Jewish teenagers, many from military families, a white southern Protestant Christian ethos permeated the place. (Many students and teachers used the word "Christian" as a synonym for "good.") Nearly all the school's academic and social honors went to white students.

Needless to say, there were no 1970s-style black studies programs, nothing of what in the 1980s came to be known as multicultural education. In my classes, we did not read a single book, essay, or poem written by a person who was not a white American or European. Even more surprising, we were not instructed about our immediate situation, about the fact that we were part of a historic effort to end a regime of racial separatism.

A great deal of credit must be given to the resilient African-American teenagers at newly integrated schools who tried to have normal high school experiences. At Baker, blacks threw themselves into sports, drama, and ROTC. Many excelled. Many did well academically too. Early in our freshman year, another black student and I were skipped to the tenth grade. Like Newt Gingrich, I received a National Merit Award and scholarships to college.

Despite successes, we African-Americans were keenly aware of our minority status at Baker and of the low regard in which blacks were held generally in our school and town. We could not put such a looming reality out of our minds. We were full of bravado, but insecure, always trying to prove ourselves worthy of the white world into which we had been partly admitted. I worried to the point of numb fingers and headaches that I would not receive appropriate recognition. And sometimes I did not. One year, my English teacher passed over me and took a white student with a lower grade-point average to the honor banquet, to which each teacher was supposed to invite her best student. Newt Gingrich secretly dated one of his Baker High teachers; I found it hard even to speak to mine.

Minority exclusion from the elite social realm of the school was particularly dispiriting. No black woman could hope to be elected cheerleader, prom queen, or homecoming queen. No black could expect to be voted most beautiful or most handsome. The absence of black cheerleaders (of all things) came to symbolize racial exclusion. During the 1970–71 school year, turmoil erupted over the cheerleading issue, and someone burned down the gymnasium.

A number of black students found Baker's peculiar brand of integration intolerable and transferred to one of the black public high schools across town. Black students from military families were accustomed to living and going to school among whites. But even we openly fantasized about attending one of the black schools to escape the pressures of integration.

For those of us who stayed behind, our peculiar integration had its lighter moments. Black students sometimes took advantage of teachers' xenophobic distrust. Once, a black student ostentatiously rolled something white between his fingers and, in his best imitation of a thug, asked our English teacher if she knew what he had in his hand. Determined to take charge of a presumably dangerous situation, the teacher demanded that he turn over his "marijuana cigarette." The class erupted into hysterical laughter, and the teacher turned crimson when the suspected big, bad possessor of illegal drugs revealed that his "joint" was nothing more than a bit of twisted notebook paper.

And then there was the "Afro pik" ban. Afro piks were the combs of choice for black students wearing the natural, Afro, or bush hairdos that school officials discouraged as expressions of radical rebellion. One day the school principal announced that Afro piks were no longer permitted on campus. Why? We were told that the sharp-toothed picks, some of which resembled angel-food cake cutters, might be used as weapons. To cope with the ban, some students took to grooming their Afros with table forks.

The presence of blacks on a white campus does not alone achieve meaningful racial integration. Within my integrated high school, segregation was the social rule. The demise of my close relationship with a white friend is illustrative.

As middle-schoolers at Fort Benning, Pam Wilson and I had been neighbors and inseparable pals. We dressed alike, in twin miniskirts, poor-boy tops, and white go-go boots. Together we danced the pony and the jerk to hits by Diana Ross and the Supremes. Together we got into trouble with our parents for playing spin the bottle, the notorious heterosexual kissing game.

Shortly after beginning the eighth grade, I moved a hundred miles away to the Atlanta Army Depot. Pam and I maintained our friendship through letters. She seemed happy to learn, eighteen months after our separation, that my father had been reassigned to Fort Benning and that I would attend her high school, Baker High. Soon after my arrival at Baker, Pam and I ran into each other in the cafeteria. But after making eye contact and waving from across the room, we felt restrained by the unwritten rule against racial intermingling. She sat at a table with white friends. The trapped look in her eyes pushed me to a table of blacks. Unable to resume the old relationship, we had none at all.

The racially segregated character of my life in the putative era of integration moved beyond Baker's walls in 1969, when my father was sent to Vietnam. We had to leave Fort Benning once again. This time we moved just a few miles, to Columbus, to await his safe return. Columbus neighborhoods were still de facto segregated. We moved to Dawson Estates, then a shiny new middle-class black neighborhood. For some time thereafter, the close human contact that constituted my social world—the neighbors, friends, dates, parties, and telephone calls—were overwhelmingly with other African-Americans.

This life of rigid black-white segregation was typical of the lives lived by residents of Columbus. But it sent me to war against myself. My multicultural preferences could not be reconciled with my segregated behavior. I had no problem with having African-American friends and neighbors; my problem was with being forced to exclude and deny feelings for people who were not African-Americans.

The U.S. military is often thought of as a conservative force in American society. My college classmates viewed it that way in the early 1970s, when "military-industrial complex" was a ritual sneer. In key respects, the military is a conservative institution. But the comparative social equality of the races among military families in the 1960s cultivated liberal expectations in me. Integrated housing, schools, churches, swimming pools, health care, friendships—they got under my skin. They became norms against which I continue to judge social arrangements.

For southern black families like mine, taking up military life in the 1950s and 1960s meant an opportunity to taste what America could be like if everyday life were not ordered around principles of discriminatory racial segregation. I had had plenty of white, Hispanic, and Asian friends in the past, but then and now I was cut off from all such people. I was not comfortable with segregation in the way that civilians seemed to be. Segregation felt unnatural. Because I subjectively experienced my social choices as constrained by segregation, my relationships with most people seemed dictated. I felt more caged than free.

In the last semester of my senior year, the war within was complemented by a war without. A friendly whisper escalated into a major battle with Baker High. While in study hall, an hour-long period of monitored individual schoolwork, I whispered a few words about a Latin homework assignment to a classmate. Talking was against the rules, and I was ordered to write the sentence "I will not talk in study hall" one hundred times. When I refused the silly punishment for what I thought was a technical and justifiable breach, the study hall teacher sent me to see our principal, Oscar P. Boyles. I expected Mr. Boyles to side with me. Instead he ruled as insolence my articulated disdain for repetitive sentence writing. He then meted out the most severe punishment within his powers, a week-long suspension from school.

I had not imagined anyone could be kicked out of school for so minor an infraction. It was 1969! Young people were burning down buildings, abusing drugs, carrying weapons. At Baker, suspension was a devastating sanction usually reserved for recidivist bullies and thieves. Because suspension was normally handed out to serious offenders, many campus organizations had a rule that suspension meant an automatic ban from further participation. Moreover, teachers were not required to permit suspended students to make up missed examinations. I faced all these harsh consequences.

I believed I was suspended because of my race. I was smart and cooperative. I had done too well at Baker. I had to be brought down a notch or two. "Anita," Mr. Boyles explained, "I've got to make an example out of you for the sake of the other nigra [sic] children." When Mr. Boyles announced my suspension, I flew into an emotional rage. I initially refused to leave his office. I left only after my mother arrived, promising that she would immediately appeal to the local board of education. But she did not know how to go head-to-head with white officials. She broke her promise to me and tried to shield me from shame by attributing my intransigence to stress over my father's absence in Vietnam.

The suspension transformed me. Thereafter I had nothing but contempt for Baker High administrators. I began to associate closely with the school's few self-described rebels, existentialists, and atheists, most of whom were white. Once or twice I invited my white friends into my black neighborhood. My poetry turned political, my clothing outrageous, my Afro large. I knew almost nothing about the civil rights movement, the women's movement, the black power movement, the antiwar movement, or radical youth culture, but I began to look as if I belonged to all of them.

I graduated from Baker in June of 1970 at commencement exercises held at the Columbus Municipal Auditorium. I was still feeling wronged. It was all I could do to balance the mortarboard atop my Afro for the duration of the ceremony. Three months later, I headed to college. My mother hoped I would accept a scholarship from Emory University, an established white school in Atlanta. Instead I chose New College, an experimental college in Sarasota, Florida, with a radical philosophy of personal freedom.

Despite the "good-bye and good riddance" sentiment with which I had left Baker High, something drew me to my twentieth class reunion in 1990. Maybe I was curious. Maybe I felt especially good about myself and wanted to show off. Baker had not ruined my life! I was prepared to forgive and forget. I was happily married. I had a Ph.D. from the University of Michigan, a law degree from Harvard, a tenured position on the faculty of Georgetown Law Center, and a long résumé.

The officers' club at Fort Benning was the reunion site. One other black alumna, a Hollywood actress named Peggy Blow, showed up for the event. My integrated high school's twentieth reunion, like my integrated high school itself, was a white affair. Undaunted, I moved about the ballroom, starting conversations with people who looked trapped. I left early, wondering how these graduates of Baker felt about the fact that their white school, in the years after integration, had become rundown and mostly black.

In 1993, I went back to Columbus yet again, this time to give a speech at the public library during Black History Month. I was stunned by the celebrity treatment I received in the hands of the African-American community. The day before my talk a chauffeur-driven stretch limousine transported me to a reception at Columbus State University. Prominent local black lawyers, judges, and politicians came to shake my hand. Some of my black classmates from Baker came by as well.

Among the sprinkling of whites at the reception was Oscar P. Boyles, then retired, the unprincipled principal of days past. I was stunned to see him. Boyles made a point of saying that he had been planning to do some house painting that day but had postponed the task just so that he could come to congratulate me. I could not resist asking the old man for his views on school integration in Columbus. Without waiting for his answer, I gave him mine. After listening to me for a while, he smiled wryly and said, "Y'all taught me a lot; yes, y'all did."

The next evening I spoke to a full auditorium at the main branch of the public library. After my talk, the black mayor pro tem of Columbus presented me with a rolled parchment signed by the white mayor, citing my high moral character and declaring the last week in February as Anita Allen Week. Little girls shyly asked for my autograph. A local television station covered the event, which was the number-two story on the evening news. My photograph ran on the front page of the local black newspaper.

This exalted VIP treatment was all due to black citizens' extraordinary pride in the modest successes of an African-American graduate of the local school system. They thought it remarkable that a black graduate of Baker High School was a published scholar and had appeared on national television. Although Columbus has produced numerous black professionals, black residents of the city are demoralized by the frequently low achievement of young blacks. When a black librarian learned about my accomplishments from a chance encounter with my father, she spearheaded the effort to bring me to

Columbus as a guest of the city and as a role model for young people. I was genuinely touched and appreciative.

Columbus does not seem so bad anymore, although it remains a profoundly segregated city. Many neighborhoods, schools, churches, and businesses serve only one race. But there has been a major change for the better since the 1960s: African-Americans have a little political power. They share power with whites and other groups, enjoying black political representation in local, state, and national government. It is not clear how much power and influence blacks in Columbus have acquired with respect to the things that trouble them most. But by 1993, they had achieved just enough political clout to persuade the Muscogee County school district to celebrate Black History Month, to finance my visit, and to extract a flattering declaration from the mayor's office.

Ben Bates

Ben Bates is the head of the English department of Langston University in Langston, Oklahoma, where he lives with his wife and two children. He is the author of several published short stories and a play.

Having grown up in a racially segregated environment in Chicago, Ben says that he was conditioned early on to see things from a racial perspective. "I think I paid too much attention to race when I was younger," he says. "When I went to college I wanted to be a lawyer because I felt obliged to serve 'my people.' I think black people are too diverse and have too many interests for such a simpleminded notion. I would have been better off pursuing more personal concerns. Anything black people do is a black thing."

In this personally revealing story, Ben describes the particular challenges of his coming of age as "an affirmative-action baby."

BOOMERISM, OR
DOING TIME IN THE IVY LEAGUE

My friend Jackie made partner in a big Chicago law firm a couple of years ago. She started with nothing; now she needs tax shelters. She thinks the story of "those hoodlum children who went to the Ivy League in the sixties and seventies" has not been told. I think Jackie is right, but I am not the one to tell the story. I haven't maintained much contact with my Yale classmates. I think of Yale as I think of my first marriage. (Yes, I actually married a Yale woman.) From courtship to marriage to dissolution, we spent about five years as a Yale couple. Yet, at this writing, we haven't spoken in at least ten years. I wouldn't know where to find her—or why I might want to. Back then I thought she would be the most important person in my life.

The hoodlum children are also known as affirmative-action babies. When the elite institutions opened their doors to us thirty years ago, it was a symbol of liberation. Today, having a handful of black lawyers and doctors doesn't seem quite so revolutionary. The hoodlum children have come a long way. But it has been a strange trip—more hallucination than dream.

In high school I wasn't even a hoodlum. During the winter and spring of 1968 I was the first-ever junior class president at

Harlan High School in Chicago, immersed in plans for our first-ever junior prom. Before 1968, only seniors received such privileges as proms and presidents, but our class was *different*. Change was in the air. We were breaking new ground. I was a young black boy at an almost all-black high school, thinking, "Today the junior class, tomorrow the nation!" I wore an iridescent blue Nehru jacket to that first prom.

I was in tune with the times. Nineteen sixty-eight was perhaps the only time in American history when a young black boy who expressed such an ambition was as likely to be encouraged as ridiculed. Martin Luther King, Jr., had expressed dreams far more grand five years earlier. Lyndon Johnson had said, "We shall overcome." Congress and the courts had attacked the separate-but-equal doctrine. Hundreds of thousands of my elders had negotiated, marched, sung, shouted, demanded, and died. Why couldn't I be president? If I played my cards right, a talented young fellow like me could even—go to Yale!

And so it came to pass. A man named G. H. Walker, stockbroker and Yale alumnus, employed a black lawyer named Benjamin Duster as his scout. Duster knew Silas Purnell, who ran a college counseling agency out of his basement in the Dearborn Homes housing project. Purnell knew the guidance counselor at Harlan High School, Ms. Richey, who knew me: junior class president, owner of a set of killer (for a young black boy) SAT scores, son of a factory worker and a postal clerk. Me, who didn't know what a stock was or why people broke them.

G. H. Walker took the Branch Rickey approach. In 1947. the Brooklyn Dodgers already had a (segregated) system for player development. Rickey could have scoured his own minor leagues for years and never found a Jackie Robinson. Instead, he removed his blinders and stepped into a new talent pool. Soon, other owners signed Negro Leaguers because they wanted to compete, not to do favors for black men. Rickey took affirmative action to improve his team; G. H. Walker did the same. I was one of eight young black boys who met with Duster in Purnell's basement office. They encouraged us to apply to Yale and told us that Walker's sponsorship could make the difference between admission and rejection.

I don't recall ever meeting Mr. Walker. Perhaps we shook hands once. When I think of him today, a blend of the Wizard of Oz and Mr. Norton from Ralph Ellison's *Invisible Man* comes to mind: pale, frail, with thinning white hair and watery blue eyes behind rimless glasses, charcoal-gray suit, white shirt, striped tie, working the strings on my shoulders. But this is not a real memory. As a high school senior, I had not read Ralph Ellison. And I'd never been to Oz until a fine September evening in 1969, when I walked through the Vanderbilt Gate onto the Old Campus of Yale for the first time and saw on my right a group of about twenty students, kicking up dust in competition for a huge blooper ball; on my left, fluid groupings of two and five and eight and ten, talking, laughing, hugging, whistling, waving; and the air full of boomerangs, Frisbees, and balls. Oh, my.

I knew I wasn't in Kansas anymore, but then I'd never been to Kansas, either. I'd never been much of anywhere beyond Chicago's south side. My father, from Alabama, and my mother, from Arkansas, came to Chicago with millions of other migrants before World War II. They learned, as did most southern blacks who came north, that their lives in the north were no less separate and no more equal than they were in the south.

My parents met, married, and raised three sons during an era when Chicago was known as the most segregated city in America. We were not isolated on the South Side, any more than the slaves were truly isolated from the slave owners, but our excursions—to Wrigley Field or Comiskey Park, to the museums, to the Loop—always had the feel of maneuvers behind enemy lines. We learned to shrug at the snarled insult of some bus driver, to feel guilty when some matron's knees buckled as we brushed (barely!) past her on our way to the toy department at Marshall Field's. On family outings and school field trips—especially those that would bring us in contact with whites—we were scrubbed, groomed, and pressed to the hilt, and ordered to be on our best behavior. Kindnesses from whites were not uncommon, but we always anticipated bigotry. Nevertheless, we were happy.

Our happiness could be measured in part by the relief we felt after a foray into the city, when we returned to the comfort and security of segregation.

But in the late sixties, change was in the air. Today, we remember the events as catalysts. We say that the assassinations, or the riots, changed our way of thinking. But maybe change spreads like a virus. And events are signs of infection. First the virus infiltrates the emotions. A strange mood takes hold of the victim. He feels *different*. Destined for greatness. All things seem possible. A poor black boy can become president. Then the victim is overwhelmed by a mix of ambition and despair. He feels inspired, when in fact he is quite ill. Deviant behavior follows.

If this seems too speculative, consider a comment Lyndon Johnson made when *Time* named him Man of the Year for 1967:

In all candor, I cannot recall a period that is in any way comparable to the one we are living through today. It is a period that finds exhilaration and frustration going hand in hand—when great accomplishments are often overshadowed by rapidly rising expectations.

("LBJ as Lear," *Time*, 5 January, 1968: 13-22)

Johnson describes the early stages of the "boomerism" syndrome. The illness is characterized by paradox. For my parents' generation, their children's bright prospects were a source of joy and, when they thought of their own separate-but-equal experience, bitterness. Sometimes the contradictions were too much to bear. This may explain why calls for fair treatment, for equal opportunity, could sound like threats. This March, 1968, report of events in Memphis is boomerism full-blown.

Last week Memphis simmered on the rim of racial rampage . . . What began a month ago as a walkout by city employees is now a black and white confrontation. Memphis garbage collectors, most of them making $1.80 an hour, went on strike . . . Nearly all of Memphis's 1300 garbage men are black . . . Mayor Henry Loeb has spurned the strikers' demands . . . Invoking Tennessee court decisions banning strikes by public service workers, the mayor brought in some 150 strikebreakers. The Negro community countered with a boycott of downtown stores with the slogan: "No new clothes for Easter." Seven hundred Negroes picnicked in City Hall. A few youngsters tried to overturn a police cruiser. Nervous cops sprayed the kids' *faces with Mace. Injunctions were brought against union leaders. When a contingent of Negro ministers and militants returned to City Hall, a raucous exchange of words resulted in the arrest of 117 protesters . . . 200 youngsters invaded the steps of City Hall to hold a mock funeral, solemnly burying justice in a borrowed gray casket. Young raiders broke into a Beale Street department store. Fires were set to the garbage piling up at a rate of nearly 500 tons a day . . . "I am not in favor of violence," said the Rev. James M. Lawson, Jr., an erudite militant who leads much of the Negro struggle. But "if I were inclined to advocate burning, it would be in East Memphis [where the mayor lives]—I think we've had enough talk of this burning down our own neighborhoods."*

("Memphis," *Time*, 15 March 1968: 19-26)

In this setting, Martin Luther King, Jr.'s, assassination during the first week of April in 1968, seems more climax than catalyst.

After King's murder, I found the nerve to tell my parents that I wanted to wear an Afro. We spent most of my senior year of high school debating haircuts. My parents also objected to my involvement in the Black Student Federation, a short-lived spin-off of Operation Breadbasket, which later became Operation PUSH. I traveled the South Side and the West Side making speeches to whomever showed up. Our mission was to organize the high school students in the struggle against racism. I even made a speech, that spring of 1969, to the Operation Breadbasket Saturday morning meeting and had an across-the-lunch-table conversation with the Reverend Jesse

Jackson. I don't remember a word that was said, but at the time I felt as if I had been anointed. I would really let my hair grow when I got to Yale.

My uncle Dudley came to visit me that first semester in New Haven. In my family, Uncle Dudley was the prosperous one. He drove a Cadillac and always wore a coat and tie. He was the first person I knew who had a flash timer and could get into his own photographs. As I was growing up, he had never consistently gotten my name right, but that day I was the apple of his eye. He made good use of the flash timer, setting up his shots and then throwing an arm around me in front of my Famum Hall entryway, in the Pierson College dining hall, in Beineke Plaza . . . . In every shot my bushy head sits atop a sweatshirt that looks three sizes too small. It was my only clean article of clothing that said "Yale," and my Uncle Dudley insisted I wear it. At home, he was a dignified, autocratic figure, but that day he was thrilled just to walk the campus with me. He looked as if he had been in the Negro Leagues for years and finally, vicariously, he was playing in the majors. I didn't know what his business was, but I thought he would have given up everything he owned for the chance to be a Yalie.

In retrospect, Uncle Dudley's infection seems obvious, but at the time I didn't see it. I couldn't understand how he could be a somebody *and* a nobody. This disorientation (Uncle Dudley's and mine) is another symptom of the virus.

Many of the young black men and women who arrived on campus that fall shared Uncle Dudley's enthusiasm. They cultivated white friendships, let the brothers and sisters slide. They told themselves: "Now you can be a doctor, a lawyer, a doctor-lawyer! This is your chance. Make your connections. Now you too can have a Yale degree. Now you can join the corporations. Now you can have a suburban, no, a country home. Now you can live. Like white people." Some of the blacks I met at Yale had escaped the Negro Leagues long ago, knew better than to look back, yet were still vulnerable to infection. Once, I spent most of my time at a freshman mixer stalking a woman who, according to campus lore, had never been seen speaking to another black person. "She must think she white!" was how some folks put it. You couldn't call what we had a conversation, but I breathed all over her.

Some of us knew we could never be white and feared that we would never measure up, that we didn't really belong in the major leagues. In the summer of 1997, we celebrated the Negro Leagues, but nobody, then or now, thinks of the Negro Leagues as first class. Josh Gibson may have hit 972 home runs, but he is not the home run king. The affirmative-action conflict revolves around a shared assumption about the difference between first class and second class. On one side is the idea that privileges (such as the chance to "play in the majors") should be shared, or at least distributed fairly; on the other side is the idea that privileges must be preserved and protected. Both sides are concerned that first-class institutions not be "watered down" by people who "don't belong." A comment in *Newsweek* from Supreme Court justice Clarence Thomas on his experience at Yale Law School expresses the tension created by this debate:

> *You had to prove yourself every day because the presumption was that you were dumb and didn't deserve to be there on merit.*
>
> ("Supreme Mystery," *Newsweek,* 9 September 1991: 27-34.)

When the virus strikes, the ambition to "prove yourself" feels exactly like the fear that your inferiority will be exposed. Thomas is a walking illustration of the fine line between inspiration and illness. Some affirmative action babies found the "compensatory" programs, the "remediations" that enabled them to partake of privilege, quite salutary. Other carriers of the virus found these same "support services" debilitating. Then there were those, such as the justice, who suffered a dual effect, and found themselves simultaneously uplifted and insulted. Paradox is the signature of boomerism.

Some of us at Yale knew that we could never be white and celebrated. In a swift series of roommate swaps and evictions, one group of brothers resegregated an entryway in Wright Hall that fall of 1969. This area became known as the Ghetto. The brothers from the Ghetto ate together, partied together, chased women together, played cards together, studied together (occasionally!), and kept each others' backs against the white menace. They told themselves: "These people don't want us here, except maybe as entertainment. They think we can all sing, dance, or bounce a ball. We ain't going for it. The white man lies. Been lying about black people, lying *to* black people, since day one. We ain't going for it." In the Ghetto, they refused to believe that the Ivy League—Uncle Dudley's Ivy League—was real; more likely, it was some kind of trick. The Ghetto brothers were more than college students—they were revolutionaries. One of the Ghetto's leading residents meticulously redesigned the "Yale" on his notebooks and folders to read "Jail."

Blame it on the virus. The college student who sees himself as political prisoner is a classic victim of boomerism. In him we see how the syndrome clouds the judgment, causes delusions of grandeur. I speak as a survivor of the plague.

My personal crisis began when I visited the Yale Co-Op for the first time. I was out of my element. The best measure of the distance between the South Side and the Ivy League is that I had budgeted one hundred dollars for my books and figured I'd have spending money left over. When I spent seventy-five dollars that first time through the line, on books for *one course*, I felt like a fish flapping around on the dock. In rapid order, it occurred to me that my parents couldn't help me, that I was in class with the sons and daughters of rich white folks, that I could never make it without my books (my books!), that my glorious future was in jeopardy, that maybe, somehow, I had been tricked. Very shortly thereafter I learned that the brothers from the Ghetto also stole books together.

As I write this, the Yale Co-Op, like every other college bookstore, is a marvel of electronic surveillance, but in the days of the hoodlum children this was not so. Back then, the Co-Op was a garden, the fruit was ripe, you could pick it yourself. The managers of the Co-Op believed in an honor code; the brothers from the Ghetto thought the whole thing was stupid. You could enter the Co-Op empty-handed, pick out a high-priced leather briefcase, fill it with books, and walk. I was never that flamboyant. I preferred to take two or three books at a time and leave the store openly with the books in my hand. I could do just as well as the briefcase boys by making multiple trips.

This was revolutionary shoplifting. I reasoned that if I was expected to compete with rich Yalies, my access to the textbooks should be as easy as theirs. I was merely compensating for my disadvantage. I only stole books (and high-quality plastic playing cards, which were the rage), but I didn't limit myself to assigned readings. I stole books with titles that intrigued me. I stole books for my less revolutionary friends. I stole books to impress women. I stole the books that I thought an educated young man should have, two or three at a time, no fidgeting, no skulking looks behind me as I exited the store.

They didn't stop me until my sophomore year, when I was on the way out of the store with two books: *The Triumph of Conservatism,* by Gabriel Kolko, which I needed for a U.S. history course, and *Passing,* a Harlem Renaissance novel by Nella Larsen. Just outside the Co-Op door, a security guard said, "Wait a minute. Did you pay for those books?"

"Yeah."

"I don't think so."

"What are you talking about?"

"You're going to have to come with me."

I was taken to a back room and left to sweat. A few minutes later, the security guard came in with a manager. I stuck to my story. After I went back and forth with the guard a few times, the manager spoke. "You were seen taking these books from the shelf."

"I don't know what you saw, but I came into this store with these books."

"You just walked into the store with two new books, then turned around and walked out?"

"That's right."

"So why did you come into the store?" The manager thought he had me. One corner of his mouth turned up.

"I need a couple of other books, but I can't afford them."

Now the manager looked as if his fish had gotten off the

hook. He motioned to the security guard, and they left the room. Then the security guard returned. "You can leave now."

"Can I take my books?"

"Take them and get the hell out of here!" The security guard looked at me, but I don't think he saw me. I took the books and left, calmly. Somehow I had turned a lie into the truth. Or maybe it was the other way around.

I told my story in the Ghetto and received congratulations from the brothers. I tried to convince myself that I had won a battle. I continued to steal books from the Co-Op, refining my technique, becoming an expert literary shoplifter. When I was stopped again in my junior year, and spent a few hours in a jail cell, it was just the price of doing business. Somebody from the college bailed me out. I was on my way to great things. As a senior, I met my first wife.

Today, whenever I walk through a sensing device in a library or bookstore, a department store at the mall; whenever I walk through a metal detector at the airport or in a public high school, I consider it a tangible legacy of the hoodlum children. It appears that the affirmative-action debate has already been decided. We want protection from the virus. This is no time for stories about the ambitions of poor black youth.

LeVan D. Hawkins

LeVan D. Hawkins, who lives in West Hollywood, California, has written for the *Los Angeles Weekly,* the *Los Angeles Times,* the *Sacramento News and Review,* and the *Santa Fe Reporter.*

In this story about his freshman year of college, he exposes the racial humiliation that he endured at the hands of his white roommate, Fred [a pseudonym]. Still, even though his focus is on white racism, LeVan carefully points out that he had felt the same kind of humiliation in the past, when black high school classmates frequently told him he was "too white." "Black people had given me a tremendous amount of grief, too," he says, "and I'd become accustomed to abuse."

LeVan is very clear that he doesn't want to be pitied for being black, and he doesn't want to live his life in reaction to racial oppression. "If I constantly find myself reacting to it, I will never be free," he says. "I still stand up to any injustice I experience; I just stand up from a position of strength."

LeVan believes that he has an obligation to serve as "a bridge between races, sexes, sexualities, and religions," and that it is especially important to reach out to young people.

FRED

When I was a freshman in college, I could only listen to the music I loved when my roommate, Fred, left the room. This was in the mid-seventies. We used record players—stereos—then. I didn't have one; Fred did and he hated black music.

"Don't want to hear it. Don't have to—it's my record player."

I couldn't understand why he was so opposed to hearing my music. My taste in music wasn't radical, nor did the singers sing lyrics denigrating whites. I liked black pop—The Stylistics, Barry White, Aretha Franklin, Marvin Gaye—great music made by black artists that appealed to people of all colors. Fred, however, was the exception, and he had the power—he owned the stereo. If I wanted to play the few albums I owned or to listen to the rhythm-and-blues radio station that played the music I enjoyed, I had to wait until he was out of the room to do it.

I suppose some people wouldn't have used his stereo under those conditions, but I loved music—I had to hear it. Every morning, I woke with a song playing in my head, and I listened passionately to the radio and kept top-ten lists of my favorite current records.

Fred loved music, too. On numerous occasions, he excitedly played his favorite music for me. His choice of music was white rock and pop.

"This is good stuff."

Some of it was. I enjoyed it and told him I so. When I tried to share my music with him, he derided it.

"All that hoo-hooing and stuff!" He would make sounds and dance around the room. "Hoo-hoo! Hoo-hoo!"

Once he grabbed one of my Aretha Franklin albums and spotted white pop star Elton John's name listed as one of the songwriters. "These people can't even write their own music."

Aretha is one of the most acclaimed singers in the history of contemporary music, but to Fred she was inferior. For him, a black singer or group's singing songs written by white rock and pop stars was proof of the superiority of white music. My way of responding was to say, "I like what I like. You like what you like." I wish I had known what I learned as an adult: The singers and groups he was telling me to listen to, the "classics"—the Rolling Stones, Eric Clapton, and the Beatles—all based their sounds on African-American musicians who had gone before them.

When I was completing my application for college housing, I came across the question, "Do you have any preference in roommates?" I wrote "no." It never occurred to me to write "black," as I later discovered many blacks had. I had attended an integrated high school of blacks and whites in my junior and senior years and had many white friends, so the idea of a white roommate didn't alarm me; I would take whatever roommate I was assigned—it would be an adventure!

It was. A bad one.

If Fred wasn't ridiculing my music, he was ridiculing the way I spoke.

"I thought you were going to the library," he said to me one day when he entered the room.

"I have to go downtown. I figured I'd go then."

He moved toward me.

"You'll go when?" he asked smiling.

"Huh?" I had no idea what was so humorous.

"You'll go 'then.'" He mocked me. Eyes gleaming, a big smile spread across his face, he bobbed his head as he stood in my face and exaggeratedly pronounced "then" as if it was the exact rhyme of "tin."

"'Then,'" he laughed, his body rocking in spasms.

One night, around the same period, I sat at a dinner party, the lone black, and told a story about my grandmother. A woman interrupted me and corrected my grammar.

"My God, speak the King's English," she said indignantly. Angry and embarrassed, I became quiet. The room was silent; all eyes were on me. I awkwardly continued and hurried the story to its conclusion. I didn't know what king the woman was referring to, but I knew that she and Fred had the same one. Their message was clear: The way I spoke was wrong.

That was the same message I received when I started high school, except the bullies who beat and harassed me (all black) accused me of trying to "sound white." At that time, I had never been around any white people—I lived in an all-black town and went to all-black schools until I was in the eleventh grade.

Fred's constant ridicule wore me down. I began to speak at a slow, deliberate pace to make sure I didn't make any mistakes. Speaking became a chore.

"Boy! What's wrong with you!" he'd ask, accenting the "boy."

Boy was the nickname he assigned me, always said with a laugh and a smile. I knew he knew enough American history to know that years ago black men had been mistreated and had been called Boy by white men half their age. Never Mister, never by their names. Boy. It was demeaning. The word "boy" spoken by a white man to a black man carries memories of degradation and oppression. Those days were supposed to be over. And here was this white man doing it to me, except he did it with a smile, and when I told him to stop, he'd tell me it was a nickname and that I should "feel like part of the group."

I wrote a term paper for my English class entitled "The Immigrant." In it, I wrote that since I started college, I felt like an immigrant in my own country—a man without a land; displaced behind language and cultural barriers. I handed Fred the paper, hoping he'd understand how I felt and change his behavior. Instead he flew into a rage.

"It's a pack of lies! I don't treat you like that! I treat you like one of the guys. Guys razz each other."

I didn't mind being teased. I resented that the names and jokes were always related to color. I had been stripped of my identity.

In high school, I was recognized as an honor student; an actor. The bullies called me a sissy. All these identities were based upon my personality and behavior. When I was Fred's roommate, I was reduced to just a color, something I possessed from birth.

Out of the thirty thousand students who attended my college, only three thousand were black. Whenever I saw another black student, I would nod or say "Hey" or "What's happening?" It helped us feel less lonely. Blacks also ate at the "black table" in the cafeteria, a table where all the blacks sat and had conversations without being ridiculed about the way they spoke. That is, as long as they sounded "black."

I don't know why I didn't sit there.

I think some of it had to do with spending the first two years of high school fighting off bullies who were black like me. When I moved to an integrated school, where whites made up seventy-five percent of the enrollment, I was relieved; most of the bullies dropped out, and the remaining ones started terrorizing the white students, who wouldn't fight back, so I was left alone. Still the beatings, the harassment, had left their impact. I knew that every black person was not my friend. Race was not the only requirement for friendship.

The idea of separatism bothered me. The black table was such a visible antisocial statement. Still, if the others had relationships with their roommates like the one I had with Fred, I understood.

If I could have stopped Fred from the actions I thought were offensive, we would've had a great relationship. We had long discussions about life, told jokes to each other, and had common goals. I knew it was possible for us to get beyond race. Doug, one of my best friends in high school, was white. Occasionally, we would discuss race or he would tell me some stupid racial joke he heard, but we never ridiculed each other because of our cultural differences.

I usually went to dinner with Fred and the people who lived in the rooms near us. The idea of sitting at a table full of strangers horrified me, so I stayed where it was familiar.

Some of the blacks didn't like it and wrote graffiti on the study-hall wall calling me an Uncle Tom and a traitor to my race. It hurt. I was ashamed and I questioned whether it was true. When I went home for the holidays, I constantly talked to my brother about it.

"I wouldn't worry about it," he told me. He also attended an integrated high school. "Just be true to yourself. You can't care what people think." It was good advice. Unfortunately, I cared.

I should have expected the ostracizing. I knew the rules. At the integrated high school I attended, there were unwritten rules regarding associating with white people. One of them was that a black person should never sit alone with a white person or a group of whites at a public gathering; you had to have another black person with you. In high school, I never disobeyed that rule. In college, I was always the lone black at our dinner table.

One day, Fred came home and told me that he had seen the graffiti in the study hall. He found it amusing. I looked at him in hatred and amazement.

You're the reason they call me that, I thought. And you're not worth it.

When winter break neared, I called home and asked my exboss if I could work at my old job during my vacation. It was a harsh Midwestern winter; sub-zero temperatures and heavy snows. I worked the midnight shift and drove to work when the mercury dropped to its lowest. One night, my car slid on the ice that blanketed the street and I ended up stuck helplessly in a ditch.

I would rather have been in my warm home resting in my comfortable bed, but I was determined to make some money: I was going to buy a stereo. I drove to work fantasizing about turning it up to its highest volume and blasting Fred out of the room. Aretha Franklin blasting out the Rolling Stones. It was what motivated me during those cold midnight rides.

The stereo I bought was flashy, with blue, yellow, and red fluorescent lights that moved with the music. It was loaded down with knobs and gadgets I had no idea how to use, and it was huge—one of the reasons I bought it. It dwarfed Fred's tiny, plain black stereo when I placed it on his desk.

I sat on my bed, put my hands behind my head, and waited for him. He entered the room, said hello, and put his coat and suitcase in the closet. I smiled and waited patiently. When he turned, he saw it. He looked at me. I smirked. He smiled in pain and walked toward my stereo.

"Wow." He looked at me again.

The smirk was still on my face.

"I'm sure you'll be fair," he said. He unplugged his stereo and placed it in the closet.

He was right. I was fair. I listened to my music whenever I wanted and allowed him to listen to his. I no longer had to wait until he left the room. No longer had to ask for his permission. The power had shifted.

When I think about that day, I ask myself why he assumed I would be fair. It would have been a very human reaction to treat him as he had treated me. But I let it go because I knew how it felt. It was degrading. It hurt: waiting until he left the room to listen to the radio; being called Boy; watching him while he ridiculed my writing ability; listening to him mock the way I spoke. I knew how unfairness felt, so I was fair.

I learned valuable lessons from Fred. I learned to listen to music with my heart and ears open. I learned to respect people's differences and that differences don't mean a person is inferior—or superior, for that matter. I learned that if you have to depend upon another person to supply you with what you need, it gives that person too much power. I also learned that people in power usually wait until they're losing it before they start talking about fairness.

Crystal Ann Williams

A widely published writer who lives in Ithaca, New York, Crystal Ann Williams says her work is about "personal revolution through revelation." In this short short story she spotlights a painful, racially motivated event in her childhood. "What happened to me that day was horrible and shameful," she says. "And, more important, it still happens— every day to colored people in every city, every state in these United States of America."

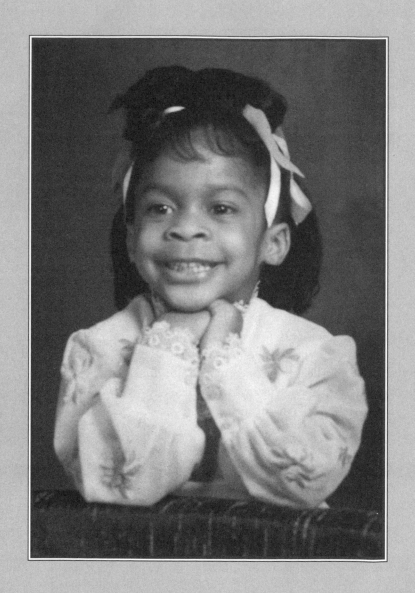

IN THE BELLY OF A CLOTHES RACK

The air is sweet with a new clothes smell, still, and so dry your nostrils contract.

Whenever we shopped, Momma and me, I would hide in the bellies of clothes racks. I liked sitting there looking up at the dropped ceiling as the dimmed fluorescent light filtered down through clothes that people had tossed. And I counted. I counted how many tags pushed their way toward me, how many one-armed hangers fell on me, and how many manicured nails twisted hangers off the rack.

I liked listening, too. There were heels clicking, muted voices whispering, and Momma's voice, humming softly, drifting over the racks to my cocooned ears. I pretended to be a crouched tigress, unseen and unheard, but hearing and hunting, placing myself at the throats of shoppers, trying to anticipate their next move. That day, a daughter pleaded, her voice gathered at the edge of hysteria, "But, Mother . . . I just can't wear that." It was a good game, to wonder from whose lips the words had come.

Saks Fifth Avenue was my favorite because it was library-quiet. There were no children shrieking or threatening to encroach on my world of beige sleeves and price tags. There was no being bumped by elbows, no trailing behind my mother as she shopped. It was a good deal—Momma knew where I was and I knew where she was, her humming a buoy.

I should have been listening for Momma, but I was too busy pouting about the cold ice and the blood I could still taste on the inside of my lip after my failed attempt at a double lutz. So when I readjusted my ears and realized that there was no humming, I scrambled out of the clothes rack and stood on tiptoe trying to find her. But I was too short.

So I jumped up and down, my feet pounding the vanilla tile. That didn't work either, so I stood and called until all sound shrank, in a receding crouch, from my body. She wasn't there. I couldn't see. There was nothing but my shrill voice begging for Momma.

Frozen in the middle of the ladies' dresses department, I remembered Momma's words: "If we ever get separated, just stay put. I'll find you." So that's what I did. My eyes searched the aisles, finding only a little girl in a pink-and-blue sundress who collided with her mother, who had stopped short to glare at me. A security guard who looked like my cousin Mack, his dark face surrounding Barbie-doll-red lips, stood at his post near the down escalator, a short distance away, beckoning. And then my pupils darkened and were filled with a stern-faced, spectacled white woman.

"Little girl, what is it you're doing?" she hissed.

"Looking for my mother."

"Your mother is not here."

"Yes she is. She's here. She was just here."

"Girl!" Her head tilted down, allowing her eyes to peer over the racks and then back to me. "There is no one here who could be your mother. She certainly isn't here." And then under her breath she whispered, "And what would she be doing if she were?"

Her face was angular. Her hair was brown and short and haphazardly placed. Her suit was blue. A delicate Jesus swayed across her chest. The lapel pin she wore glinted in the faded light.

It was then, when I was seven, on that Saturday afternoon at the Saks in Fairland Mall, in Dearborn, Michigan, that I knew that the clarity of my family—my father's black, leathery skin, the smooth milk of my mother's white skin, and the brown sugar of my skin—was obscured. The saleswoman didn't understand, but I did. I knew the implication. I'd seen it before, but I hadn't known what it was, hadn't known it was directed at me.

Even as I could hear Momma's "Cris? Crissy?!" I understood what being lost meant. Being lost is to look in the face of a spectacled white woman and wonder what the gnarled ball making its way from your stomach to your throat is called.

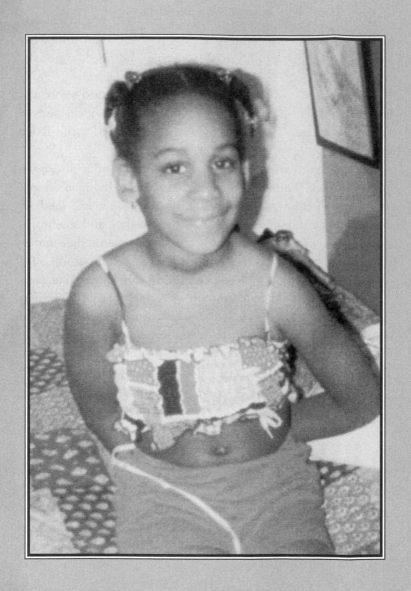

Erica S. Turnipseed

Working as an administrator at a major university in New York City, Erica S. Turnipseed is also completing a graduate degree in anthropology. She is a native of Brooklyn, New York, where she lives today.

In this story, Erica, like many black children, discovers that she is being discriminated against because of European-influenced hair standards. She is ostracized because of the texture and length of her hair.

The title, "Hand Games," characterizes both childhood games and the tactile adoration of "good hair."

HAND GAMES

It was lunchtime, and the sooner we finished eating lunch the sooner we could go out to play. I brushed the crumbs off of my desk and into a neat pile on the skirt of my Catholic school uniform, the green plaid creating peculiar frames for the oddly shaped crumbs. Deftly grasping opposite ends of my skirt, I held it out in front of me, creating a temporary bowl for the contents. I walked gingerly over to the trash can and let the crumbs fall into the growing mound of discarded lunch scraps. Brushing off the crumbs that clung to the fabric, I asked permission to go to the restroom.

Standing in the line for the girls' room was a test of my eight-year-old patience. The girls ahead of me tugged at themselves and at each other or jiggled in place, demonstrating how badly they had to "go." I stood quietly and meditated on the fun games I would play with my best friends in the school yard. I anticipated the exhilaration of Tweedle-leedle-lee, *Una dos y eso,* Miss Mary Mack, and other hand-clapping games. We would play for the entire recess time—maybe half an hour—and my hands would sting from our overzealous claps.

When I returned to the classroom, my fellow third-graders

were preparing themselves for the gaiety that awaited them outside. Donning jackets and storing our lunch boxes, we formed a line and filed out of the classroom. Anticipation overcame some, and the bold ones burst forth with giggles and bouts of fidgeting in the line. After minutes upon minutes of quieting down and straightening up, our procession made its much-awaited trek to our concrete slice of heaven.

Sequoia and Michelle were already outside, waiting for Inez and me to join them. Sequoia, with her ruddy complexion glowing from vigorous activity and her golden hair a frizzy tangle grazing her shoulders, looked like she had already been outside for a while. At eight, she had been granted her mother's permission to do her own hair, and it showed. Michelle was a little less shock-worn, but her three long braids hung lopsidedly from her head, and her plump brown cheeks gleamed with perspiration. As if we were members of a secret sorority, we conspired about which hand-clapping game we would play first, weighing the merits of each. No sooner had we made our decision than Inez skipped up to us, completing our quartet.

> *Una dos y eso, hit it.*
> *My mama told me, six years ago,*
> *There was a lady knockin' at the door,*
> *Sayin' ooh, aah, I wanna piece of pie . . .*

We played passionately and without reserve, singing the rhyme with the conviction of eight-year-old prophets. Girls played jump rope and boys tackled and pushed each other all around us, but we were oblivious to them and spun our tale with vigor.

Pie too sweet, I wanna piece of meat.
Meat too tough, I wanna ride a bus.
Bus too full, I wanna ride a bull.
Bull too black, I want my money back . . .

My eyes and hands synchronized with the rhyme, moving left and right and over and under to the beat of Inez's swinging ponytails.

Money too green, I wanna jelly bean . . .

My muscles tensed with fatigue and the anticipation that the game would soon be over and we would play another.

Bean too round, I wanna go to town . . .

We played and played, and then the game was finished. Invigorated, I adjusted the skirt of my uniform, and Michelle pulled up her kneesocks. Inez threw her two powerful ponytails back over her shoulders, while Sequoia tried in vain to place the misplaced strands of hair that haunted her face.

It was then that I saw a "lunch mother" approach our circle. "Lunch mother" was a euphemism for parents (usually women) who volunteered to help control the children at lunchtime and patroled the school yard as part of their Christian charity to the school. Unlike most lunch mothers, this one was young and pretty. Her curly black hair hung in spirals around her face, framing her dark, almond-shaped eyes and contrasting with her butterscotch skin. Attracted to her eyes that glinted softly in the sunlight and the gentle Spanish cadence of her words, I deduced that she seemed nice.

She offered us the steps to play our game on. Standing on the steps meant occupying the coveted landing in front of the school's back door, a privilege that could only be secured through a lunch mother. We would be above the masses, away from the noisy crowdedness of the childish mob below. We accepted her invitation eagerly. But apparently, her kindness was not without a desire for reciprocation. She herself wanted to engage in our hand games.

We began our game, haltingly, but became distracted by her. Murmuring Spanish terms of endearment to Inez, the lunch mother fondled her thick ponytails, tightening the baubles that secured them. That done, she moved on to Michelle's thick braids, which formed an irregular pattern against her back. Unbraiding and rebraiding them, she complimented their length.

The lunch mother imparted a mother's love to Sequoia's unkempt tresses, sectioning her golden frizziness with her fingers, creating styles replete with bangs, braids, and hair left loose. My hair lay in obedient cornrows on my head, the handiwork of my own mother. The lunch mother didn't speak to me. She reserved her adulation for my friends and offered me pinched looks when I tried to resume the hand-clapping game. My friends, for their part, did not miss our hand games. They were held within the lunch mother's orbit, adored and adoring.

Satisfied at last with Sequoia's new hairstyle, the lunch mother offered to play a hand-clapping game with the triumvirate. Assuming my former position, she launched into a game with them. Together, they exhibited a fervor that I thought only we had known. Displaced, I watched the alien game unfurl in front of me. Each clap accentuated my inexplicable hurt. I felt myself retreat from my friends, me in my painful ignorance, they in their bliss. I wondered what I had done wrong.

Touré

Touré, a Boston native, now lives and writes in Brooklyn, New York, and he is a graduate student at Columbia University. He has written for *The New Yorker, The New York Times Magazine, Callaloo, Playboy,* the *Village Voice,* and *Rolling Stone.* Currently he is collaborating on the autobiography of rapper KRS-ONE.

In this prose poem, Touré writes about his father: "His way of walking—infused with pieces of the tough posture of a street kid, the stiffness of a military man, the smooth of a city hall veteran, the bounce of a proud father—it was nothing less than lionly. I had to write about it."

BLACKMANWALKIN

Woooooooooooooo my daddy must be cool or I don't know what is
what I think while he, along wit little me just up to somebody's
knee, peacock around Blue Hill Ave in Mattapan Square like he
got some political office or pulpit or crown in his back pocket
and wave to somebody every third step like he the center of a
big ol ticker-tape puh-rade. And Dad can struuut. He did his
graduate work at UCLA (the University at the Corner of Lenox
Avenue, in Harlem) back when they had professors named
Duke and Count and Cab, so you know he learned from the
best the way to really do Blackmanwalkin.

Now, you might say that no people's style of cookin or talkin
or dancin is really better than another's, and you might be right,
but once you get to walkin? You got to give it up to
Blackmanwalkin. Hands down. Say mos people's walkin is the
color red, then Blackmanwalkin is a brighter, sharper, mo
vibrant, sexy, brilliant fire-engine red. Course, them sorta differences is visible only if you can see. But seein as everythin
started in Africa, the comp ain't really fair cuz in walkin our
lead on all y'all is, oh, a few million years.

When Dad strut he hold his head and torso up hiiigh and
do his hands swayin round his hips and keep his motion smooth

but compact cuz he been in the army and throw a slight straight-strictly-out-of-Brooklyn bounce in every other step (cuz that's where he did undergrad studyin on Blackmanwalkin). If you see him you'll jus know he in control of everthing round him. And if you a irresistible force you would get bashful in a quickfast. Every time I sit up in the window at home and watch him strut out the door, from the way he do Blackmanwalkin I jus know he Somebody. So I know I am, too. Watchin him, I'm a young-ass-know-I'm-somebody somebody. And then I see my Somebody strut out the door and I ask my little self, What is it about that strut that makes him strut that strut that he strut so baad? What is this Blackmanwalkin about? And then, one night, with Dad and his brother Herbie gone out the house, I get a lesson from Mom and my Auntie Wendy.

Mom and Auntie Wendy push aside the livin room table and the rug and turn up the Earth, Wind & Fire and tutor little me and my little sister to move like them; followin the rhythm. Little me, jus up to somebody's knee, don't know I'm gittin a lesson on Blackmanwalkin, don't see that Mom and Wendy ain't really talkin bout dancin, they talkin bout everythin in the world your black butt might do, cuz everythin in the world your black butt might do gots to be done with rhythm.

The next day I start lookin out the window, watchin the bigger boys do they Blackmanwalkin. Bein little, I'm not sure who some of them is, but I can see they have it goin on. There's that fightin man who beat up on everybody, but only after tellin em how and when he gon beat em up, and that doctor dude with the big Afro who swoop into the basket with that red, white, and blue ball and slam it on through. They Blackmanwalkin is loose and fluid like they could slide through any hole, could turn they bodies to liquid if they wanted, could do that word Dad said to do when you didn't know nothing else to do: improvise. And, there's that brother from that movie everyone love who never smile and always wear black leather and always tellin off some whitey or layin it with some woman (they got a whole song bout him bein a bad mother). He strut slow and tough, like he jus come from seein one girl and takin his time gittin to the next. Who know where he really been, or what he really got in his pants, but jus from the way he do his Blackmanwalkin you think he got a big old thing loosenen up all them women. And there go that prior cat that say the dirty words and make everyone laugh, the one who say the N word all the time. He move like that dude in that Albert Murray book that Mom used to read to us where the guy had a "sporty-blue limp-walk which told the whole world that you were ready for something because at worst you had only been ever so slightly sprained and bruised by all the terrible situations you had been through." After a lot of watchin I see all them bigger boys do they Blackmanwalkin with a smooth syncopation, with everythin right in place, with they tops and bottoms workin back and forth like counter rhythms and they left sides and right sides groovin in a cool call and response and the whole thing jus rhythm, rhythm, rhythm, rhythm, jus movin down the ave makin visual music.

Then I see the best of them bigger boys ain't jus soundin off. They Blackmanwalkin about gittin somewhere and makin a statement at the same time. A journey and a destination, too. The way they strut it, it about always bein somewhere even while you goin somewhere cuz you so baad don't no party start til you get there so there's no rush to get there cuz where you is you already somewhere jus cuz you there. So after I think that up I sit my little self up in the window and watch Dad do Blackmanwalkin out the door and off to where the wild things are and jus from seein his Blackmanwalkin I know he will return and the crown will never fall out his pocket and the parade will never end and little me jus up to somebody's knee stay up in that window and see the day's curtain come down and down and down and get to wonderin if my little totem is real and maybe he strong and not strong enough to stop the men ridin six white horses with flamin crosses in they hands who bash in the face of that little Till boy who whistled too loud and maybe bash in Dad's face or maybe bash in my face and maybe he liquid and not liquid enough to slide by them who brought them bad liquids to that man next door whose wife be screamin and screamin sometimes and maybe he big and not big enough to hold back the world who pushed Martin to his back and maybe he rhythm and not rhythm enough to keep his rhythm from never, never stoppin and then the day's curtain is all coverin everythin and I am dragged off to bed not knowin: When the wild things strolled up, had Daddy's Blackmanwalkin been baad enough?

Then mornin come. And he wake little me up with kisses on my face and his big red robe rubbin on my chest and Mom is callin *brek-fast* and I piece together my clothes and I watch him do Blackmanwalkin out the room and I piece back together my tattered little faith that when Dad get to Blackmanwalkin and get to leavin, he gon always, always Blackmanwalk on back to little me jus up to somebody's knee.

Charisse Nesbit

"**I**t seemed that I was too black for the white people, yet not black enough for the black people," Charisse Nesbit says in her account of growing up in Maryland in the 1970s and 1980s. Echoing a familiar theme, Charisse depicts her search for a community in which she could be herself—free to dress, act, and talk as she saw fit. After a stint at the University of New Mexico, where she continued to suffer at the hands of those who called her "white girl," she finally found solace in Atlanta's black community.

CHILD OF THE DREAM

I was always called "white girl" as a child—and maybe I was. After all, I was a product of my environment. I was brought up with white Barbie dolls of impossible proportions and long silky blond hair—neither of which I possessed. As a child, I believed what I was taught, and I wasn't taught to love myself for who I am—an African-American.

Growing up in a mixed neighborhood in rural Maryland, I had to deal with white people all the time. Although we all interacted on a daily basis, the white children in my classes knew nothing about me as a black person. This revelation occurred to me one day when I was in the sixth grade. I was talking with three classmates, two white girls and one black boy. We were talking about washing our hair, when the boy mentioned that I didn't wash my hair every day. I began to explain why, but the girls cut me off.

"You don't wash your hair every day? I would feel so dirty if I didn't wash my hair every day. Ewww!"

I went on to explain that my hair was different and that I couldn't wash it every day, but it didn't matter. Being a kid, I didn't have the knowledge to explain the difference in our hair types and the fact that my hair didn't make enough natural oil to be washed every day. (Later I understood all this from having to deal with my hair and its complications.) All my classmates understood, in that five minutes of conversation, was that I was a black girl with bad hygiene.

This made me question myself. Was I dirty? I knew I wasn't, but because I couldn't explain myself well enough, I began to feel as though I was and that those girls had unearthed something about me that I had just never realized. It wasn't until much later in life that I realized that their thinking was wrong but, in the meantime, I tried to convince myself that a whole race of people, most of whom only washed their hair once a week, could not be wrong.

In middle school I discovered magazines that featured black women. It was important for me to have these images of glamorous black women, which I'd craved so long, and I would sometimes carry the magazines to school. One day in eighth grade I had one of the magazines open to a relaxer ad featuring a woman with very smooth, beautiful hair in my opinion, anyway. A white classmate looked over my shoulder and pointed out the picture to another classmate. "Do you think she uses thirty-weight or forty-weight on her hair?" Thinking this very funny, he howled with laughter.

Previously, when this boy had touched my hair and found it somewhat slick, I'd tried to explain to him why I used hair grease. This time, I simply told him that African-Americans didn't use car oil on their hair and that our hair wasn't naturally oily like white people's hair. I was tired of blatant ignorance and having to constantly justify who I was and why I did the things I did.

Nevertheless, I used to pray every night that I would somehow miraculously wake up with long, silky, wash-and-go hair like my Barbie's. I would even go so far as to put a towel on my head, pretending I had hair that would swing like the white girls' hair at school—far different from my Afro puffs, which wouldn't budge when the strongest winds would blow.

Just washing and combing our hair, when it is in its natural state, is a chore that can take hours. As a child, getting my hair done became a bonding process between my mother and me, mainly because it took so long to do. We'd spend the time together talking and swapping stories, learning a lot about each other. My classmates could never have known how much it hurt me to have them criticize my grooming habits and ridicule something that meant so much to me. And because I wasn't able to explain, I just held it inside and tried to work it out within myself.

I constantly questioned myself as a child. All of the positive images of people I'd seen were white. To be beautiful, you not only had to be stick-skinny, with no behind, you had to have long silky blond hair and blue eyes, a thin nose, and thin lips. I'd look in the mirror at my full lips, flat nose, brown eyes, and kinky black hair and feel like I just didn't measure up. I didn't look a thing like Barbie, not even when they came out with the black versions, which still had blue eyes and were basically just a darker version of the white one. Because I didn't fit the mold, I had a hard time convincing myself that I was beautiful.

To get away from these stark realities, I'd often turn to books. The fantasies portrayed in them offered me the opportunity to lose myself for a little while, but all the books I read growing up were about white people. I used to enjoy the Sweet Valley High series about two Barbie-like twins, Elizabeth and Jessica, who drove a fancy car and had perfect suburban lives. This series, and others like it, influenced me so much that, when I first began writing, all of my stories featured white characters. I didn't feel it was possible to have characters who were black because everything I'd read featured only white characters.

I had teachers who tried to get me to read stories by black authors, but since the teachers were white, I saw them as trying to pigeonhole me into only reading about black characters. So, if anything, instead of opening me up to a whole world of authors I could relate to, their efforts only served to push me away from black authors. I never saw them pushing black authors on the white kids, so when they pushed them on me, I saw them as trying to make me fit into yet another stereotype.

Most of the programs I watched on television were also about white people. In fact, the only time I'd see African Americans was when one of us portrayed a hooker or a criminal. Often, the black-criminal drama would be acted out in real life on the news when I'd see a black man getting hauled away in handcuffs.

Wanting something more for myself than what seemed to be my fate, I began to identify with the way of life I'd read about in Sweet Valley High. I didn't deny I was an African-American, but I decided I didn't have to talk in slang, be uneducated, or act uncivilized or unruly to keep my identity.

Everyone else where I lived felt otherwise, however. Taking their cues from stereotypes they saw on television, they began to call me "white girl" or "wannabe" because I refused to be a stereotypical African-American. These names hurt, as did the ignorance I'd gotten from the white kids, only more. I could understand the white kids' ignorance regarding who I was. They had never been forced to learn about my culture the way I was forced to learn about theirs. What I couldn't understand was how my own people could purposely say things to hurt me. We had all been through the same thing. Why did they hate me for being a little different? Sounding educated and being interested in things other than what they were interested in didn't make me any less black, did it? It seemed that I was too black for white people, yet not black enough for black people.

I thought that if I was going to be free to be myself, without having to feel bad for it, I was going to have to go away to school and experience a different culture. I thought I'd be able to do that in New Mexico. But going to a different place, especially one with a very low number of African-Americans, only served to make me start the process of proving myself all over again. Because I wore my hair differently from the other African-Americans on campus and dressed a little differently and didn't speak slang, I came under scrutiny by my people once again.

It wasn't enough for them that I was obviously black and made no effort to hide or deny my blackness. They still pointed the finger and accused me of being white-washed. Even though most of them had been raised by white people and knew less about our shared heritage than I did, they still decided to make up their minds about who I was before they actually got to know me. Once again, I was not "black enough."

When I confronted a guy at a black student union meeting about this, he said, "You're just trying to be white. You talk white, you look white, you smell white." Everyone in the room was shocked, and most of them tried to stifle their surprised laughter, but it didn't matter. The damage was done. Once again I was the victim of ignorance and misunderstanding. I "smelled white"?

I began to hear echoes of voices from my past—accusations of trying to be something I wasn't—only they weren't from my past. It was bad memories repeating themselves all over again.

Finally, after going on an academic exchange for a year to Atlanta and taking a break from the University of New Mexico, I experienced things that transformed me, and I finally saw images I thought only existed in my wildest dreams. It was there that I realized that, although people I'd met had treated me as though I were a stranger to my own race because of my differences, I really wasn't.

Atlanta taught me that there were African-Americans who knew of a world beyond what was shown to them on television. There I met and made friends with entrepreneurs, medical students, and aspiring musicians—all black. My friends and I would stroll through the most expensive malls in Atlanta, stopping to play the pianos in the stores without thinking twice, even though most of the patrons in the malls were white. This was something that would never have happened anywhere else I'd lived. I had always been self-conscious about being black—especially when shopping anywhere expensive.

In Atlanta I realized that it is okay to know who you are and what you want and to actively and aggressively pursue your dream, regardless of what it is. I realized that even the most far-fetched dream is available to me, not just reserved for white people. Meeting the people I met in Atlanta made me realize that I wasn't alone in wanting more out of life than what was offered to those of my race on television. They made me realize, finally, that wanting and getting things by using my intellect did not make me any less black or any more white.

Despite what is shown on television and in magazines, successful, educated black people (some of whom have no sense of rhythm) do exist. Their success doesn't make them any less black or mean that they have forgotten who they are as black people. Seeing them, I no longer feel bad about trying to do something with myself and leaving my friends behind in Maryland to do nothing with themselves.

I'm proud of who I am as a person and what I'm doing with my life. Because I am graduated from college and speak the way I do, I still hear the occasional talk of "white girl"—but it is only occasional now. I have to do what's best for me by being me and not what someone else feels I should be. I've learned to love myself for who I am, a black woman who is beautiful in her own right and who looks nothing at all like Barbie.

Shilanda L. Woolridge

"**I** think we're too monolithic in our thinking as a community sometimes," says twenty-five-year-old Shilanda L. Woolridge, "which explains why there tends to be controversy if someone is black and a Republican or gay or non-Christian or anti-affirmative action. As a writer, I see myself as an agitator . . . addressing taboos and debunking the status quo regarding black culture."

Currently living in Austin, Texas, Shilanda works as a writer and self-professed "computer geek." She is a contributor to the anthology *Does Your Mama Know?*

RITE OF PROCESSES

Kids aren't stupid. Well, I don't think I was, anyway. Kids notice everything. They may not understand what they see, but they notice. However, when you are a black kid growing up in America you notice more because you have to. Especially if you grew up as I did, in majority-white situations where there were only a handful of black kids around.

I always noticed things about myself that were different from everyone else. My skin color, the shape of my nose and lips, the music I listened to, the food I ate, and the vibe and energy I felt when I was around other black people.

But there was one thing that stood out from the rest. The thick, kinky, explosion of hair upon my head. I could look at the Asian and Latino kids and see that they too had their differences from the white American mainstream. Still, they all had similar hair—which left people like me out in the cold. I noticed very early on that no other race of people on the planet had the springy, kinky, temperamental hair that black people did.

Unfortunately, many black women, like my mom, were taught traditions that involved taming the personality of their hair as much as possible. Taming and grooming meant the same thing in black households. In fact, there are seven words that send chills down the spine of most little black girls . . . "Its time to get your hair done."

Several times a month I sacrificed entire Saturdays for the sake of my hair. No amount of whining or dragging of feet would change my mom's mind as she began to clear the kitchen in preparation for the monumental task ahead of her.

Once she was ready for me, I'd lie across the kitchen counter with my head dangling over the sink while my mom worked her hands through my hair. After the washing and conditioning, my hair would be thoroughly tangled, and she would do her very best to rake a comb through it and part it into sections. After the parting, she would run a blow-dryer with a comb attachment set on (very) high heat through each section and then liberally apply pomades, affectionately known as grease.

As my mom pomaded my hair, the straightening comb would be heating on a burner on the kitchen stove. A straightening comb is a big ugly black metal iron with teeth shaped like a comb and a wooden handle. It would get heated directly on the stove top and would begin smoking when it was too hot.

When my mom was ready, she would carefully lift one of my greased, parted sections of hair and run the hot comb through from the roots to the end. (I can still hear the hiss, sizzle, snap, and crackle of the melting grease. Nor will I forget the wonderful pungent smoky odor of my frying hair.) Then she would go from part to part, ironing my hair into its straight alter ego.

Things got really tense when she was working on my hairline or behind my ears. When told to hold down my ear, I would practically fold it in half. It would only take one sneeze, cough, or twitch at the wrong moment and I'd get branded like a heifer. However, the absolute worst was the "kitchen," an area of short hairs on the back of my neck. The dreaded kitchen was one of my ticklish areas. So I would put my head down so far that my chin would touch the middle of my chest. Then I would shut my eyes and grit my teeth as I tried not to fidget.

After hours of hard work, my mother would release me with a temporarily tamed head. The house would reek of burned hair from the downstairs basement to the second-floor bedrooms, but it's a smell that most black families get accustomed to after a while.

When my mom decided that I was ready to start visiting a beautician, she asked me if I wanted a relaxer, or a Jheri Curl. Not knowing how to style my hair, I figured that a Jheri Curl would be the wiser choice. Hey, if it was good enough for Michael Jackson, it was good enough for me!

Little did I know that curly perms required their own kind of grease, called an activator. An activator is a type of lotion that is used to moisturize hair done in curly perms. Moisture was the key to keeping an attractive Jheri Curl. If you dared to let your hair dry out, it would frizz into an unruly bush-like mess. To help retain this moisture, the Jheri-curled would wear plastic baggies on their heads when they slept at night and when they were in the privacy of their own homes.

Even though I immensely enjoyed the effortless grooming that a curl gave me, I hated the mess. At the time, every collar of every shirt or jacket I owned had a permanent stain. In addition to that, one of my favorite jackets had an oily streak that trailed all the way from my neck to the small of my back. I honestly don't know how I allowed myself to walk around in public looking that way.

Even though the curl was a mess, my hair flourished and grew long. I liked having the longer hair, but I couldn't take the wet look anymore. So I told my mom that I wanted to get my hair relaxed. I figured that I could learn how to style my hair in no time. I just had to get away from that awful oily curl!

Needless to say, getting my hair relaxed had its drawbacks as well. Coarse hair like mine required chemical treatment for about twenty to thirty minutes. If the kink-killing chemicals weren't left in long enough, then various patches of hair would be straight while others would still be nappy.

So I had to sit in the beauty shop, breathing in the pungent ammonia-like fumes, while the chemicals did their job. The beautician came and checked on me periodically to see if the hair close to my scalp was lying flat. When fifteen minutes had passed and the tingling had begun, I knew I was in trouble. After twenty minutes the tingling began to feel hot. The beautician checked, but no, I still wasn't ready. At twenty-five minutes the beautician grabbed a fine-tooth comb and began to pull it through my hair.

Since my hair was thick to begin with and was made thicker by the chemicals, it was hard for her to comb it without scratching my scalp. This was bad. Every sista knows that you don't scratch your head for twenty-four hours before a relaxer. If you messed around and forgot, you'd get a reminder when the relaxer chemicals started working on that tender skin. So there I was with a chemically burning scalp that was actively getting scratched.

I knew I couldn't take it any longer—she had to take this shit out and she had to do it NOW! Fortunately, she was done, and I was led to the shampoo bowl. Ice-cold water streamed over my head and I sighed with grateful relief.

As I lay in the shampoo bowl I wondered why we had been given hair like this. Having kinky hair didn't serve any biological or evolutionary purpose at all. Obviously God did it because he didn't like us. My hair was so much trouble and I hated it. I knew that I couldn't handle chemicals and beauty salons for the rest of my life. I just wanted to be able to deal with my hair as it was. What the hell could I do—cut it all off? I certainly couldn't stop perming it. Later that day, my entire scalp scabbed over, effectively gluing my hair to my head. I had to wear a hat for more than a week and put Vaseline on my hair to help the burns heal.

Once my hair was straight, I didn't have to worry about Jheri Curl juice anymore, but I was preoccupied with the scabs and welts left behind by the relaxer chemicals. It was horrible, but black women all over the country would grin and bear it as a part of the process of taking care of their hair. What other options did we have?

After that I knew I was through with relaxers and got a curl perm again a few months later. This was the beginning of the cycle of the damned that many sistas like me traveled on. Curl perms don't take too well on relaxed hair, so my hair broke off. Then I grew my curly hair out again. I got rid of the curl and got my hair relaxed. I was sick of growing my hair out and having it break off over and over again. I was sick of shelling out fifty bucks every six weeks to get my hair tamed. I came to the conclusion that I didn't want to perm my hair ever again, but I was terrified to take action. After two years of careful consideration, I decided I was ready to deal with my black hair on its own terms, not someone else's.

At the university I went to I encountered proud black women with unprocessed hair for the first time in my life. These confident women held their heads high, sporting their unprocessed hair in various styles ranging from skin-bald heads and short, close-cropped naturals to Afros and dreadlocks of various lengths and thicknesses. I also encountered black men with breathtakingly beautiful dreadlocks down to their waists and beyond.

For the first time, I encountered black people with long hair that was truly theirs, not fake hair extensions. These folks stared boldly in the eye of the traditions and childhood experiences that told us our African-textured hair was bad and needed to be altered. Every time I encountered one of these brothas or sistas I asked them about their hair and how they took care of it. As I learned more, I began to love my hair for what it is, and not hate it for what it wasn't.

I realized that my hair wasn't meant to shine, blow in the wind, or lie down straight. I decided that I would grow my hair out in dreadlocks, and I have been doing so for the past two years. I absolutely love the freedom that being natural gives me, and I plan to grow my hair out in locks until the day I die.

People of all races stop me in the streets to compliment and inquire about my hair, especially sistas who are as tired of chemicals as I was. If I ever have any daughters, I will teach them to take care of their hair the way it's supposed to be taken care of. The black female rite of passage involving pressing, chemicals, and shame claims an unworthy place in our heritage. There are some childhood traditions that shouldn't be passed on to future generations, and I believe this is one of them.

Winston Eldridge

Born and raised in Richmond, Virginia, Winston Eldridge says his biggest inspirations have been his mother, the aunt with whom he lived after his mother's death, and the teachers of the Richmond public schools, who, he says, "never let segregation be used as an excuse for demanding less than excellence."

Now in his forties, Winston lives with his wife and four daughters in Mount Rainier, Maryland, where he works as a data-processing supervisor. He has recently co-written a memoir, *Better Than Good: The Story of Adolph Newton.*

The following story, Winston says, depicts the first time that he talked with a white person and almost felt sorry for him. "This was important in my development," he says, "because I truly felt that this man had more problems than I did. . . . It seemed to me that he had given up on everything, and in a sense had already stopped living."

Asked for his thoughts on the future of race relations in the

United States, Winston said, "If one day we can talk among ourselves without keeping score of which culture suffered most, which contributed most, and which should be studied at the expense of others, maybe we can begin to make real progress. The key lies in our children and the freedom we give them to define themselves and the world."

Dr. Martin Luther King, Jr.'s, life and his dream were important in shaping the future, Winston says, "because they gave African-Americans a sense of possibility . . . but too many of us were content to let the dream die with him, rather than see it as the foundation upon which to build other dreams. The challenge for us all is to recognize that, as great as Dr. King was, and with all that he did, he was but one of the many bridges to our future. The greatest honor that we could give him is to try to continue his work."

HAVE A NICE DAY!

I was feeling good as I walked across Jefferson Davis Highway. The interview had gone great, and I got the job. It's going to be worth giving up Saturdays and Sundays, I thought to myself. I'll be able to pay for school trips, buy clothes, and take care of some things for myself. Because I had turned sixteen, I could get a driver's license. High school was more than half over; I was a junior, and I would be making ten dollars a week more than on my last job.

The only problem would be working for the U.S. government. My parents thought a government job was the most secure thing in the world; to them, a black person with a government job had a future. My cousin Sandra, who was twenty-one and more like a sister, said that the U.S. government was the world's biggest slave owner. She was attending Boston University, and she knew a lot about black history, so she knew what she was talking about. Sandra said that everyone who worked for the government was a part of the military-industrial complex. She also said that it helped to keep black people enslaved in South Africa and other parts of the world. I didn't know a whole lot about the military or the industrial complex, and I didn't want to hurt her feelings, but I planned to take this job. I put some of those Florsheim shoes and a couple of Italian knit shirts in layaway. I didn't see how my shipping light bulbs and toilet paper from a warehouse in Virginia had anything to do with a war on the other side of the world.

I looked back at the other side of the highway. There was a fence that ran as far as you could see, big gates with cannons on either side, a garrison flag that was bigger than my bed, and a sign. The sign was the first thing that caught your eye as you rode past. White letters on a blue background jumped out at you: DEFENSE GENERAL SUPPLY CENTER. For the first time, I really read it—DEFENSE, as in Department of Defense.

I remembered some of the things Sandra had talked about. Those Vietnamese people never called me nigger, or chased me on Halloween, or disrespected my family, like some white people right here in this city had. Why should I help America when I knew that black people weren't Americans? As Malcolm X said, "If a cat has kittens in an oven, does that make them muffins?" On the other hand, Mom and Pop would point to people like Ralph Bunche or Adam Clayton Powell, who were accomplishing things by being in the system. They talked about the people who had died in order for black people to have the vote, and how stupid it was to waste that vote. It got very confusing, and I was starting to get a headache. I started thinking about things I could handle, like how good our football team was going to be.

A car pulling over in front of me interrupted my thoughts.

"Need a ride?"

My eyes followed the voice into the '61 Ford Fairlane, settling on the driver. White guy, about twenty-two, medium build, didn't look too dangerous. Probably military—his hair wasn't too long. Voice wasn't too redneckish. The car was clean—no power locks. Windows were down (it was mid-April, after all), and I could get out if something strange happened. And the bus wasn't due for twenty-five minutes.

"How far you going?"

"All the way to Broad Street," he answered.

"I'm just going to Decatur, this side of Hull," I said.

"Yeah, I know where that is. Get in." He leaned over and popped the lock on the door. "Where you coming from, Bellwood?" he asked as I settled into the bucket seat. As soon as I was in, he eased off the clutch and pulled back into traffic. Bellwood was what we commonly called the supply center.

"Yep, gonna be working there on the weekend. Part-time job."

"Congratulations. My name's Joe." He stuck out his right hand.

"Thanks, I'm Winston. Thanks for the ride, too." I shook his hand as I looked over the white rolled and pleated upholstery. "Nice car, what size you running?"

"Thanks, took me a while to fix it up. It came with a 289, but a couple of my buddies and me worked on it till now she's running 325. Turns eleven in the quarter, but I don't run her anymore. You know cars?"

"Not too much. Just watch guys work on theirs. Should be getting my license soon, though. Then I'll be able to get one."

"That's a good idea. Man should have his own car; he can come and go like he needs to. Man without a car ain't really a man. Still in school, Winston?"

"Yeah, junior this year."

"You look a little older than that. What school you go to?"

"Maggie Walker." Joe was asking a lot of questions, but I figured he was just making conversation to pass the time.

"Hey, y'all always have a helluva football team. You play ball?"

"Not at school—too small. Just at the playground. How 'bout you?"

"Played a little baseball. I went to Manchester. Got a partial scholarship to a school in the western part of the state, but only stayed there a year. Kinda hard to study when you're racing cars and chasing girls. You gotta girl, Winston?"

I jerked my head around from the passenger-side window. "Yeah, why?"

"Hey, I didn't mean nothing by it. Just talking. I ain't trying to get in your business. You thinking about college?"

"Don't know where I want to go yet; all depends on where I can get some money, I guess." I leaned back in the seat and relaxed a little, surprised that my right hand was gripping the door handle.

"Go to school. That's your best bet. Gotta watch out for the draft, though. Soon as I stopped school and lost my deferment, Uncle Sam was there."

"I got a couple years before I register. I should be in college by then. You thinking about going back?"

When Joe didn't answer, I looked at him. He was staring past me at a restaurant we were passing.

"See that restaurant there—Daisy's Grill? That's where my wife works." Joe pointed to a green building on the east side of the road. It was kind of a redneck hangout, one of those places the cops and ambulance drivers learned to find as soon as they came on the job. There were always fights there on weekends.

Some black men worked in a paper-bag factory on the other side of the highway; they'd go in there to pick up lunch, but they wouldn't stay to eat.

"Maybe I should say ex-wife, 'cause that's what she is," Joe said. "Can't get used to saying that though."

"Divorced, huh?" I felt like I had to say something to keep the conversation going. Joe had a strange look in his eyes, like he was looking at something way down the road. I had seen a man look like that once before, when I was downtown with my uncle. We had passed a man on the street who was being arrested after fighting some cops on the street. His head was bleeding and he was cursing, but he never raised his voice. Uncle Bob told me that the man was probably shell-shocked from Korea. He said that he called that look the thousand-yard stare.

Joe began to talk again, even though I don't think he even realized who I was. He probably didn't even care who he was talking to. I was glad the car didn't have power locks.

"It ain't final yet, but it might as well be. Matter of fact, I'm on my way to my lawyer's office now."

"Paperwork, huh? I heard lawyers always have you signing something." I wasn't too far from where I needed to go, so I figured my best bet was to keep him talking, maybe take his mind off whatever was on it.

"Naw, bro. I'm going to kill the sumbitch."

I stopped breathing, remembering all of the stories about people getting killed by hitchhikers—or while they were hitchhiking. Suddenly, sixteen didn't feel almost grown.

Joe looked at me and smiled. "Don't worry, you're cool. It's a long story, man. I'm gonna go kill that sumbitch, kill that bitch I married, and then I'm going back to Nam. I can't deal with it over here no more. People over here are crazy as shit." He started tapping on the steering wheel.

Since I couldn't think of anything to say, I let Joe keep talking. I didn't really want to hear this stuff, but I didn't want to take a chance on interrupting him, either.

"Guess I'm more used to it over there than here now; this'll be my third tour. People here losing their damn minds. Guys walking 'round with hair longer than women, damn hippies walking around not taking baths, then calling me an animal and baby-killer and shit when I wear my uniform. Hell, I didn't want to come back this time, but Uncle Sam made me."

"Where were you? I got a couple of cousins over there . . ."

"I was all over—Da Nang, Chu Lai, couple places where there weren't any American troops, you know? Where's your cousin at?"

"I can't remember the name of the place, but I think it's close to Saigon."

"He'll probably be okay, then. Biggest thing he gotta worry about is one of them women having a razor blade in her stuff. If he's been over there a while, he knows how to handle himself. Lots of guys go over there and fall in love, though. Course if you got to fall in love, it might as well be with one of them. 'Cause those women don't mind satisfying a man. It ain't like it is over here now. Looks like women wanna get in a pissing contest with you every time you open your mouth. Like they wanna prove they got more balls than you or something. That liberation shit is almost as bad as them damn hippies."

We were close to my stop. "Yeah, a lot of stuff is changing."

"Don't get me wrong. All of it ain't bad. Take some of the things y'all black folks doin'. Now, growing up here, I didn't know nothing 'bout y'all, 'cept when we got to fighting at the park. I just didn't know any black folks, and that's the way it was."

"Same here, I guess. Up until I took a math class in summer school last year, I never went to school with any white people. Only white people I ever see in my neighborhood are cops and insurance men."

"That's what I mean. But when I got to Nam and got to the bush, my unit was almost all black guys. There was only one other white guy in my squad, and he was an asshole. Got himself killed before he'd been in country two months. Dumb motherfucker made Gomer Pyle look smart. But anyway, I found out that black people are people. I learned a lot. After a while you start to learn what's really important and what's really bullshit. That's what I can't take about being back in the States. So much of what you deal with is bullshit."

I waited for him to go on.

"Like this shit the politicians and everybody else running on people about the war. Don't nobody over there know what it's about. The biggest thing is you trying to keep your ass in one piece, and when one of your buddies gets blown away, you gotta take it out on somebody, so you're just waiting for a chance to blow the other guys away, but it ain't personal. It's bad, Winston. If you can stay away from there, don't go. Only reason I'm going back is it's the only place where I know how to act. 'Specially after this thing with my wife."

"What happened with that? If you don't mind me asking."

"No problem, man. She sent me a letter talking 'bout wanting a divorce. That was kinda cool, 'cause I was over there, and she was over here not knowing if I was gonna come back or not. So that was all right. It's not like we had kids or nothing, you know. So I got in touch with a lawyer I knew, and he was sposed to take care of the paperwork, and I thought everything was cool. Then I find out she's screwing him."

"Damn."

"Naw, that ain't all. Bad enough they screwing in my house, in my bed, but I wasn't too bent out of shape 'bout that. The motherfucker was driving my car—my '64 Vette that I wouldn't even let her drive. Hell, I didn't even drive it myself 'cept on Saturdays. She sent me a picture of my car with this asshole behind the wheel, and it wasn't at the house, either, so I knew this mutherfucker was *driving my Vette*. Some shit a man just can't let happen, Winston, know what I mean?" Joe pulled over and stuck out his hand. "Here's your stop. I got a seven o'clock flight out tonight. Good talking to you, Winston. Good luck with the job and school."

I couldn't really think of anything to say as I got out. I shook his hand. "Thanks a lot for the ride, Joe. Good luck to you, too. Have a good one." I didn't look back as I walked away.

The lead-in to the late news that night was a double homicide, but I changed the channel. High school was half over, I was a junior, and my only problem would be working for the U.S. government.

This incident has stayed with me for thirty years. It was my first real experience of talking with a white person in a setting other than school, a job, or business. As a result of this encounter, I began to realize that white people had as many problems as we did, and that being white did not make one exempt from life's struggles.

This was also my first exposure to the effect that Vietnam

would have on race relations, here and over there. For a long time after that day, whenever there was a report of a domestic dispute that ended in homicide, I thought of Joe—especially when it involved white people. I remembered that while we were in the car, for just a brief time, I had thought of him as not white, but as just a guy with a lot on his mind.

Tess Alexandra
Bennett Harrison

Now almost eleven years old, Tess Alexandra Bennett Harrison is an elementary school student who lives in Athens, Georgia.

Asked about Dr. Martin Luther King, Jr., she said, "I think he had a very good dream, and he tried to make it real, until somebody white killed him." Still, she thinks things are going to get better with regard to race relations. "People aren't going to be so prejudiced, and they'll get along with each other."

"MIXED" EMOTIONS

Hi. My name is Tess. I live in Georgia. I'm ten, and I want to say something about growing up black. Actually, I'm not all black. I'm mixed. I'm adopted and my biological mother is white and my biological father is black. I have a black adoptive family of two mothers and two sisters. I say I'm mixed, but Mother told me that if I have any black blood I am black. That's fine with me.

When I was little, I didn't think anything about this race stuff until one of my mothers told me about it. She told me about slavery and how black people were treated here, and how they were beat up after slavery was over when they tried to do things like vote. She came to my class and showed us pictures of how slaves were packed into ships. It was awful what people went through. My mom said that white people would just come pick up black folks from the jungle and say, "Come with me," and the people wouldn't know where they were going or be able to tell their families where they were.

When Mom told me this, it made me feel really bad. What if I was in that position and somebody took me from my home? And what if I was in that ship and didn't have room to move and had to lay in my doo-doo and was so sick that I was barfing all over myself and no one would help me? What if you were in that position? Wouldn't you feel bad?

A few weeks ago, I told my mom that I was glad that I was adopted into this family. I was adopted when I was a second old. My mom gave me my first feeding. I am glad I was adopted by black people, I told my mom, because I wouldn't want to have a white family because I would feel like I do with some of my white friends. I'm glad I was adopted into this family also because my mother teaches me a lot about black people and about black history and how white people treated black people. I would not want to be white and be part of a group who have treated people so bad.

Mia Threlkeld

With an honesty that might astonish many adults, fourteen-year-old Mia Threlkeld of Birmingham, Alabama, writes of her experience of having other black teenagers label her too white. While she has moved beyond caring about her peers' racial remarks—chalking them up to ignorance—she thinks that black and white people have a long way to go in regard to racism.

Still, Mia says, she doesn't want any special privileges. "I actually think affirmative action adds to the racism problem today," she says. "I don't want white people to start thinking that blacks can't get anywhere in this world without special treatment."

All the names in her story, except her own, have been changed.

A TRUE FRIEND?

My name is Mia, and I am a fourteen-year-old black female from Birmingham, Alabama. I like all people no matter what their skin color. I'm against racism, and it really upsets me when I see racists because it is like they are missing out on meeting a lot of great people just because they are afraid of anything that is different from themselves. You can't blame the people themselves, though, because you are not born racist—you are raised that way by your parents or you are influenced by your friends. I think if we all could see everyone through our hearts instead of our eyes then the world would be a much nicer, not to mention safer, place to live.

I had never experienced racism toward myself until I was in seventh grade. I was starting a new school and didn't know too many people. Kim, my best friend from kindergarten through fifth grade, was going to the same school, and that made me less worried because at least I would already have a ready-made friend. We didn't have one single class together, not even lunch, but we still made an effort to see each other before and after school and between classes, and we talked on the phone. I'm pretty shy, so I hadn't made many friends, but Kim had. I haven't told you yet but Kim is white and so were the friends she made. I quickly became friends with Kim's friends. They were great. They were funny and sweet, but then I would hear the black kids talking: "Yeah, Mia—she always hangs around with those white girls. She must think she's white." They would come up to me and ask me why I hung around with white people—and not even beat around the bush with the question. I mean, what was the big deal?

Then I got called such names as white girl, cracker, and Oreo. I didn't understand why they were making such a big deal out of my having white friends. Not too long after that, I also became friends with this black girl, Ashley, but she was always asking me why I hung around with those white girls instead of with her and her black friends. I usually just shrugged my shoulders and tried not to let the question bother me, since Ashley was my good friend.

Then one day, near the end of the school year, I was talking to Kim and our friends Leslie and Misty when Ashley took me by my arm and told Kim that I was going to hang around with her friends today. So that day I did, and I felt a little out of place. But I felt better because no one was calling me names, and I knew it looked like I fit in. I didn't feel so—I don't know the word—different, I guess.

So I tried to become friends with them, and little by little Kim and I started drifting apart. First I didn't hang around her at school anymore, and we just talked on the phone. But pretty soon I was busy with all my new friends, and all of a sudden, like *boom*, Kim and I weren't friends anymore. I felt ashamed because all the time she had been such a good friend to me, and all of a sudden I just stopped being there for her and being her friend.

I liked some of my new black friends, but I couldn't act the way I wanted to around them or laugh the way I wanted to around them or even listen to the music I liked around them because it was "being too white." So it was like I had to put on a show when I was around them. And now I'm so used to doing that, I really don't know who I am. But soon I hope to find out.

Another school year has come, and when I walk down the hall and pass Kim I put my head down or pretend to be busy talking to someone and act like I don't see her because I'm full of shame that I would just "betray" her, if that's the word I'm looking for, like that. Sometimes I give a friendly "hi," but then it brings up memories and I feel even worse. If I could go back and change things I would have stayed Kim's friend, but now I feel it's too late to try to be her friend again. If I were her, I wouldn't even want me as a friend.

It still seems that, whatever I do, I can't please the black people because I talk and act "too white" and my skin isn't dark enough.

I think what I learned from this whole experience is that you don't have to try and please anyone but yourself, and you don't have to be anyone but yourself. And don't be afraid to be yourself because it doesn't matter what people think of you, just what you think of yourself.

Anne Alexis Bennett Alexander

Nineteen-year-old Anne Alexis Bennett
Alexander is a student in Athens, Georgia. She began writing
when she was eleven years old, and has already had a portion of
her diary published in an anthology called *Life Notes: Personal
Writings by Contemporary Black Women.*

In this story, Anne says that there really is no one "black
experience." Growing up in a mostly white world as she did, she
had different experiences from many African-American children, but, as she points out, that doesn't make her any less
black.

At the root of racism is the stereotyping of people according
to their color, Anne says, and sometimes black people are guilty
of it as well. "I think that race plays too large a part in human
interaction," she says, "and I don't feel it should determine people so much."

THE BLACK EXPERIENCE . . . ?

When I was asked to write something about what it is and was like growing up black, a question popped into my head. The question was, "Should I bother to submit anything, seeing as how I didn't grow up with the 'black experience'?" I didn't grow up with bunches of black friends, doing black things, going to black schools, living in a black neighborhood, or hanging out with black people. Instead, I grew up in a pretty small southern college town in a white neighborhood, going to a white school, with white friends, hanging around white people. I grew up as a black person with the white experience. In thinking of this fact, I realized that it is all the more reason to contribute.

Although I grew up in the south with the white experience, it was not the same as the white experience that white people grow up with. Because I am black in a white world, I encountered racism and prejudice.

A specific incident that is my first recollection of being different, being black and encountering racism and prejudice occurred when I was about six years old and in elementary school. I was with my class, eating lunch outside, and a girl in my class was passing out candy. She skipped over me and I asked her if

I could have some candy like everyone else. She replied, "No, my mother said that I can't share with niggers."

I didn't know what a nigger was, but if it meant I couldn't have candy when everyone who was white could, I knew it could not have been a good thing. It didn't occur to me then the profundity and meaning of such a thing, but when I think of it now, I can't help but realize and see the ignorance of so many people, and the way that it gets passed down to their children, and then when they grow up, they pass it to theirs, and so on.

I attended a private elementary school, junior high, and high school, and children called me nigger all the time. They told "nigger jokes" to my face, and called me a monkey, among other derogatory things. It affected me greatly to encounter such prejudice, racism, and ignorance. Not only did it make me feel like an outcast, but it made me feel bad about who I was and where I came from. I remember going home and crying because I knew that I had to go back to school the next day and put up with more of the name-calling and teasing. I didn't want to tell my mother and have her go to the school and do what any mother would ordinarily do (only my mother does it better) because I wanted to handle it myself. I didn't want to make it worse by having my mother fight my battles for me. But taking it all on myself made me feel an even greater sense of isolation and pain because I didn't have my mother for comfort. To make matters worse, I hated my mother for sending me to a school where this would happen, but I wouldn't even tell her what was going on. I was miserable.

I realize now that what doesn't break you makes you stronger and even more knowledgeable. Because of these experiences, I have grown and realized much beyond what my counterparts realize. I went to school with people who actually believed that there is no prejudice in the world. I was part of a student body made up of 99.9 percent whites, most of whom believed that if a white person and a black person went out for a job, both having equal credentials, there would actually be competition. I also went to school with a bunch of people who lived in counties where the schools were barely integrated and racial crimes still existed. Part of me knew this and wanted to ignore it, but my mother constantly reminded me of it when the need arose. She reminded me that just the act of riding in a car with my white friends in the next county over could start trouble.

Although I did encounter a lot of these racist and prejudiced attitudes from white people, it did not make me view all white people in a negative way. I had been brought up by my mother to treat people as their actions warranted, but it was not always easy to live that way. Sometimes I wanted to treat them all the same, as if they were all racist, but I fought the urge. After the ninth grade, for the most part the name-calling and teasing stopped because the kids just grew out of that stage, so it became easier to live by what I had been taught. I started to date a white guy at that point. I really didn't think a lot about his race. I was just attracted to him as a person.

While race wasn't a factor for us at the beginning, we discussed it a good bit after he became more comfortable with me. I think we both realized that, having grown up in a southern society, we both initially experienced some level of discomfort and ignorance about racial issues. I think it made a difference that we both were originally from the north.

I also think there was some initial hesitation on his part about having certain conversations because he did not have the same exposure to blacks as I had to whites. This was, in a way, odd, because he had gone to Africa with his parents several times, and they had lived there at some point, but he understood that the cultures were vastly different and that his exposure to Africa did not give him an automatic understanding of American blacks.

I think it is also interesting that he would be as accepting as he was of his feelings for me, considering the fact that his parents, brother, and sister had spent a good deal of time in South Africa before he was born in New York. Don't think that little piece of info didn't send my mother into a swivet. But there was never any indication that there had been a negative influence on his family during the time they had spent there. This was amazing, considering the impact that such a complete immersion in a culture like apartheid can have.

My boyfriend was a junior in high school and attended school with me. I found all of his friends very accepting of our interracial relationship. Being in a relationship with him (that still continues today) helped me to see that all white people are not the same. He took me out and treated me just as he would have any other girl. In a lot of ways he treated me even better. When we went out together he freely held my hand, feeling no shame, and did such things as kiss me in public. That's a lot for a white boy living in the south.

Having the experience of an interracial relationship, and seeing how people viewed us from the outside, was very informative. I noticed that, for the most part, even though we live in Georgia, blacks were the ones who tended to be put out by the interracial situation, whereas the whites were accepting—both those who knew us and those who didn't.

Mostly it was black males who would make rude comments, though black females did as well. At times, when my boyfriend and I were out together, black males would approach me to get my name and number, totally ignoring the fact that my boyfriend was right there. When I told them I was taken, they would then proceed to bad-mouth me about having a white boyfriend.

One time in particular stands out in my mind. It was the first time the two of us had ever encountered negativity about our relationship. We were downtown one night and an old man approached us while we were sitting on a bench talking. At first he told us he was glad that the two of us were in a relationship. He said that it was a good thing if we loved each other. Then, all of a sudden, he totally switched gears and said things like "Martin Luther King would roll over in his grave if he saw this."

Why I felt the need to deal with a perfect stranger being rude to us I do not know, but I challenged him by asking why he thought that when it was Martin Luther King who wanted us all to get along. We continued to go back and forth, and of course, he was never able to back up his ignorant statement. He finally left feeling very stupid, I am sure, because he never produced an argument that made sense upon closer examination.

After the incident, my boyfriend and I talked about what happened and we realized that the man had never said anything to my boyfriend. From the very beginning the stranger only directed conversation to me. It was an odd experience, as the tables had turned and it was the black person looking down on the white person as not being worthy to talk to, rather than the white person looking down on the black person. Of course, this upset my boyfriend very much, and I remember thinking, "See, they [whites] wouldn't like it if they were in our position."

Nevertheless, I understood that this interchange wasn't about me and my boyfriend in particular; rather, we were being viewed as part of a whole societal issue. But it's hard not to take it personally when someone is standing in front of you dogging you out, even though they don't know anything about you or your circumstances.

Seeing all of this and taking all of this in is what has, I think, made me a more intelligent person, among other things. I took the ignorance of the people around me and turned it into my intelligence. I took their weaknesses and made them my strengths. The simple realization that these people did live in ignorance was the first step to helping the problem. In class debates and casual encounters, I talked to these people and schooled them in the ways of reality and in the ways of the world—mine and theirs. I turned their ignorance into intelligence by spreading the knowledge of the realities I knew.

I have had white people say such things to me as "You aren't really black," or "You are very inappropriate." Even though I may get angry at first, I try to patiently explain to them that the fact that I am black should not, in their minds, automatically make them think of me as ignorant, violent, trashy, valueless, amoral, or inappropriate, as they seem to think. As soon as you can express to people that their preconceived notions of something are wrong, despite what their parents or friends say, the sooner you can teach them how to work together and have the knowledge they need to survive as socially successful people.

I was lucky because, as my fellow students got older, they began to become interested in me and my reality versus theirs. They began to ask questions like, "What is the difference between African-American and black?" and "Why is it that you don't look and act like the other black people that we see around town?" and "Why don't they look and act like you?" Though they seemed like stupid questions, I had to realize that they simply wanted information that they had not had access to. My classmates began to inquire about my culture and my feelings and my world because they began to realize it wasn't the same as theirs. Answering them and teaching them helped me to discontinue the cycle of ignorance that tends to flourish here in America.

My black experience was as a black girl in a white world, rather than as a black girl in a black world that was in turn surrounded by a white world. But I wouldn't change it for anything. Those white people were a reality check for me, just as I was for them. If I had been a black girl growing up in an all-black world, I feel that I may have suffered the same ignorance that comes from growing up as a white person in a white world. That is, if I had not been exposed to people different from me, I would not have had a chance to learn about them.

That is not to say that I have lived in a *totally* white world. My family is black and I have had the wonderful experience of growing up in a black family and all that it traditionally means. I attended a public school with a fifty-fifty mixture in the first grade and from the third through the seventh grades. My family is black in the usual sense of the word. That is, we go to a black Baptist church, we have wonderful family times with my aunts, uncles, and cousins, we have the traditional wonderful, homey big dinners around the table, with traditional black fare like potato salad, greens, ham, fried chicken, cornbread, etc. And my mother never misses an opportunity to teach us about our history as blacks, as well as the history of my family. I have had many black friends and enjoy the wonderfully different way we talk with and relate to each other in our own special language.

The reality is that I am black, have always been black, and will always be black, though some of my experiences have involved more contact with whites than some other blacks have had. My mother tried hard to make sure that being in a white school did not crush the cultural differences that are almost inherent in me. I can't count the times she has had to talk to my headmaster about not treating me differently because I may approach things differently from the white kids, or sound different from them. She has told him time and again that I am me and she did not raise me to be an automaton or a cookie-cutter copy of anyone else, including the white kids at my school, who all tend to talk, walk, dress, and act alike.

One of my cousins who grew up in Washington, D.C., where my family is from, used to tease me and my sister about going to white schools and having white friends. After he came south to go to Morehouse College and spent a good deal of time with us, he finally told my mother that if the truth was to be told, he teased us a lot, but felt that we were more black than he was. He said that in D.C., because it is a predominantly black city, being black was simply taken for granted and was not given much thought. He realized that my mother's constantly working to expose us to black experiences gave us more of an awareness and appreciation than he had.

Ignorance is not the key to successful living or a successful life, and the knowledge that I obtained, no matter how tough it was to get, was worth it, and it is nothing that I would ever contemplate changing. It may not have been what people think of as the "black experience," but I'm black, and it was my experience, and things can't be much simpler than that. When we say "black experience," we have to make sure that we take in the full range of experiences that black people have. Mine may not be what comes to most people's minds, but it was truly my black experience. One I wouldn't trade.

Linnea Colette Ashley

A self-described military brat, Linnea Colette Ashley was born in California in 1976, but she has lived many places since then. She recently earned a bachelor's degree at Florida A. & M. After a summer internship at the _San Francisco Chronicle_, she hopes to study South African literature in South Africa for a year, and then she wants to teach creative writing to high school students.

In this story, Linnea conveys the anger she feels toward blacks who have judged her by the color of her skin. From fifth grade on, she says, she knew she was never "black enough."

A WASTE OF YELLOW:
GROWING UP BLACK IN AMERICA

Mama never taught me high yella; she was too busy teaching me the differences between black and Negro, darkie and African-American. Who had time for all the shades in between —shades like "swirl" and "sellout" and even that "biracial" name tag that would have been okay if both my parents hadn't been black born and black bred, black loved, and black wed.

Mama sighed, knowing that I would encounter a white world far from friendly sometimes. She had me on the ready, though. She knew it would hurt, but she knew I wouldn't tumble under the weight of ignorance-packed words.

What Mama didn't know, or Daddy either, was that ignorance doesn't see color, and sometimes the word that cuts the deepest isn't a shade of midnight but closer to emerging dawn.

'Cause I was born with gray eyes and a head full of hair that rivaled Diana Ross's and Tina Turner's. And when Mama spit me out I was about as pink as those white babies emerge, enough to make a person question if there had been a mix-up at the hospital.

But no, a few weeks at home and my color filled out to a nice, half-baked yellow-toned brown. So there I was, a potential high-yellow heifer who forgot she was a Negress. What I actually turned out to be was a long-haired, light-eyed, light-skinned tomboy who thought no more of being yellow than I did of being a girl. It was just one of those things that happened to me. I had ovaries (some people told me), and I was lacking some pigment (said some others).

But high yella didn't mean anything more to me than suntan-colored stockings for Sunday morning service and a burning scalp from the relaxer Mama pulled through my longer-than-shoulder-length hair. It was nothing variant from black to me.

Somewhere along the line, I discovered "black power"—and self-hatred. As much as my mother had tried to ready me for the stateside war of the races, she couldn't have prepared me for the soldiers who had been in it so long they became a product of it and lost sight of the true goal.

The first time I remember being ambushed, I was a freshman in high school. I was new to the scene and shy among a school full of strange voices and faces. Even the scent was foreign to me. But what surpassed all else in strangeness was the other students' coldness and the way they avoided me.

People I didn't even know walked close enough to almost jostle me but, instead, jostled me with whispers carefully aimed in my direction:

"High-yella heifer thinks she cute."

"Too good to speak, I guess, with her cat-eyed self."

All I'd done is be new and shy, but I'd managed to commit the greatest offense—I'd been born bright-skinned, light-eyed—and, to top it off, I talked like a white girl.

How dare I?

How dare I be new and anticipate that my own people would embrace what I had always thought was something they could understand—my pigment. They were supposed to be my sistas and brothas. They were supposed to be my family. Instead, they were the source of self-doubt and intimidation.

And it had always been that way. From fifth grade on—that point when we all started discovering whether or not we were colored—I had always been alienated.

I was never black enough. In the seventh grade, when I mingled with the white kids in my "talented"and "gifted" classes and spoke with traces of an Anglo accent, I was the black girl who wasn't black.

Among whites, I was a swirl (their rationalization for me not being a dumb Negro). To blacks, I was an Oreo (their answer to me not fitting a stereotype). And the older I got, the more pronounced the alienation.

Freshman year at my second high school taught me to resent my no-longer-gray but almost hazel eyes. I began to despise the long brown hair and the lighter-than-caramel skin that linked me to the loathsome phrase "high yella."

Sistas spit "high-yella" at me when I walked by. Brothas leered at me and oozed "high yella" into a phrase of perversion. And the "blacker-the-berry-the-sweeter-the-juice" people made it an insult.

Again there was the question—how dare I? How dare I not understand that an apology should follow me everywhere—an apology for the massa's blood that was obviously pulsing through my veins, obviously giving me life? How dare I not apologize for having features that mark me as anything except a straight-up-broad-nose-full-lipped-kinky-haired Negro? How dare I not apologize?

I began to question myself. I walked more quickly. I lowered my eyes. I anxiously pulled at my hair. I began to apologize, and I never even realized it.

I'm sorry.

I'm sorry.

I'm sorry that you think I'm beautiful, despite my coloring.

I'm sorry that your boyfriend has been brainwashed to think that high yella can be beautiful at all.

I'm sorry I don't look more like . . .

More like what? That was the question.

I looked just like my father. Who else should I look like? I had hair like my mother's—who else's hair should I have? Daddy's eyes and Mama's lips. Who else's features should I have requested of God before being plopped down on earth?

My insecurities followed me to college. Some at the university regarded me as beautiful. They never saw past my brown eyes, hinting at hazel in the sun, but they regarded me as a beauty anyway. And then there were the other voices, the ones I had become accustomed to hearing:

I wasn't black enough.

I had it easier because America smiled on me and my likeness to whiteness.

Even friends questioned whether or not I shared their plight as a black woman, as if there were a shade of brown that was revered and respected. As if the slightly looser kinks in my hair were noticed and tolerated better than the tight kinks in my darker sistas' hair.

If truth be told, yella was harder on me than black ever was. Not because I received special treatment. Quite the contrary. Yella was harder on me because it robbed me of a haven of acceptance and understanding.

I've always been too dark for white America and too light for black America. Caught in the middle, some strange medium color on a canvas of extremes, I stand out against the rest of the painting, not out of beauty, but out of oddity.

In a world full of extremes, where we're given little boxes in which to classify the American experience, what can I do when I can't fit into them? I'm forced to write my *own* story and tell the truth as I've experienced it. And how should I begin?

"My name isn't important, just know that I'm a waste of black"? Or, maybe more appropriately, "I'm a waste of yellow"?

Sometimes I have to struggle not to believe that. At those times, I remember that someone once told me I was the color of a Hawaiian sunset. All I could do was smile. It was the nicest way I'd ever heard high yella put.

Caille Millner

Now twenty years old and a student at Harvard University, Caille Millner grew up in San Jose, California, where she interned as a writer for the *San Jose Mercury News* when she was a teenager. She had two articles published in the *Washington Post* in 1997 and, since 1995, she has been a writer for Pacific News Service.

"I was lucky enough to receive lessons about the history of American race relations from an early age," she says, noting that white children used to call her nigger and ask her to explain why she looked "that way." Still, she retained her hope in Dr. Martin Luther King, Jr.'s, dream. "I think that with today's subtle, insidious prejudice, blacks will have to find a different way to achieve Dr. King's dream than the great upheavals of the 1950s and 1960s. But the dream is still worth fighting for."

As she recounts in her story, Caille found herself embroiled in a battle at her high school when she was sixteen years old and had an article published in the *San Jose Mercury News*

about racism at her school. Despite the humiliation and the pain of her experience, she says, "I am proud of the way I handled the situation. It helped me learn, among other things, strength and confidence in the power of words." Now, she intends to use her gifts as a writer to serve her community and to change the system from the inside.

BLACK CODES: BEHAVIOR IN THE
POST–CIVIL RIGHTS ERA

Five hundred and fifty-seven dollars. That's how much it cost me to get my left fender fixed after someone smashed a large object into it. For a fender replacement, the bill wasn't so bad. What hurt more than the bill was the feeling I had when I walked out of school to find the car smashed in what was obviously not an accident.

When I was fourteen, I left an elitist public school with no racial sensitivity and went to an elitist private school with very few people of color. The logic behind this decision was that, while I wouldn't receive much racial support at the new school, at least I would receive a good education. Being one of the only black students was nothing new to me; being one of the only black students who wanted to be black did not come as a surprise either. I had the (mis)fortune of growing up in a tiny black community that strived to distance itself from other black communities as much as possible.

Racism was never overt at my school. It rarely is anymore—which is one of the travesties of the post–civil rights era. It's difficult to explain to a group of white liberals how the absence of overt hatred does not mean the absence of racism. So when I asked the administration why Black History Month didn't exist at my school, they didn't consider it a deficiency on their part.

"There's really so much else going on right now," they said politely when I asked two years in a row. "But maybe we'll put an announcement in the bulletin."

And when I sat in the back of my freshman world history class, crying because the teacher had said slavery really wasn't that bad, no one thought it constituted a problem.

"It's been hard to integrate blacks into the curriculum of this course," said the teacher. "But I am trying."

As I struggled to maintain a positive sense of identity at school, I was simultaneously forging an idea about my role in the black community. Bourgeois black society wasn't for me, I knew that. Whist and debutante balls didn't fit on my packed agenda of writing, dancing, and thinking. I couldn't meet the gossip requirement, and I wasn't interested primarily in men with the three C's: car, cash, and career.

At the same time, I could never fit into the "other" black community—the "others" on the margins, looking in on society as a whole with hungry eyes. I wasn't streetwise. I had no concept of how to fulfill the complex social requirements for gaining status as a marginalized member of the black community.

I suffered from the isolation of Du Bois's talented tenth. I knew I wanted to serve a community that had no use for me as an individual. There is a psychic peculiarity of being an outsider to an outsiders' group, and I spent most of high school feeling very peculiar.

The summer before my junior year, I met a woman who

wanted to know about that psychic peculiarity. Her name was Nell, and she was an editor for Pacific News Service in San Francisco. She was working on a youth newspaper that hired writers from all facets of society: homeless teenagers, skater punks, and high school valedictorians.

I tried to describe what I was going through to her, but I wasn't articulate enough to express my overwhelming alienation from every major group I had ever had contact with. She listened and then told me to pour my emotion out on paper.

I wrote about the racial slights at my school and the difficulty of going to a place where no one understood, or wanted to understand, what it was like to look like me. I wrote about the black community and my struggle for its acceptance. Finally, I wrote about struggling to accept myself and how my real goal for high school was to get a good education and to understand who I really was.

The article took seven or eight major rewrites and a lot of heartache. Some nights I would stay up, exhausted after hours of homework, and cry with frustration over the feelings I couldn't put into words. I did a lot of crying during the writing of that article. It was eventually titled "When Worlds Divide" and was published in a full-page feature in *West*, the Sunday magazine of the *San Jose Mercury News*, on February 11, 1996. I was sixteen years old.

The day the article was published, I read it carefully. My words were there, and for the first time I felt I might have given voice to the emotions I was feeling. But I was also scared. Writing the article had been a catharsis, an act that was bigger than I was and, therefore, out of my control. The fact that it was actually published meant that I would have to suffer the consequences. And from what I knew of progressive white environments, the response would not be kind.

The immediate reaction was a faculty meeting at seven o'clock the following morning to discuss how the school should handle "the situation." The immediate reaction was being called a liar and a slanderer in the halls, being pointed at with anger and hostility. The immediate reaction was what I had steeled myself for. Although I had intended the piece as an article about my identity, the school took it as a personal attack.

The consequences of my article were bigger than either the newspaper or I had expected. *West* received more letters about my piece than they had received for any single article in months. Most of the public was horrified that I had continued to attend my school. Although I had not named the school, it couldn't have been that hard for readers to figure it out. There weren't many schools like the one I had described in the city of San Jose.

My freshman world history teacher confronted me shortly after the article was published. "You have slandered me and called me a racist," she said. "You don't know what you've done. This is going to affect my career, my family, my entire life."

"I didn't even name you in the article, and I certainly didn't call you a racist," I stammered.

"You took what I said out of context," she said.

"What kind of context can that be put in? You said slavery wasn't that bad. There's no way I can live with that."

The incident with that teacher shook me up, especially when she began talking about me in her classes. I told the principal, who sensed a public-relations disaster and put a stop to her talking about me at once. But that didn't stop her from encouraging one of her students to start a petition against me.

About three days after the article came out, I heard rumors about a petition circulating through the school. I actually managed to get hold of the document for a few minutes. It was a petition to "support" the school administration; it also called for disciplinary action against me.

What surprised me the most about the petition was the number of people who had signed it. At least seventy-five students— the majority of the senior class—had signed the petition over the course of the two days it had been circulating. These were people I knew, people I had been friendly with, even some I had grown up with. I found out later that very few of them had actually read the article, much less thought about what I had said.

The next week an unsigned threat arrived in the mail. "You had better watch out, driving that big yellow car with your name on the license plates," the letter taunted. (I drove a "character car," a 1983 mustard-yellow Volvo.) I gave the letter to my mother for posterity and didn't think much about it.

Then I walked out of school a few days later and found my car smashed.

After the petition came out, I wasn't sure I could make it. I was frightened by the amount of hatred my words had stirred up. I was also afraid. Would the administration take action against me, as they had intimated they might? I was also sick of being hated by all the students. I didn't regret publishing my article by any means, but I didn't know if I could last another year and a half at my school.

Fortunately, I got angry. The destruction of my car stirred me to act. I came to the conclusion that if I was going to be a pariah, I would at least teach the school who they were dealing with. My friend from Pacific News Service, Nell, and my mother went to talk to the principal and warn him that any "disciplinary" action against me would result in a swift lawsuit. We alerted the local branch of the NAACP, who immediately assured us that they would support us. The editor at *West* also pledged her support. Sure enough, the hostility died down. No more threats. No more petitions.

I kept writing, which was my response to the threats. I was extremely prolific for the next year and a half, publishing in newspapers around the country. The greatest irony is that the administration wound up loving me when I became the first student ever from my school to get into Harvard University, where I'm now finishing my first year.

Jenniffer Dawn
Bennett Alexander

After the painful experience with racism at Duke University that nineteen-year-old Jenniffer Dawn Bennett Alexander describes in her story, she is doubtful that Dr. Martin Luther King, Jr.'s, dream will ever come true. "I believe his dream is just that, a dream," she says. "I do not think we will ever get past the racial prejudices in this society."

Jenniffer does not blame whites alone for the plight of blacks in the United States. She is careful to point out that her problems at Duke University began with what she sees as the black women students' unwillingness to support each other. "But this is not to say," she says, "that whites are not primarily at fault for our racial discord."

BETRAYAL, IN BLACK AND WHITE

As a freshman at Duke University, I was finally among blacks who spoke like me and came from virtually the same background as I did. For the first time in my life I was with blacks who totally understood what it was like to have to change and adjust in order to be accepted as black. There, the black students understood that I could have white friends as well as black friends; that I could speak "regular" English as well as Ebonics; and that I was just as black as anyone else, even though I could traverse two worlds.

About a month into school, rumors about me started circulating regularly. A friend and I kept track, and it was literally a new rumor every week, all of them pertaining to one male or another. I was doing nothing to be ashamed of, but had to cast down my head because of the awful things that *black women* were saying about me. I thought that I had left the days of jealousy and pettiness behind me in junior high and high school, but that was not so. I found that deceit and bitterness had nothing to do with class or upbringing, but were rampant among virtually all the black women at Duke. And for no reason other than men (who, I might add, were far from being worth the effort).

Because there were far fewer men than women, and because

the higher the women went in achieving their educational goals, the slimmer the pickings of black men were, the women on campus were ridiculously petty and small-minded. We didn't matter to each other as black people or women, or even as fellow students. Instead, every female was viewed in terms of her potential impact on the male population. Because I was viewed as being poised, intelligent, articulate, personable, thin, confident, and good looking, I was in big trouble. I was quickly accepted by the males, none of whom I had the slightest romantic interest in, so I became a prime target for the reputation shredder.

I was friendly with many male upperclassmen, and this made the other women on campus jealous. Though I was nothing more than friends with these men, it was assumed that something more was going on. My best friend, Deon (a pseudonym), and I would often be invited to our male friends' apartments for games of spades and just hanging out. Because most ladies were not invited, for reasons I will go into below, the only reason they could imagine for our being invited was that we were sleeping with them. This was just not so, and my male friends defended me to the utmost (which made them no friends among the women casting aspersions).

The girls would surely have cut the nonsense short if they had realized how juvenile, insecure, and just plain stupid the men thought they were for acting as they did. But I suppose they thought that by ruining my reputation, they could somehow boost their own. What they failed to grasp is that the men they said I was doing all manner of evil with were the ones that they wanted, and these same men were angry for having their names besmirched (not to mention having to watch me be hurt by all of this) and thus much less likely to start relationships with the women.

As a Taurus, I have always been comfortable around males, and find it easy to communicate with them. I was never cursed with the giddiness and silliness that a lot of girls my age find themselves succumbing to when around those of the opposite sex. It was because of this fact that I was popular with males. I knew how to "just chill," as they put it. But the women's resentment or misconstrual of my knack for being able to do this severely sullied my reputation.

I was hurt and confused and needed my friends to support me. They knew what I had and had not been doing, and I looked to them for comfort when my world started to crumble. Unfortunately, it did not come.

Because of my newly earned reputation, I began losing my girlfriends one by one. In retrospect I realize that they probably were not my friends in the first place, but to this day that fact only minimally eases my pain.

By the time all of my so-called friends dispersed, it ended up being just me and Deon, and that was how it was to remain. Both Deon and I came to the conclusion that it was best to rely only on each other, and we ended up being much happier because of it. We did everything together. My name could not be mentioned without hers, and vice versa. As time passed, we rebuilt our reputations and were known as the girls on campus that everyone wanted to know, or say they knew. We were just fun to be around. Every party we had was packed, and people we didn't know were coming up to us all the time telling us that they wanted to get to know us. We finally thought we had regained our reputations. This feeling would be short-lived.

One afternoon in early spring I walked into the Burger King on campus to meet Deon for lunch. This was the usual lunchtime hangout for the black students at Duke. When I walked in I noticed that everyone kept looking at me strangely. I didn't give it a lot of thought, but sat down to wait for Deon. It was then that an associate of mine walked up to me with our school newspaper and stated that there was an article she thought I should read, so I did.

The article was about two females painted as sluts, arriving at a party uninvited because they were strictly there to have sex with the men. Though there were two characters, it was mostly about one. The other girl was described as a sidekick. The author wrote it in first person, as someone observing the goings-on, and she spared nothing in making it clear how disgusted she was by it all. The author stated how pretty, intelligent, graceful, friendly, well-spoken, and popular the girl was, and that she realized that she (the author) was probably just jealous.

After reading the article I looked at my associate questioningly. She told me that everyone thought that the article was about me and Deon. I was mortified. I laughed, thinking she must have been joking. I read the author's name: Katrina Daisy Patron [a pseudonym]. It was in no way familiar to me (though I knew everyone in the black community). Katrina had described the woman in the article in such incredible detail that every single black student who knew me thought the article was about me. I didn't know what to say or do, so I waited for Deon.

When Deon arrived, I told her about the article and she read it. Afterward she laughed as I had, and said it was ridiculous. How could she have been describing the two of us? We did not put together all the clues until later that evening.

The article stated that Katrina Daisy Patron had taken pictures of her article's main character, who had braids, for a fashion show at school. This was our first clue. I had been in a fashion show for the big campus Black Weekend just a few weeks before, and everyone knew it. I was the only one with braids. A girl named Katrina had taken the pictures for the program. But that girl was white, and I didn't remember ever having any contact with her after that brief encounter.

Then Deon remembered a small gathering that we attended at which Katrina was present. But we had been invited and did not have sex, or want to, with anyone there. Deon remembered that immediately upon our arrival, Katrina had gone into an adjoining room, and did not come out the whole time we were there. This explained why I had not taken note of her presence. We later found out that because of the reputations we had gotten earlier in the year, it solidified the notion that the article was about us. This was outrageous! Needless to say, I got very upset.

Katrina called that night, crying, and saying that she had heard that everyone thought the article was about me, and how awful that must be. She said that the article was not about me, and she was sorry that everyone thought it was. I cussed her out, and hung up.

That night my phone rang off the hook. Most of the calls were from my male friends, lending their support. We found out from some of the men that Katrina had been after a few of them at the gathering, and had been quoted as saying, "Why don't they [the men] like me? Deon and Jenniffer get invited to all the parties. What's wrong with me?" That night, unbeknownst to us, Katrina got several anonymous phone calls from our supporters berating and threatening her.

Though the calls we got from our friends were somewhat comforting, it did nothing to alleviate my anger and sadness. I reached the lowest point I have ever reached. "How could someone, especially a white girl I did not even know, do this to me? Why would she do this to me? What was the point? What did she think she would gain?" Deon and I sat late into the night wondering and crying and trying to make sense of it all. There were lots of questions, but no answers.

For the next few days we were both too emotionally drained and mortified to go to class, so we sat and lamented. We eventually got calls from some of the deans at the school saying that they wanted to meet with us. Deon and I agreed, but were a bit wary about the meeting. The deans had asked for the meeting not because they had heard what had happened to us but because Katrina had called them saying that she was being threatened! I was enraged, to say the least. We were the victims here, and she was the one whining to the dean about being threatened! Deon and I weren't even the ones threatening her, and we had not told anyone to do so. What were we to do?

For me, the answer was easy. I called my mother (who just happens to be a lawyer). As soon as she heard my voice, she knew that something was wrong. I told her the whole story. Though I did not say it, she could tell that I needed her, and she drove up immediately. I have never been so glad to see her in my life. Relief just swept over me. I felt like everything would be all right. We stayed in a hotel because she thought that I needed to get away from the campus for a while. Deon's parents came up too after my mother convinced Deon of the necessity of a united front.

My mother and I spent the weekend, before a scheduled Monday meeting with school officials, discussing the article, events, and my social life in minute detail. As an attorney, Ma wanted to know of any possible trouble spots in our position as it related to the article. But there were none. I simply had not done what Katrina Daisy Patron portrayed, and there was no reason for her to say those things about me. When we weren't talking about the issue, we were going to every movie in the mall (I learned to appreciate the escape value of movies), eating great food, and drinking lots of tea. Ma understood that I didn't always want to talk, and she left me alone at those times. It was a wonderful comfort to have my mother with me, even though I had been so anxious to go off to Duke in the fall, and since then she'd constantly been after me to call home and let her know I was okay.

Monday morning rolled around and my dad, also an attorney, arrived from D.C. The meetings, which lasted virtually all day, did not go well. In the first, Katrina, two deans, the editor of the school newspaper, Deon, me, both sets of parents, and a friend of Deon's and mine were all gathered in a small office, squeezed around a small table. Katrina vehemently denied all of the accusations and insisted that we were behind the threats. She posed as an innocent victim fearful for her life because of the savage black people calling and threatening her.

I was on automatic pilot. I couldn't even get up the strength to talk. While Deon was angry and spoke, my feelings were more internal, and I shut down. My mother became my mouthpiece. Without me even telling her all I felt, she knew it in every minute detail and beautifully, eloquently, passionately, and powerfully conveyed it at the meetings. Basically, we were told that the school felt bad about what happened, but there was nothing that they could do to reprimand Katrina. They said that the newspaper was not a part of the university, and they had no say in what was printed. Though my mother questioned Katrina about every truth in the article (i.e., taking my picture for the fashion show, my coming to the party and her being there), Katrina still maintained that the article was total fiction. Even though she had been at the party and had seen that we did nothing but watch television and leave before she did, she had intentionally let the article imply that we came to the party and had sex with the men there.

All this, and the school said there was nothing they could do! The newspaper was our school newspaper, and everyone knew it to be our school newspaper, but the school was hiding behind the legality of it being an independent newspaper and saying there was nothing they could do. It would have come as a great surprise to everyone I knew to find out that our school newspaper was not our school newspaper after all. What b.s.!

Deon and I were extremely hurt and disillusioned. This great institution, which boasted of its academic excellence, was still incredibly inept socially. Despite the fact that the article was written by a white girl who did not know me, and basically painted black women as indiscrimately sexually available, the school did not see the incident as a race issue. They maintained that the article could have been written about any girl. Maybe it *could have* been written about any girl, but it *wasn't*. It was written by a *white* girl about two *black* girls on a campus in the south. No matter how academically cosmopolitan Duke was, it was still a southern school.

Once again my reputation had been denigrated by a jealous female. I learned that the conniving, malicious ways I thought were only characteristic of black women were not determined by color. Thoroughly humiliated and beaten, I left two weeks before my first year ended, without finishing the semester.

In the weeks before the newspaper story appeared there had been several racial incidents on campus. The television show *60 Minutes* had run a piece on the segregation of the Duke University campus. A black student at Duke had been arrested by the campus police because they wrongfully assumed that he had stolen a computer. There had also been a recent cartoon in the school newspaper (?!) depicting the all-black janitorial staff watching television, with a caption to the effect of, "Duke cleaning crew mopping floors." After the article written by Katrina Daisy Patron appeared, which blacks took as a calculated attempt at smearing the virtue of black women, the campus erupted in racial tension.

While at home, I was constantly in touch with people at school. In the two weeks before school ended, there had been a sit-in in our honor, and in honor of the victims of the other two racial incidents, in which all of the black students participated. Newspapers and television covered the story. More than two hundred white professors signed a letter to the Duke president basically telling her that they were embarrassed to be associated with a school that had the racial reputation Duke did, and the president must commit to doing something about it. Black professors wrote a similar letter. A meeting was held with black women and Duke administrators to discuss the problem of their degenerating relations. The incoming freshman class had a big dose of racial topics in the president's convocation address, and it was thoroughly covered in the press. It did not help that a national poll found Duke to have the ninth worst racial climate of any campus in the nation. At the same time, Duke tied for second place (up one ranking) in the national college ratings.

I felt good that what had happened to me had brought

about some good, and that the establishment finally had to face up to their prejudice and rectify it. As painful as it was to go through, it was good to know that something good came out of it. I had the distinct feeling that I was only a pawn in a much larger game, much like Anita Hill, who played such a crucial role in the process of bringing to light the problem of sexual harassment in the workplace. I would never deign to think of myself in such important and exalted terms, but the same kind of reasoning applies. I had been hurt, terribly hurt, by the incident, but it had taken on a life all its own that outweighed and overshadowed what had happened to me.

I had started out at Duke to learn a profession. I had so much passion for what I wanted to become, but along the way I lost it. I was so caught up in what was happening to me socially that I lost sight of what I was really there for. I went back to Duke the next semester, but realized that it did not hold the same attraction for me as it once did. I decided not to return after my third semester there. In my absence from school, I have been working at a doctor's office to get my finances together. The black doctor I work for specializes in treating the elderly.

I am mending my wounds, and working with the patients has reminded me of why I began the long, hard journey toward medical school. My spark of passion is beginning to burn again, and I am at last at peace with what happened. I still am determined to reach my goal, but now I realize that it is going to be far from easy. I thought my only challenges would be academic, but those were a walk in the park compared to the emotional stress I endured, at the hands of whites as well as blacks.

The comfort I initially felt at finally finding a group of blacks like me was short-lived. I now realize that comfort doesn't just come from skin color. Of course, oddly enough, I had already learned that lesson in reverse. That is, there were whites I had been comfortable with despite their skin color, and then I learned that there were blacks I could not trust even though their skin was like mine.

I guess my lesson is that we can be hurt by anyone. We can be comforted by anyone. Race isn't necessarily an automatic indicator of some of the things we might think it is. I think I would rather have been hurt only by whites instead of knowing that although someone white wrote the piece, the groundwork had already been laid by my black sisters and their vicious rumors.

I felt betrayed by my black female peers at Duke, a group for which I initially had such an affinity. They had shredded me for no reason other than jealousy over what they thought the males felt about me. I also felt betrayed by Katrina Daisy Patron, a white girl I didn't even know, who, society had taught me, was the most likely person to betray me. And I felt betrayed by Duke University. I had longed to go there and be a part of that esteemed institution, and they had committed to me through early acceptance, but in the final analysis, they didn't care what happened to me.

Ultimately, I learned that betrayal hurts no matter what color the betrayer.

SUGGESTED READING

BOOKS

Adler, Bill. *Growing Up Black*. New York: William Morrow, 1968.

Angelou, Maya. *I Know Why the Caged Bird Sings*. New York: Random House, 1969.

Archer, Chalmers. *Growing Up Black in Rural Mississippi: Memories of a Family, Heritage of a Place*. New York: Walker Publishing Company, 1992.

Beals, Melba Pattillo. *Warriors Don't Cry: A Searing Memoir of the Battle to Integrate Little Rock's Central High*. New York: Pocket Books, 1994.

Bell-Scott, Patricia. *Life Notes: Personal Writings by Contemporary Black Women*. New York: W. W. Norton, 1994.

Bray, Rosemary L. *Unafraid of the Dark: A Memoir*. New York: Random House, 1998.

Brown, Cecil. *Coming Up Down Home: A Memoir of a Southern Childhood (The Dark Tower)*. Hopewell, N.J.: Ecco Press, 1993.

Campbell, Bebe Moore. *Sweet Summer: Growing Up With and Without My Dad*. New York: Putnam Publishing Corporation, 1989.

Carroll, Rebecca, and Ntozake Shange. *Sugar in the Raw: Voices of Young Black Girls in America.* New York: Crown Publishers, 1997.

Cary, Lorene. *Black Ice.* New York: Alfred A. Knopf, 1991.

Davis, Angela. *Angela Davis: An Autobiography.* New York: Random House, 1974.

Dunham, Katherine. *A Touch of Innocence: Memoirs of Childhood.* New York: Harcourt, Brace, 1959.

Fulwood, Sam, III. *Waking from the Dream: My Life in the Black Middle Class.* New York: Anchor Books, 1996.

Gaines, Patrice. *Laughing in the Dark: From Colored Girl to Woman of Color—A Journey from Prison to Power.* New York: Crown Publishers, 1994.

Gates, Henry Louis, Jr., ed. *Bearing Witness: Selections from African-American Autobiography in the Twentieth Century.* New York: Pantheon Books, 1991.

Gates, Henry Louis, Jr., *Colored People: A Memoir.* New York: Alfred A. Knopf, 1993.

Gibson, Aliona L. *Nappy: Growing Up Black and Female in America.* New York: Writers and Readers Publishing, 1995.

Halberstam, David. *The Children.* New York: Random House, 1998.

Holland, Endesha Ida Mae. *From the Mississippi Delta: A Memoir.* New York: Simon & Schuster, 1997.

hooks, bell (Gloria Watkins). *Bone Black: Memories of Girlhood.* New York: Henry Holt, 1996.

Hunter, Latoya. *The Diary of Latoya Hunter: My First Year in Junior High.* New York: Crown Publishers, 1992.

Hurston, Zora Neale. *Dust Tracks on a Road.* New York: J. B. Lippincott, 1942.

Jay, David. *Growing Up Black.* New York: Morrow, 1968.

Kozol, Jonathan. *Amazing Grace.* New York: Plough, 1995.

Lincoln, C. Eric. *Coming Through the Fire: Surviving Race and Place in America*. Chapel Hill, N.C.: Duke University Press, 1996.

Mabry, Marcus. *White Bucks and Black-Eyed Peas: Coming of Age Black in White America*. New York: Scribner Publishing, 1995.

McDowell, Deborah E. *Leaving Pipe Shop: Memories of Kin*. New York: Scribner Publishing, 1996.

McKinley, Catherine E., and Joyce DeLaney. *Afrekete: An Anthology of Black Lesbian Writing*. New York: Anchor Books/Doubleday, 1995.

Moody, Anne. *Coming of Age in Mississippi*. New York: Dial Press, 1968.

Morris, Willie. *North Toward Home*. Boston: Houghton Mifflin, 1967.

Njeri, Itabari. *Every Good-bye Ain't Gone*. New York: Random House, 1982.

Peery, Nelson. *Black Fire: The Making of an American Revolutionary*. New York: New Press, 1994.

Pemberton, Gayle. *The Hottest Water in Chicago: Notes of a Native Daughter*. Boston: Faber and Faber, 1992.

Reeves, Donald. *Notes of a Processed Brother*. New York: Pantheon Books, 1971.

Staples, Brent. *Parallel Time: Growing Up in Black and White*. New York: Pantheon Books, 1994.

Tarpley, Natasha., ed., *Testimony: Young African-Americans on Self-Discovery and Black Identity*. Boston: Beacon Press, 1995.

Taulbert, Clifton L. *Once Upon a Time When We Were Colored*. Tulsa, Okla.: Council Oak Books, 1989.

Thompson, Becky, and Sangeeta Tyagi. *Names We Call Home: Autobiography on Racial Identity*. New York: Routledge & Kegan Paul, 1996.

Thompson, Gerald. *Reflections of an Oreo Cookie: Growing Up*

Black in the 1960s. Monroe, N.Y.: Library Research Associates, 1991.

Wickham, DeWayne. *Woodholme: A Black Man's Story of Growing Up Alone.* New York: Farrar, Straus and Giroux, 1995.

Wideman, John Edgar, and Robert Douglas Wideman. *Brothers and Keepers.* New York: Henry Holt, 1984.

Williams, Gregory Howard. *Life on the Color Line: The True Story of a White Boy Who Discovered He Was Black.* New York: E. P. Dutton, 1995.

Woodson, Jacqueline, ed. *A Way Out of No Way: Writings About Growing Up Black in America.* New York: Henry Holt, 1996.

ARTICLES

Bloom, Lynn Z. "Coming of Age in the Segregated South." In *Home Ground: Southern Autobiography,* edited by J. Bill Berry. Columbia, MO.: University of Missouri Press, 1991.

Cary, Lorene. "A Children's Crusade: The Journeys of a Black Prep-School Grad." *Newsweek,* November 4, 1991 (118:19), p. 46.

Cureton, George. "My Ghetto: A Backward Glance." *Partisan Review,* winter 1993 (60:1), p. 143.

Edwards, Audrey. "Sisters Under the Skin," *The New York Times Magazine,* September 19, 1993, p. 34.

George, Lynell. "Crossing the Color Line." *Utne Reader,* July-August 1992, p. 121-122.

Holloway, Karla F. C. "The Thursday Ladies." *Sage,* fall 1987 (IV:2).

Jackson, Kai, and Catherine E. McKinley. "Sisters: A Reunion Story." In *The Adoption Reader,* edited by Susan Wadia-Ells. Seattle: Seal Press, 1995.

Lebret, Martine. "A Self-Reflective Essay." *Journal of Education,* fall 1990 (172:3), p. 156.

Minerbrook, Scott. "My Father, Myself: A Story of Hope and Reconciliation," *Emerge,* October 1995, p. 52-57.

Nauden, Gloria. "Finding My Place in Black America." *Emerge,* July-August 1997, p. 67.

Quant, Brenda Dyer. "Cloak of Darkness." *African American Review,* spring 1993 (27:1), p. 29.

Russell, Karen K. "Growing Up with Privilege and Prejudice." *The New York Times Magazine,* June 14, 1987, p. 22.

Schultz, Elizabeth, ed. "Dreams Deferred: The Personal Narratives of Four Black Kansans." *American Studies,* fall 1993 (34:2) p. 25.

Senna, Carl. "A Catholic Boyhood." *Boston,* December 1989 (81:12), p. 113.

Smith, Vern E. "College Street, Pink Duck and Nightmares." *Emerge,* June 1994, p. 38.

Touré. "Black and PC on Campus." *Essence,* October 1993, p. 42

Wallace, Michele. "Memoirs of a Premature Bomb-Thrower." *Village Voice,* February 13, 1996, p. 35-36.

Williams, Gaye. "Somewhere Under the Rainbow Coalition . . ." *Ms.,* October 1984, p. 80-82.

Williams, Gaye. "Reminescence of a Post-Integration Kid." *New Directions for Women,* March 1985 (14:2), p. 8.

Zinn, H. "Young Ladies Who Can Picket," Z, February 1996 (8:2), p. 42–46.

TEXT CREDITS

PHOTO CREDITS

CHRONOLOGY

1929   January 15—Martin Luther King, Jr., was born.

1938   The U.S. Supreme Court ruled that black students must be given equal educational facilities.

1942   The Congress of Racial Equality (CORE) was founded.

1954   May 17—In the case of *Brown v. Board of Education of Topeka,* the U.S. Supreme Court banned segregation in public schools.

1955   Rosa Parks, a seamstress, refused to give up her seat to a white person on a public bus in Montgomery, Alabama, leading to a black boycott of buses by the Montgomery Improvement Association that lasted more than a year. Dr. King's leadership of the boycott led to his national prominence.

1956   December—Martin Luther King, Jr.'s, home in Montgomery, Alabama, was bombed. The Montgomery bus boycott was successful and city buses were desegregated.

1957   The Southern Christian Leadership Conference was organized with Martin Luther King, Jr., as its president.

The governor of Arkansas, Orval Faubus, called in the Arkansas national guard to prohibit students from desegregating a white high school in Little Rock. President Dwight D. Eisenhower called in one thousand federal troops to restore order and to escort nine black students into Central High School.

1960 February 1—Students in Greensboro, North Carolina, arranged sit-ins at all-white lunch counters. Student sit-ins and nonviolent demonstrations in many southern towns and cities followed.

1961 May—Freedom Riders, both black and white, rode buses throughout the south to challenge racial segregation.

1963 May 3—Dr. King and other ministers were arrested during a demonstration in Birmingham, Alabama. The police then turned dogs and fire hoses on the boycotting schoolchildren. June 12—Medgar Evers, leader of the Mississippi NAACP, was assassinated. August 28—250,000 people attended the March on Washington for Civil Rights where Dr. King delivered his "I Have a Dream" speech. September 15—Four little African-American girls were killed by a racist's bomb in the basement of a church in Birmingham, Alabama.

1964 The Civil Rights Act, guaranteeing blacks the right to vote and authorizing government to sue to desegregate public facilities and schools, was passed. Dr. Martin Luther King, Jr., received the Nobel Peace Prize. Civil Rights activists James Chaney, Andrew Goodman, and Michael Swerner were killed in Mississippi.

1965   February 21—Malcolm X was assassinated. March 7—
       Dr. King and the Southern Christian Leadership
       Conference began a voter registration drive in Selma,
       Alabama, by attempting to march from Selma to
       Mongtomery. Six hundred marchers were beaten by
       state patrolmen and a posse of men on horseback.
       March 21—With the protection of federal troops, Dr.
       King led a march from Selma, Alabama, to the state
       capitol in Montgomery. A white civil rights worker, Viola
       Liuzzo, was killed as she transported some of the
       marchers back to their homes. August 6—The Voting
       Rights Act, signed by President Johnson, opened the
       door for black voter registration. August 11–16—A race
       riot took place in the Watts area of Los Angeles in which
       thirty-four people were killed.

1966   Huey Newton and Bobby Seale founded the Black
       Panther Party in Oakland, California. The new chair-
       man of the Student Nonviolent Coordinating Commit-
       tee (SNCC), Stokely Carmichael, called for "black
       power."

1967   Thurgood Marshall was confirmed as a U.S. Supreme
       Court justice.

1968   Three students were killed as they protested segrega-
       tion at South Carolina State College. March 28—Dr.
       King led a march for striking sanitation workers in
       Memphis, Tennessee. Dr. King announced his plans for
       a Poor People's Campaign. April 3—Dr. King gave his
       last speech, "I've Been to the Mountaintop." April 4—
       Dr. Martin Luther King, Jr., was assassinated at the

Lorraine Motel in Memphis, Tennessee. In response to Dr. King's assassination, riots erupted in more than one hundred cities. The Poor People's Campaign went on without Dr. King. More than fifty thousand people marched on Washington, D.C.

1971   The Supreme Court ruled that busing for the purposes of achieving school desegregation was constitutional. Jesse Jackson was a moving force behind the founding of Operation PUSH.

1973   Mrs. Martin Luther King, Sr., was shot and killed.

1979   Klansmen shot and killed five people at an anti-KKK rally in Greensboro, North Carolina.

1981   A Solidarity Day march protesting the racial policies of the Reagan administration drew three-hundred-thousand participants.

1988   Jesse Jackson announced that he would run for President of the United States. Colin Powell became chairman of the Joint Chiefs of Staff.

1991   Clarence Thomas was confirmed as a U.S. Supreme Court justice.

1992   April 30—Riots broke out in south-central Los Angeles in response to the not-guilty verdict for four white policemen accused of the videotaped beating of Rodney King, a black motorist.

1993   Two of the four policemen who were acquitted for Rodney King's beating were found guilty of violating his civil rights.

1997   July—Two white men were charged with murder for burning and beheading Garnett P. Johnson, a black man, in Independence, Virginia.

1998   June 6—In Jasper, Texas, three white supremacists associated with the Klu Klux Klan beat James Byrd, Jr., a disabled black man, and then dragged him behind a pickup truck until his body was completely dismembered.